HOUSTON'S

TOP 100 FOOD TRUCKS

Paul Galvani Publisher

Sugarland, TX 77478 US

281.630.5127

carpaneto@aol.com

ISBN 978-0-575-09852-3

Library of Congress Control Number: 2013901613

Design-Self Design

Houston, TX

Printed in China

HOUSTON'S

TOP

100

FOOD

TRUCKS

Paul Galvani

CONTENTS

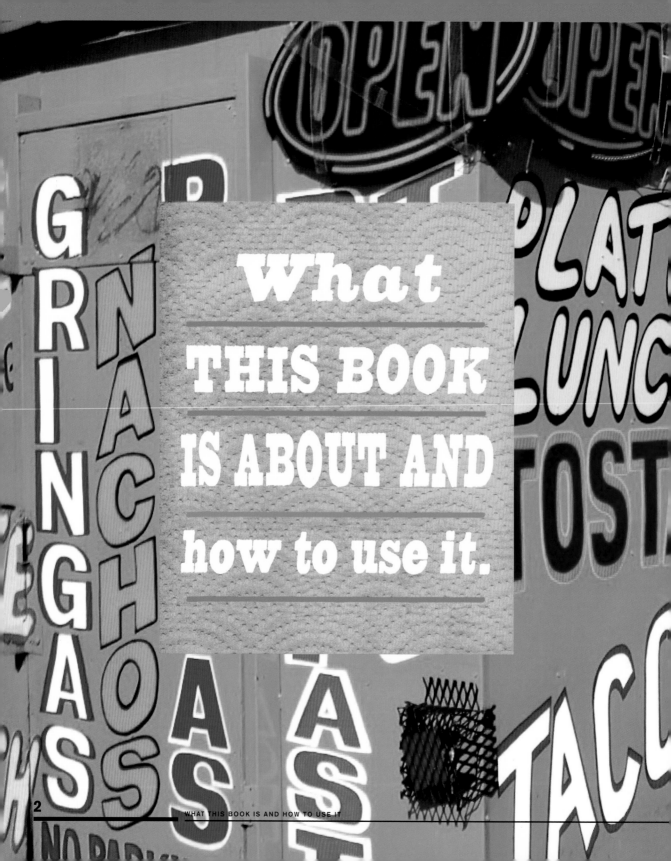

What THIS BOOK IS ABOUT AND how to use it.

If you close your eyes for a moment and drift back to your childhood, I'm willing to bet that you can re-create the sounds of the ice-cream van coming down your street and, as the sound got closer and closer, maybe even the feeling of excitement and anticipation as you begged your parents to buy you an ice cream.

While you probably didn't know it at the time, eating ice cream from an ice cream van was probably one of your first experiences with food from a mobile food vendor. Fast forward to today and you'll arrive at one of the hottest food trends sweeping the nation: the mobile food revolution.

Nearly 1,400 food trucks ply the streets of Houston and Harris County — and if you're like me, you wish you could try every one of them. This guidebook is my attempt to help you hunt down some of the best and most interesting. There is also a glossary of terms that you will find on the menus of these trucks, as well as tips on how to make the most of your mobile experience. Over the time it took me to compile this list, I personally visited every truck reviewed in this book. I

ate every *arepa*, barbecue brisket, rib, sausage, chicken, *banh mi*, *boudin*, *burrito*, *churro*, *crêpe*, char-broiled

chicken, cupcake, *gelato*, *pho*, po-boy, *pupusa*, chicken *tikka masala*,

sno-ball, *taco* and *torta* myself. I took every picture, unless otherwise credited. I wrote every review. I interviewed every owner or server. I paid for everything I ate or drank, even though many owners offered me their food for free. My answer was always the same: "Thank you, but you've got a business to run, and my reviews have to remain unbiased."

I did not get sick once. Not even the slightest queasiness or mildest gastrointestinal upset. To those who let fear of food poisoning keep them from eating street food, I say that fear can be a self-fulfilling prophecy: If you think you'll catch food poisoning, you probably will. I visited trucks in all sorts of neighborhoods from the early morning to late at night, and I never felt even mildly uneasy.

Not listed in this book are any of the pushcarts or any bicycle carts that you often find in Hispanic neighborhoods, selling *raspas* (shaved ice), *refrescos* or *liquados* (fruit drinks), *helados* (ice cream), *paletas* (popsicles) and such. This is simply because they tend to be even harder to track down than the larger trucks or trailers. If, however, these items are served from a larger mobile food unit, you'll find them documented and reviewed here.

In doing a book of this kind, it would have been easy to write about nothing but Mexican taco trucks, since the vast majority of the trucks in the Houston area serve Mexican food. What I strove for, however, was the greatest diversity I could find, from Nigerian to Venezuelan, Vietnamese, Korean, Mexican, Indian, Middle Eastern, Colombian, Honduran,

it would have been easy to write about nothing but Mexican taco trucks, since the vast majority of the trucks in the Houston area serve Mexican food. What I strove for, however, was the greatest diversity I could find

Chinese, Thai, Greek, Salvadoran, Guatemalan, Puerto Rican, Portuguese, South African, Filipino, Bahamian, Italian, Cuban, French, Texan, Cajun, Creole and Chicagoan. Even within the category of Mexican trucks, I tried to expand beyond just tacos to units selling *churros* (donuts), *refrescos* (fruit drinks),

elotes (corn on the cob), and *pollos asados* (charbroiled chicken). I sought Mexican taco trucks that had some kind of specialty, whether it was the style of Monterrey or Mexico City, or whether it was *tacos al vapor* (steamed tacos) or *tacos Tlaquepaque* (Jalisco-style tacos topped with spicy sauce). I tried to find something different to eat at every truck.

One of the best things about food trucks is the direct, personal contact you have with the person who prepares your order. I met some incredible people who quickly opened up to me. They were eager to tell their stories and spread the word about mobile food units. Most allowed me access to the interior of their units to take pictures. They spent as much time as it took to answer every question I had. Never once did I feel that someone did not want to talk to me. I didn't meet any jerks — not one. I got the feeling that being a nice person is a prerequisite for owning or operating a food truck.

My theory is that a brotherhood of sorts has developed as a result of the common challenges the mobile food vendors face in overcoming similar difficulties and ensuring that all of the complex city and county ordinances are followed. In the biz they call it "food truck love". Many of the colorful people in this business have equally

colorful names: The Taco Pimp, the Taco Nazi, Buffalo Sean, Bubba J, the Smoke Doctor, Big Daddy, The Grillologist, the Prep Artist and Cracklin' Man, to name a few. Some gave me only their first names. Maybe they had reasons. I never asked a second time.

One of the best things about food trucks is the direct, personal contact you have with the person who prepares your order I didn't meet any jerks — not one. I got the feeling that being a nice person is a prerequisite for owning or operating a food truck.

I realize that, because I sampled fewer than ten percent of Houston's trucks, someone will inevitably say, "You missed the best one." I probably have — and maybe I can add it to a future edition. So if your favorite mobile food unit isn't mentioned, or if you locate an interesting truck, please visit my website, www.houstonstop100foodtrucks.com, or my Facebook page, Houstonstop-100foodtrucks. Share your discovery with me — and with the rest of the world. We're hungry to know.

This then is a book about Houston's cultural and culinary diversity as demonstrated by the different ethnic cuisines available at the various mobile food units around the city and its environs. I was often asked "What's your favorite food truck?" to which, I replied: "I don't have one." There are certainly some trucks that I will return to before I return to others, but the reason these 100 trucks are in the book is because I believe them to be the best Houston has to offer - each and every one of them.

Where
TO FIND
THE TRUCKS

☞

Certain parts of town are more likely to have a good number of trucks than others. After a while, you will begin to notice a pattern of where you find these trucks. There are some businesses and areas that just seem to attract them.

Gas stations, flea markets, dance halls, night clubs, discos, museums, bars, used auto parts lots, certain supermarkets, parks, home improvement centers, sporting venues, certain school and college campuses and farmer's markets, all are great locations where food trucks can usually be found.

One of the questions I get asked a lot is: "Where do you find these trucks?"

Here is a list of places where trucks can be found.

1. 5th Amendment, 2900 Travis
2. Agora, 1712 Westheimer
3. Alabama Ice House, 1919 West Alabama
4. Antidote Coffee, 729 Studewood
5. Antique Bar, 2511 Bissonnet
6. Bar 5015, 5015 Almeda
7. Bar Boheme, 307 Fairview
8. Bayou City Bar & Grill, 2409 Grant
9. Bayou City Farmer's Market, 3000 Richmond
10. Beaver's, 2310 Decatur
11. Bo Concepts, 4302 Westheimer
12. Black Hole Coffee House, 4506 Graustark
13. Boneyard Drinkery, 8510 Washington
14. Boomtown Coffee, 242 W.19th St.
15. Brian O'Neill's Irish Pub, 5555 Morningside
16. Buchanan's Native Plants, 611 11th St.
17. Buffalo Exchange, 1618 Westheimer
18. Catalina Coffee Shop, 2201 Washington
19. Catbird's Bar, 1336 Westheimer
20. Contemporary Arts Museum Houston, 5216 Montrose
21. Darkhorse Tavern, 2207 Washington

22. Dirk's Coffee, 4005 Montrose
23. Discovery Green Flea Market
24. Distillery 2520, 2520 Houston
25. Double Trouble, 3622 Main
26. F Bar, 202 Tuam
27. Fairview Lounge, 315 Fairview
28. Fitzgerald's, 2706 White Oak
29. Grand Prize Bar, 1010 Banks
30. Guitar Center, 8390 Westheimer
31. Houston Museum of Natural Science
32. Inversion Coffee, 1953 Montrose
33. Jackson's Bar, 1205 Richmond
34. Karbach Brewery, 2032 Karbach
35. Khon's Bar, 2808 Milam
36. Kung Fu Saloon, 5317 Washington
37. Liberty Station, 2101 Washington
38. Little Woodrow's, 2306 Brazos
39. Lizzards' Pub, 2715 Sackett
40. Mango's, 403 Westheimer
41. Mapleleaf Pub, 514 Elgin
42. Marquis II, 2631 Bissonnet

If you own a smart phone, there are a number of different apps that will help you locate food trucks near you. Eat St., Roaming Hunger and Truxmap are three of the best apps for this.

43 Memorial Wine Cellar, 7951 Katy Freeway

44 Mugsy's on Richmond, 2239 Richmond

45 Museum of Fine Arts, Houston, 1001Bissonnet

46 Nance Street Studios, 1707 Nance

47 No Label Brewing Co., 5373 1st St., Katy

48 Numbers, 300 Westheimer

49 OTC Patio Bar, 3212 Kirby

50 Petrol Station, 985 Wakefield

51 Phul Court, 1311 Leeland

52 Poison Girl Bar, 1641 Westheimer

53 Rebel's Honky Tonk, 5002 Washington

54 Rice University Farmer's Market, 2100 University

55 Roeder's Pub, 3116 S. Shepherd

56 St. Arnold's Brewery, 2000 Lyons

57 Scorpion Studios, 1401 Westheimer

58 Shady Tavern, 1206 West 20th Street

59 Sherlock's Baker St. Pub, 1997A West Gray

60 Simone on Sunset, 2418 Sunset

61 Soap Car Wash, 3759 Richmond

62 Soundwaves, 3509 Montrose

63 Sugarbaby's Cupcake Boutique, 3310 S. Shepherd

64 Taft Street Coffee, 2115 Taft

65 The Beer Station, 806 Richmond

66 The Cellar Bar, 3140 Richmond

67 The Davenport Lounge, 2117 Richmond

68 The Houston Design Center, 7026 Old Katy Road

69 The Menil Collection, 1515 Sul Ross

70 The Plaza, Greens Road near Imperial Valley

71 The Pearl Bar, 4216 Washington

72 Urban Harvest Downtown Farmer's Market, City Hall

73 Urban Harvest Eastside Farmer's Market, 3000 Richmond

74 Wabash Antiques & Feed Store, 5701 Washington

75 Warehouse Live, 813 St. Emanuel

76 Washington Avenue Drinkery, 4115 Washington

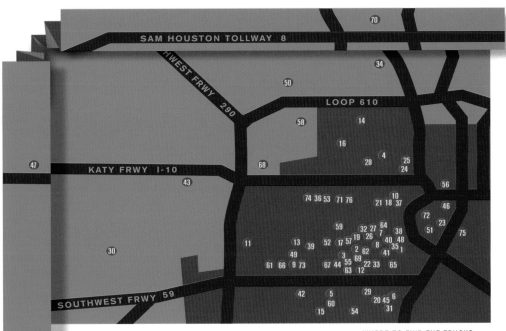

Truck
CLUSTERS

32
31
30
29

HOLLYVALE DR

28

L ROUTE RD

23

20
19
18
17

16
15
14
13

N. SHEPHERD DR

45

7 8 9 10 11 12

TRUCK CLUSTERS

LOUISE RD

SINTA FLEA
MARKET

1 2 3 4 5 6

Food truck owners have a tendency to congregate in clusters. Perhaps they feel that there is safety in numbers or maybe they're all fishing where the fish are. Regardless, where you find one truck, chances are you'll find another close by. Listed below are the various truck clusters that I located around the city, documenting and photographing every truck I found.

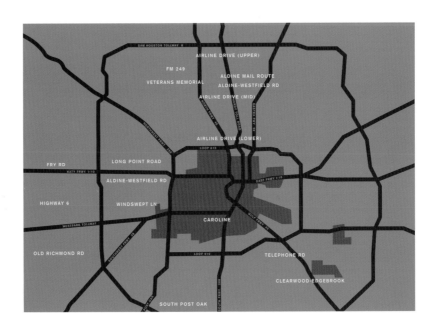

Airline Drive is base central for Houston's food trucks. This is without a doubt the most colorful street for food trucks in Houston. There are more food trucks on this street than on any other street in the city. One Saturday, I found 50 trucks on a ten-mile stretch of Airline from the 2200 block to the 12000 block, not counting the 22 that are located inside the Sunny Flea Market, the 12 located in the Sinta Flea Market next door, as well as the 6 located in the Mercado Xochinilco, on the opposite side of the road (see below), all in the 8700 block of Airline. That's a total of 90 food trucks. I photographed each one I found, but did not review all of them, since most of them are fairly typical taco trucks, I felt that I had already adequately covered this category in the book and therefore did not feel the need to review them. If, however, I found a truck that offered something a little different from all the other taco trucks, I reviewed it in the book.

This list is best approached from the bottom up, starting from the 2000 block of Airline and going north until you reach Aldine-Bender in the 12000 block of Airline. I have listed the street numbers to help you locate a particular truck and have also listed the major cross streets for added convenience and to give you some orienting points. Once you reach the Sunny Flea Market at 8705 Airline, you will need to park your car and visit the trucks inside the grounds of this flea market. You won't be disappointed. I have a separate section only for the trucks inside the flea markets

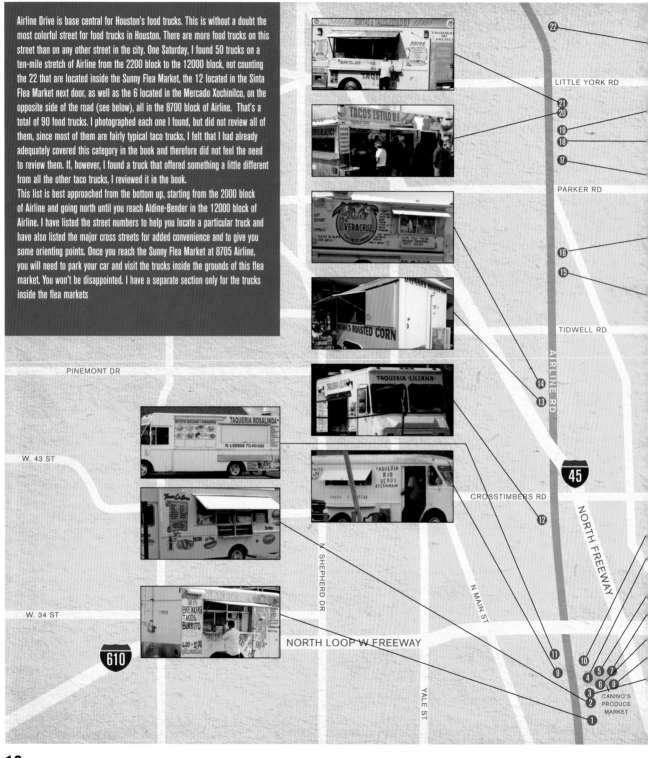

JENSEN DR

EASTEX FWY

RD

FULTON ST

610

11	2709 AIRLINE **Taqueria** **Rosalinda**	22	7804 AIRLINE **Taqueria** **La Reforma**
10	2606 AIRLINE **Pollos Asados** **El Regio**	21	7040 AIRLINE **Taqueria** **Mi Jalisco 2**
9	2603 AIRLINE **Taqueria** **Rio Verde**	20	7040 AIRLINE **Taqueria** **Mi Jalisco**
8	2520 AIRLINE **Tacos** **Y Mas**	19	7009 AIRLINE **El Manna** **Grill**
7	2520 AIRLINE **Buddy's** **Foodservice**	18	7008 AIRLINE **El Rey** **De Monterrey**
6	2520 AIRLINE **Taqueria** **Leticia**	17	7000 AIRLINE **Lindo** **Atotonilco #**
5	2520 AIRLINE **Taqueria** **Tacambaro**	16	6320 AIRLINE **Taqueria** **Mexico D.F.**
4	2520 AIRLINE **Taco's** **Sylvia's**	15	6300 AIRLINE **Taqueria** **San Luis**
3	2426 AIRLINE **Tacos El Rey** **De Reyes**	14	4903 AIRLINE **Taqueria** **Veracruz**
2	2426 AIRLINE **Tacos** **La Rosa**	13	4711 AIRLINE **Dayana's** **Roasted Corn**
1	2214 AIRLINE **El Rey Del** **Tacorriendo #2**	12	4215 AIRLINE **Taqueria** **Liliana**

GULF BANK RD

VETERANS MEMORIAL DR

45

NORTH FREEWAY

N. SHEPHERD DR

VICTORY DR

E. LITTLE YORK RD

18 8705 AIRLINE
Taqueria
Chirris

17 8705 AIRLINE
Elotes/Aguas
Frescas

16 8705 AIRLINE
Elote
Mexicano

15 8705 AIRLINE
Elotes
Express

14 8705 AIRLINE
La Pupusa
Salvadoreña

13 8705 AIRLINE
Hot Dog
Cart

12 8705 AIRLINE
Chicharron
Preparados

11 8705 AIRLINE
Hot Dog
Stand

10 8705 AIRLINE
Refresqueria
Las Brisas

9 8705 AIRLINE
Taqueno
Puro Norte

8 8705 AIRLINE
Taco De
Puro Norte

29 8705 AIRLINE
Pupusas
Express

28 8705 AIRLINE
Ricas
Comidas

27 8705 AIRLINE
Aguas
Express

26 8705 AIRLINE
No Name

25 8705 AIRLINE
Hot Dog
Stand

24 8705 AIRLINE
No Name

23 8705 AIRLINE
La Papa
Loca

22 8705 AIRLINE
Las Pollitas
Hernandez

21 8705 AIRLINE
Pupusa
La Esperanza

20 8705 AIRLINE
Ricos
Elotes

19 8705 AIRLINE
Pupusas Y Tacos
El Buen Sabor

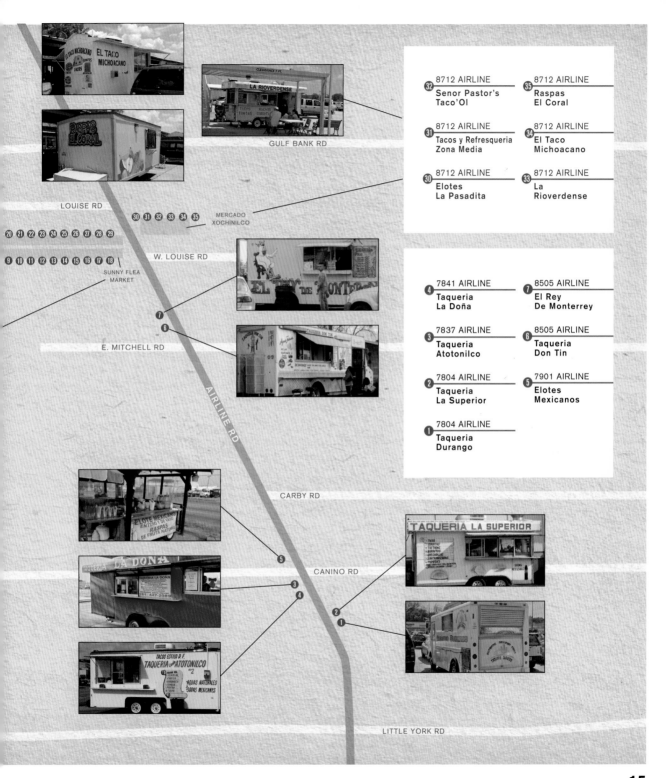

EL TACO MICHOACANO

PAPO'S EL CORAL

LA RIOVERDENSE

CLEARANCE 7 FT.

GULF BANK RD

LOUISE RD

MERCADO
XOCHINILCO

30 31 32 33 34 35

20 21 22 23 24 25 26 27 28 29

9 10 11 12 13 14 15 16 17 18

W. LOUISE RD

SUNNY FLEA
MARKET

EL TACO DE MONTERREY

7

6

E. MITCHELL RD

TAQUERIA DON TIN

AIRLINE RD

32 **8712 AIRLINE**
Senor Pastor's
Taco'Ol

35 **8712 AIRLINE**
Raspas
El Coral

31 **8712 AIRLINE**
Tacos y Refresqueria
Zona Media

34 **8712 AIRLINE**
El Taco
Michoacano

30 **8712 AIRLINE**
Elotes
La Pasadita

33 **8712 AIRLINE**
La
Rioverdense

4 **7841 AIRLINE**
Taqueria
La Doña

7 **8505 AIRLINE**
El Rey
De Monterrey

3 **7837 AIRLINE**
Taqueria
Atotonilco

6 **8505 AIRLINE**
Taqueria
Don Tin

2 **7804 AIRLINE**
Taqueria
La Superior

5 **7901 AIRLINE**
Elotes
Mexicanos

1 **7804 AIRLINE**
Taqueria
Durango

CARBY RD

ELOTE MEXICANO
RASPAS
DE FRUTA NATURAL

TAQUERIA LA SUPERIOR

5

TAQUERIA LA DONA

3

4

CANINO RD

2

1

TACOS ESTILO D.F.
TAQUERIA ATOTONILCO
AGUAS NATURALES
SOPAS MEXICANAS

LITTLE YORK RD

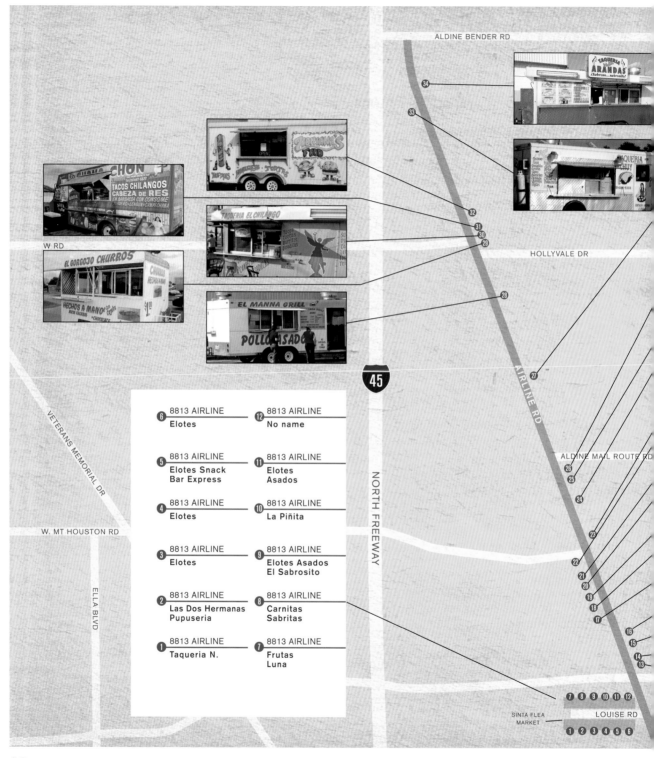

ALDINE BENDER RD

HOLLYVALE DR

45

W RD

VETERANS MEMORIAL DR

W. MT HOUSTON RD

ELLA BLVD

NORTH FREEWAY

AIRLINE RD

ALDINE MAIL ROUTE RD

6	8813 AIRLINE	12	8813 AIRLINE
	Elotes		No name
5	8813 AIRLINE	11	8813 AIRLINE
	Elotes Snack Bar Express		Elotes Asados
4	8813 AIRLINE	10	8813 AIRLINE
	Elotes		La Piñita
3	8813 AIRLINE	9	8813 AIRLINE
	Elotes		Elotes Asados El Sabrosito
2	8813 AIRLINE	8	8813 AIRLINE
	Las Dos Hermanas Pupuseria		Carnitas Sabritas
1	8813 AIRLINE	7	8813 AIRLINE
	Taqueria N.		Frutas Luna

SINTA FLEA MARKET

LOUISE RD

7 8 9 10 11 12

1 2 3 4 5 6

LUTHE RD

CHRISMAN RD

SELLERS RD

LF BANK RD

Y TOLL RD

GULF BANK RD

23 9618 AIRLINE
Antojitos
Hondureños

22 9531 AIRLINE
Refresqueria
Las Piñas Locas

21 9523 AIRLINE
Taqueria
Mi Jalisco

20 9521 AIRLINE
Delmita's
Pollos Asados

19 9519 AIRLINE
Taqueria Aguas A
La Mexicana

18 9517 AIRLINE
Refresqueria Aguas
A La Mexicana

17 9515 AIRLINE
Katrachos

16 9210 AIRLINE
La Sabrosita

15 9008 AIRLINE
Chilangos
D.F

14 9000 AIRLINE
El Semafaro
De Monterrey

13 9000 AIRLINE
Taqueria
Mexico

34 11900 AIRLINE
Taqueria
Arandas

33 11717 AIRLINE
Taqueria
Chuy

32 11006 AIRLINE
Adriana's

31 10910 AIRLINE
Chana Y Chon
(off main road)

30 10910 AIRLINE
Taqueria
El Chilango

29 10910 AIRLINE
El Gorgojo
Churros

28 10720 AIRLINE
El Manna
Pollos Asados

27 10400 AIRLINE
Taqueria
Angeles

26 10028 AIRLINE
Tacos
El Mante

25 10028 AIRLINE
Antojitos
La Esperanza

24 9822 AIRLINE
Tacos
Guanajuato

On the seven mile stretch of Aldine Mail Route from Airline Drive to Eastex Freeway, I found sixteen trucks all of which were Mexican, except for one which was a BBQ truck.

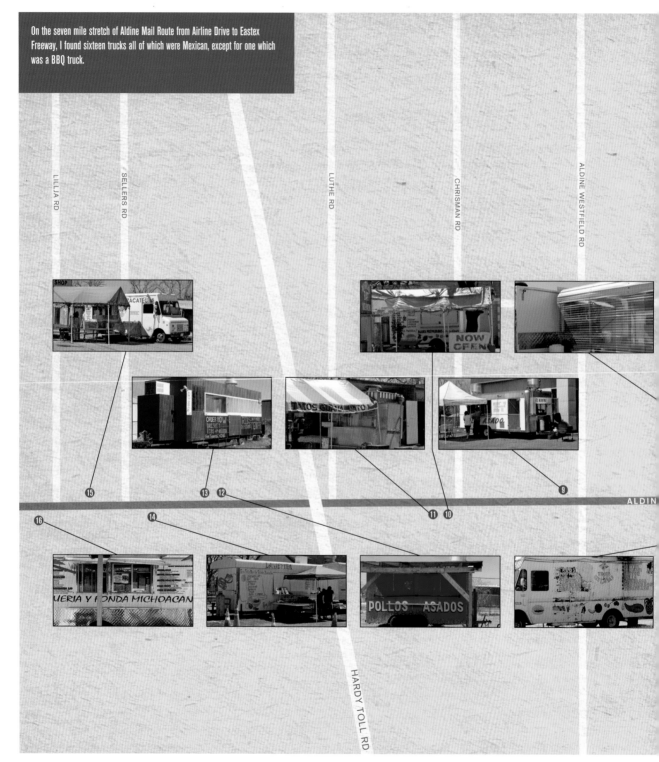

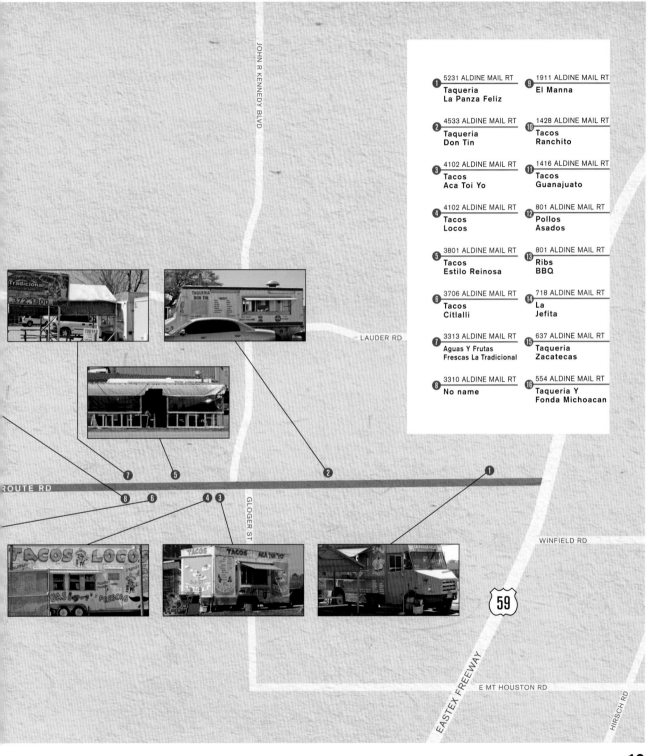

JOHN R KENNEDY BLVD

① 5231 ALDINE MAIL RT
Taqueria
La Panza Feliz

② 4533 ALDINE MAIL RT
Taqueria
Don Tin

③ 4102 ALDINE MAIL RT
Tacos
Aca Toi Yo

④ 4102 ALDINE MAIL RT
Tacos
Locos

⑤ 3801 ALDINE MAIL RT
Tacos
Estilo Reinosa

⑥ 3706 ALDINE MAIL RT
Tacos
Citlalli

⑦ 3313 ALDINE MAIL RT
Aguas Y Frutas
Frescas La Tradicional

⑧ 3310 ALDINE MAIL RT
No name

⑨ 1911 ALDINE MAIL RT
El Manna

⑩ 1428 ALDINE MAIL RT
Tacos
Ranchito

⑪ 1416 ALDINE MAIL RT
Tacos
Guanajuato

⑫ 801 ALDINE MAIL RT
Pollos
Asados

⑬ 801 ALDINE MAIL RT
Ribs
BBQ

⑭ 718 ALDINE MAIL RT
La
Jefita

⑮ 637 ALDINE MAIL RT
Taqueria
Zacatecas

⑯ 554 ALDINE MAIL RT
Taqueria Y
Fonda Michoacan

LAUDER RD

ROUTE RD

GLOGER ST

WINFIELD RD

59

EASTEX FREEWAY

E MT HOUSTON RD

HIRSCH RD

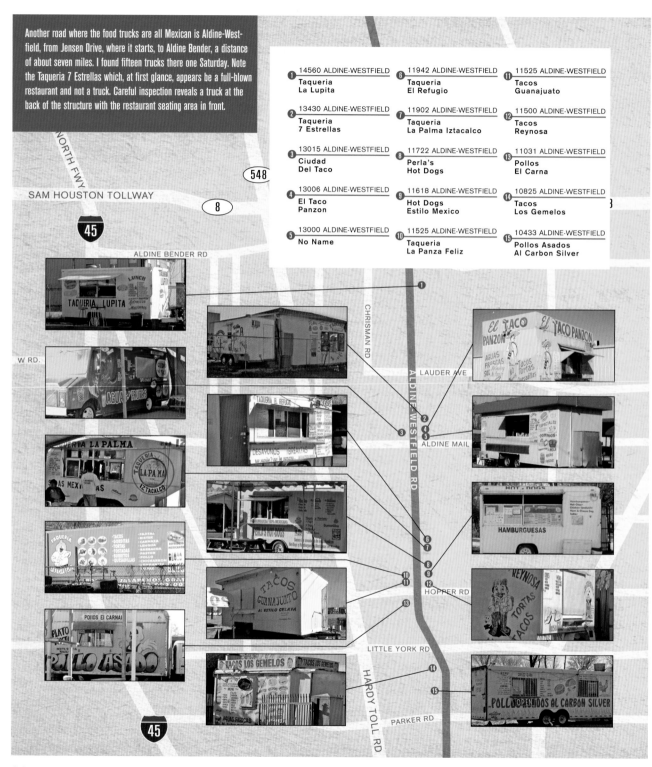

Another road where the food trucks are all Mexican is Aldine-Westfield, from Jensen Drive, where it starts, to Aldine Bender, a distance of about seven miles. I found fifteen trucks there one Saturday. Note the Taqueria 7 Estrellas which, at first glance, appears be a full-blown restaurant and not a truck. Careful inspection reveals a truck at the back of the structure with the restaurant seating area in front.

1 14560 ALDINE-WESTFIELD
Taqueria
La Lupita

2 13430 ALDINE-WESTFIELD
Taqueria
7 Estrellas

3 13015 ALDINE-WESTFIELD
Ciudad
Del Taco

4 13006 ALDINE-WESTFIELD
El Taco
Panzon

5 13000 ALDINE-WESTFIELD
No Name

6 11942 ALDINE-WESTFIELD
Taqueria
El Refugio

7 11902 ALDINE-WESTFIELD
Taqueria
La Palma Iztacalco

8 11722 ALDINE-WESTFIELD
Perla's
Hot Dogs

9 11618 ALDINE-WESTFIELD
Hot Dogs
Estilo Mexico

10 11525 ALDINE-WESTFIELD
Taqueria
La Panza Feliz

11 11525 ALDINE-WESTFIELD
Tacos
Guanajuato

12 11500 ALDINE-WESTFIELD
Tacos
Reynosa

13 11031 ALDINE-WESTFIELD
Pollos
El Carna

14 10825 ALDINE-WESTFIELD
Tacos
Los Gemelos

15 10433 ALDINE-WESTFIELD
Pollos Asados
Al Carbon Silver

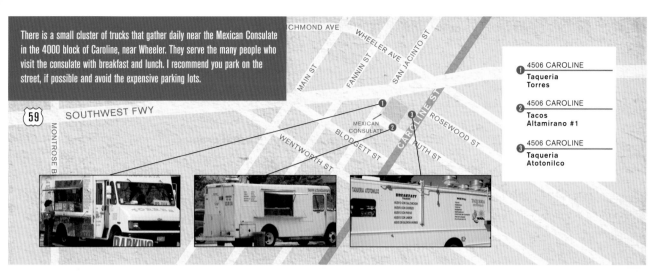

There is a small cluster of trucks that gather daily near the Mexican Consulate in the 4000 block of Caroline, near Wheeler. They serve the many people who visit the consulate with breakfast and lunch. I recommend you park on the street, if possible and avoid the expensive parking lots.

1 4506 CAROLINE
Taqueria
Torres

2 4506 CAROLINE
Tacos
Altamirano #1

3 4506 CAROLINE
Taqueria
Atotonilco

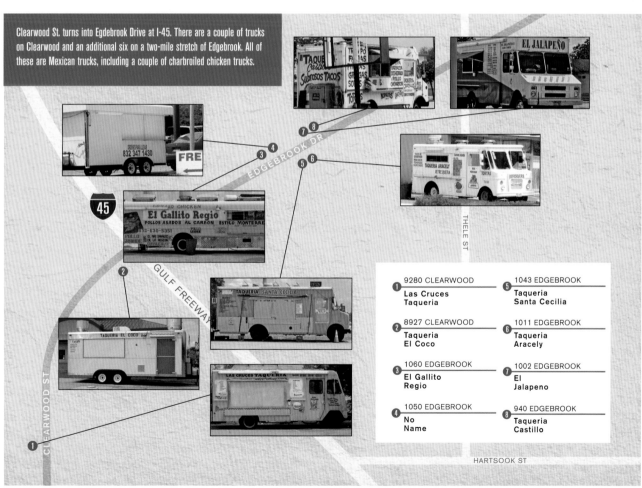

Clearwood St. turns into Egdebrook Drive at I-45. There are a couple of trucks on Clearwood and an additional six on a two-mile stretch of Edgebrook. All of these are Mexican trucks, including a couple of charbroiled chicken trucks.

1 9280 CLEARWOOD
Las Cruces
Taqueria

2 8927 CLEARWOOD
Taqueria
El Coco

3 1060 EDGEBROOK
El Gallito
Regio

4 1050 EDGEBROOK
No
Name

5 1043 EDGEBROOK
Taqueria
Santa Cecilia

6 1011 EDGEBROOK
Taqueria
Aracely

7 1002 EDGEBROOK
El
Jalapeno

8 940 EDGEBROOK
Taqueria
Castillo

Long Point, between Hempstead Highway and Gessner, is another street with a significant number of food trucks. This five mile stretch had fourteen food trucks on it when I drove down it one Saturday. Most of the trucks here are Mexican. You will also find a couple of charbroiled chicken trucks and a couple of *refresquerias*, as well as one roasted corn truck here.

1 10106 LONG POINT
El Norteño
Pollos Asados

2 10022 LONG POINT
Taqueria
D.F.

3 9893 LONG POINT
El Norteño
Pollos Asados

4 9616 LONG POINT
Salamanca
Taqueria

5 9352 LONG POINT
Tacos
Arcelia

6 9352 LONG POINT
Tacos
El Costeño

7 8355 LONG POINT
La
Fortuna

8 8355 LONG POINT
Elotes
El Regalo

9 8355 LONG POINT
Refresqueria
Rio Verde #2

10 8355 LONG POINT
Refresqueria
Rio Verde

11 8355 LONG POINT
El Norteño
Pollos Asado

12 8030 LONG POINT
El
Taconazo

13 7403 LONG POINT
Taqeria El
Ultimo

14 6850 LONG POINT
Taqueria
Juarez

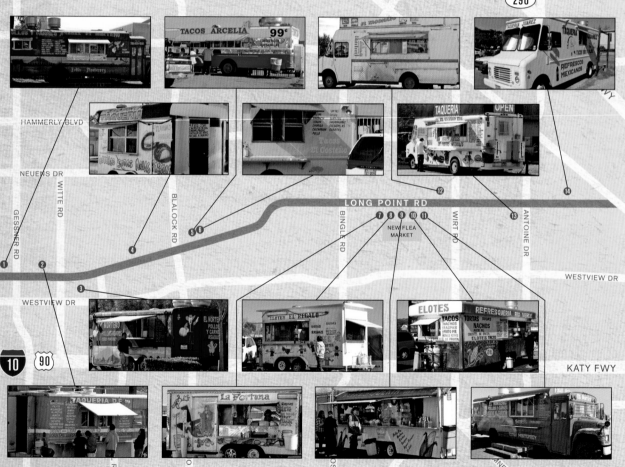

South Post Oak from US 90 (Old Main) to the Sam Houston Tollway, a distance of approximately six miles, had fourteen trucks on it one Saturday. While most are Mexican, you'll also find a Salvadoran truck, a couple of char-broiled chicken trucks, a roasted corn trailer, a *refresqueria* and a BBQ truck.

1 12355 SOUTH POST OAK
Mario's
Roasted Corn

2 13115 SOUTH POST OAK
Tacos &
Burritos To Go

3 13500 SOUTH POST OAK
Pupuseria
Ramirez

4 13717 SOUTH POST OAK
Pollos Asados
Ayala

5 13803 SOUTH POST OAK
Esperanza Pollos
Asados Al Carbon

6 13803 SOUTH POST OAK
Jus Smoken
BBQ

7 14106 SOUTH POST OAK
Taqueria
Torres

8 14109 SOUTH POST OAK
Taqueria
Sabrosos

9 14513 SOUTH POST OAK
Tacos
Don Beto

10 15541 SOUTH POST OAK
Los Pajaritos
Refresqueria

11 15509 SOUTH POST OAK
Taqueria
Salamanca

12 15500 SOUTH POST OAK
Taqueria
Tacoocho 1

13 15500 SOUTH POST OAK
Taqueria
Tacoocho 2

14 16950 SOUTH POST OAK
Esperanza Pollos
Asados Al Carbon

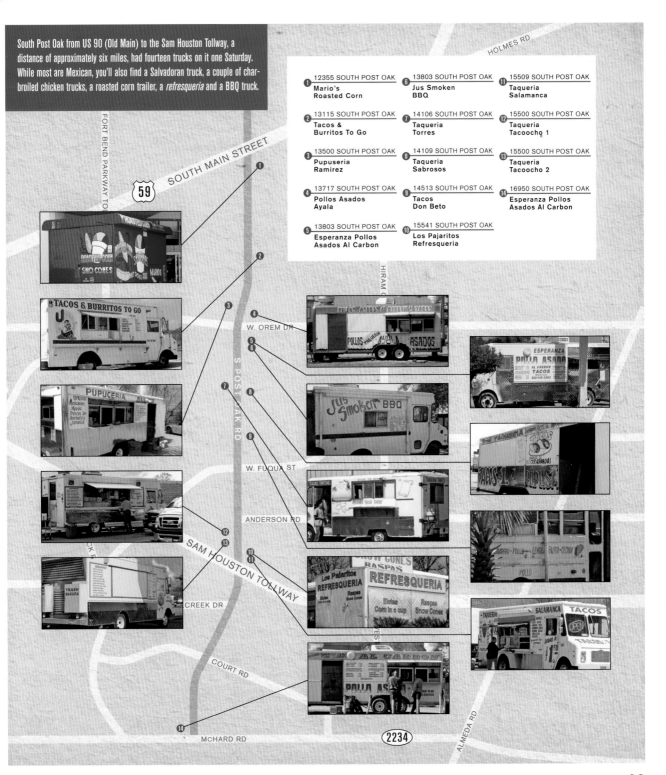

The Saturday I drove Veterans Memorial Drive from I-45 to FM 1960, where it turns into Stuebner Airline, a distance of about fourteen miles, I documented fourteen trucks, all of them Mexican, except for one Indian truck. Note El Grand Taco and Tacos Los Gemelos which, at first, appear to be restaurants with solid structures, and not mobile food units. Careful inspection reveals that a mobile unit is at the heart of the structure, around which a semi-permanent building has been constructed.

1. 13200 VETERANS MEMORIAL
Pollos Asados
El Norteño

2. 13205 VETERANS MEMORIAL
Taqueria
El Paisa

3. 12672 VETERANS MEMORIAL
Desi Grill

4. 12251 VETERANS MEMORIAL
Tacos Mayra

5. 11602 VETERANS MEMORIAL
Loz Locoz
Tacos

6. 11242 VETERANS MEMORIAL
Taquerias
Mi Jalisco

7. 10615 VETERANS MEMORIAL
El Taco
Regio

8. 10465 VETERANS MEMORIAL
Tacos
Los Gemelos

9. 10301 VETERANS MEMORIAL
El Grand
Taco

10. 10201 VETERANS MEMORIAL
Pollos Asados
Los Dos Huazteca

11. 10102 VETERANS MEMORIAL
Kike Tacos
Mexico D.F.

12. 10100 VETERANS MEMORIAL
Pollos Asados
Monterrey

13. 10096 VETERANS MEMORIAL
Taqueria
El Chilango

14. 8800 VETERANS MEMORIAL
Taqueria
Chuy 2

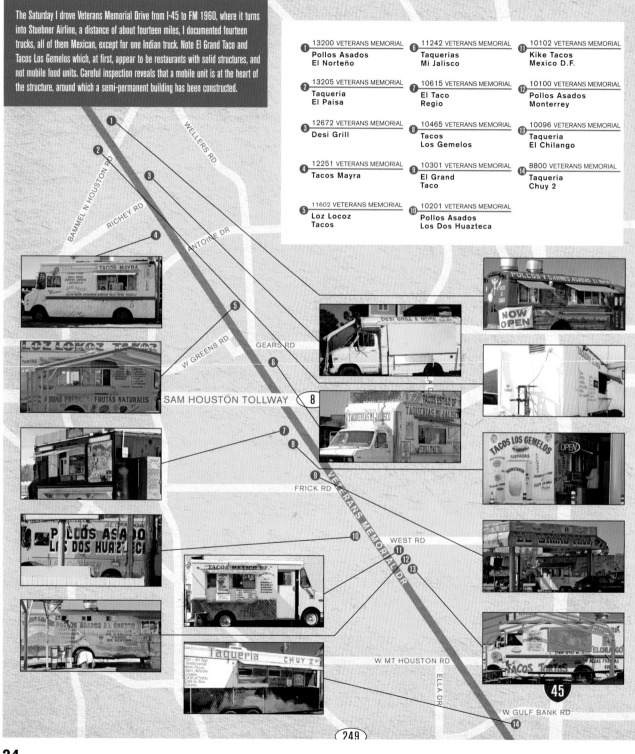

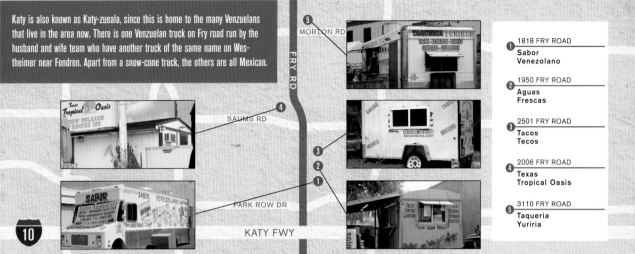

Katy is also known as Katy-zueala, since this is home to the many Venzuelans that live in the area now. There is one Venzuelan truck on Fry road run by the husband and wife team who have another truck of the same name on Westheimer near Fondren. Apart from a snow-cone truck, the others are all Mexican.

❶ 1818 FRY ROAD
Sabor Venezolano

❷ 1950 FRY ROAD
Aguas Frescas

❸ 2501 FRY ROAD
Tacos Tecos

❹ 2006 FRY ROAD
Texas Tropical Oasis

❺ 3110 FRY ROAD
Taqueria Yuriria

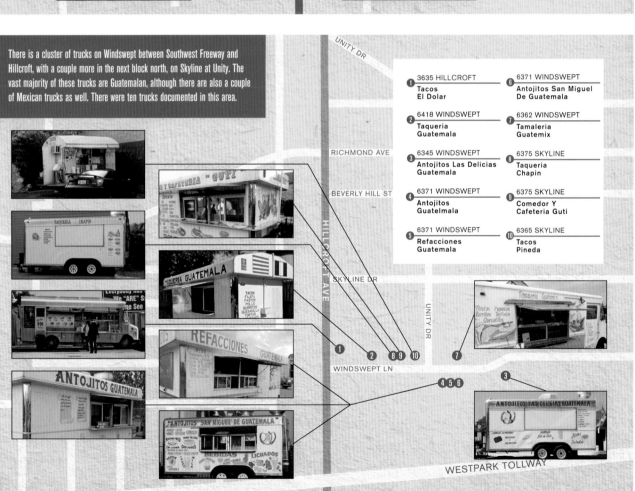

There is a cluster of trucks on Windswept between Southwest Freeway and Hillcroft, with a couple more in the next block north, on Skyline at Unity. The vast majority of these trucks are Guatemalan, although there are also a couple of Mexican trucks as well. There were ten trucks documented in this area.

❶ 3635 HILLCROFT
Tacos El Dolar

❷ 6418 WINDSWEPT
Taqueria Guatemala

❸ 6345 WINDSWEPT
Antojitos Las Delicias Guatemala

❹ 6371 WINDSWEPT
Antojitos Guatelmala

❺ 6371 WINDSWEPT
Refacciones Guatemala

❻ 6371 WINDSWEPT
Antojitos San Miguel De Guatemala

❼ 6362 WINDSWEPT
Tamaleria Guatemix

❽ 6375 SKYLINE
Taqueria Chapin

❾ 6375 SKYLINE
Comedor Y Cafeteria Guti

❿ 6365 SKYLINE
Tacos Pineda

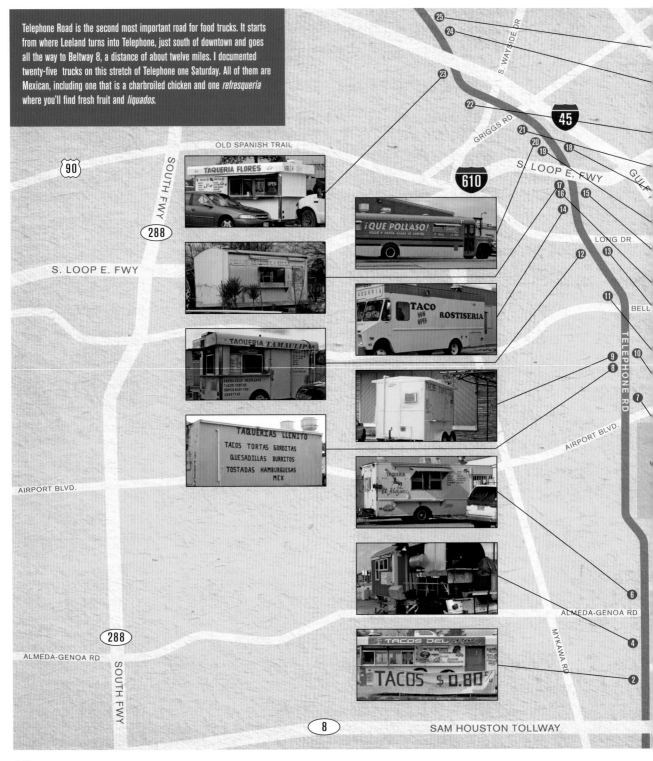

Telephone Road is the second most important road for food trucks. It starts from where Leeland turns into Telephone, just south of downtown and goes all the way to Beltway 8, a distance of about twelve miles. I documented twenty-five trucks on this stretch of Telephone one Saturday. All of them are Mexican, including one that is a charbroiled chicken and one *refresqueria* where you'll find fresh fruit and *liquados*.

LA PORTE FWY

22

OBBY
T

NOA RD

EDA-GENO
QUA ST

FREEWAY

45

SAM HOUSTON TOLLWAY

13 5603 TELEPHONE
Taqueria
Las Palmitas

12 5604 TELEPHONE
Taqueria
Tamaulipas

11 6300 TELEPHONE
Machado's
Roasted Corn

10 6719 TELEPHONE
Taqueria
Diana

9 6762 TELEPHONE
Tacos
Juanitos

8 6766 TELEPHONE
Tacos
Llenitos

7 6915 TELEPHONE
Tacos
D'Mundo

6 9708 TELEPHONE
Taqueria
El Alazan's #2

5 9715 TELEPHONE
La Unica
Refresqueria

4 10310 TELEPHONE
Tacos
Al Carbon

3 10505 TELEPHONE
Taqueria
La Silla

2 10744 TELEPHONE
Tacos
Del Max

1 10855 TELEPHONE
Taqueria
El Alazan

25 1001 TELEPHONE
Taqueria El Rey
Del Tacorriendo #5

24 1721 TELEPHONE
Pollos Asados
El Volcan

23 2680 TELEPHONE
Taqueria
Flores

22 3102 TELEPHONE
Taqueria El Rey
Del Tacorriendo #4

21 3711 TELEPHONE
Taqueria
La Huasteca

20 4002 TELEPHONE
Que
Pollaso

19 4302 TELEPHONE
Tacos Y Tortas
Tampico

18 4341 TELEPHONE
Taqueria El Sol
De Monterrey

17 4676 TELEPHONE
Pollos
Asados La Silla

16 4676 TELEPHONE
Tacos
La Silla

15 4705 TELEPHONE
Pollos Asados
Al Carbon La Silla

14 5010 TELEPHONE
Tacos
Rosticeria

The six miles of Highway Six, between Bissonnet and Westheimer has twelve trucks on it, with 6 in the parking lot of the Mercado 6 Flea Market, alone. While most are Mexican, you'll also find a Chicago hot dog truck, a BBQ trailer, a roasted corn trailer, two snow cone trucks and a Venezuelan truck. This wins the prize for the most diversity

1 4010 HIGHWAY 6
Taqueria
Basabe

2 4955 HIGHWAY 6
Taqueria
El Ranchero

3 4955 HIGHWAY 6
BB's Beef
and Hot Dog

4 7355 HIGHWAY 6
Elotes
Asados

5 7355 HIGHWAY 6
Taqueria
El Jarochito #1

6 7355 HIGHWAY 6
Taqueria
El Jarochito #2

7 7355 HIGHWAY 6
Kona-Ice

8 7355 HIGHWAY 6
Main
Kitchen

9 7821 HIGHWAY 6
Tandoori
Nite Dhaba

10 8402 HIGHWAY 6
El Punto
Criollo

11 8720 HIGHWAY 6
Big 6
BBQ

12 9449 ALDINE-WESTFIELD
Yum-Yum
Sno Balls

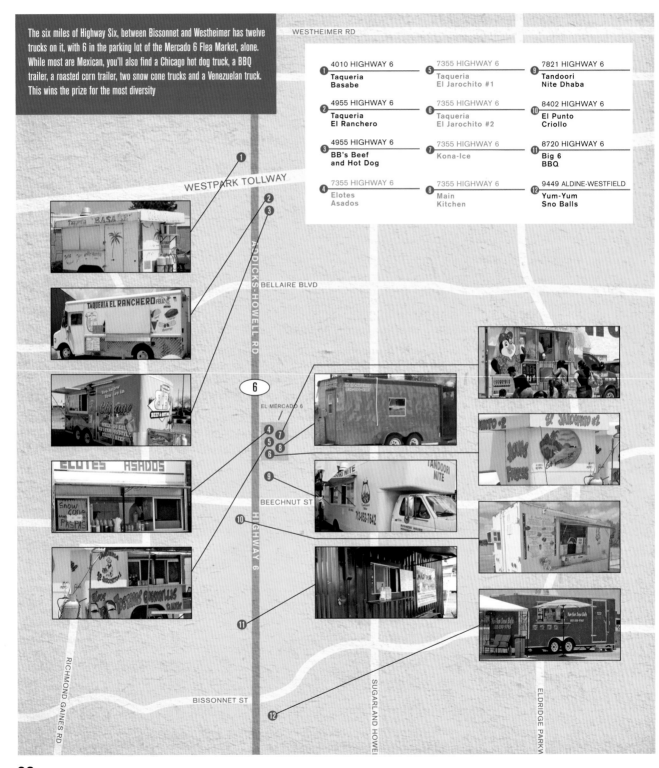

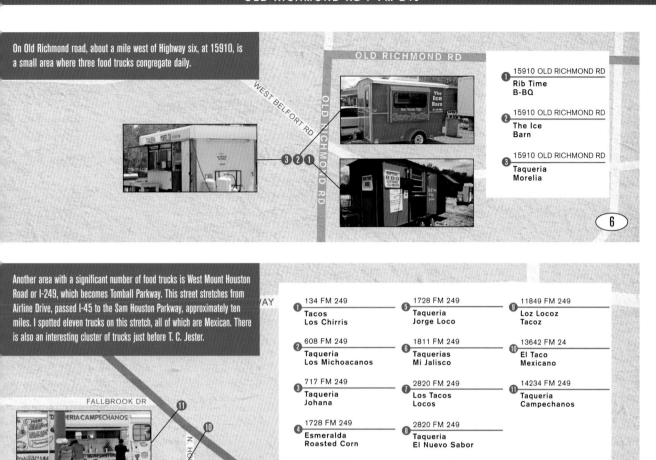

On Old Richmond road, about a mile west of Highway six, at 15910, is a small area where three food trucks congregate daily.

1 15910 OLD RICHMOND RD
Rib Time
B-BQ

2 15910 OLD RICHMOND RD
The Ice
Barn

3 15910 OLD RICHMOND RD
Taqueria
Morelia

6

Another area with a significant number of food trucks is West Mount Houston Road or I-249, which becomes Tomball Parkway. This street stretches from Airline Drive, passed I-45 to the Sam Houston Parkway, approximately ten miles. I spotted eleven trucks on this stretch, all of which are Mexican. There is also an interesting cluster of trucks just before T. C. Jester.

1 134 FM 249
Tacos
Los Chirris

2 608 FM 249
Taqueria
Los Michoacanos

3 717 FM 249
Taqueria
Johana

4 1728 FM 249
Esmeralda
Roasted Corn

5 1728 FM 249
Taqueria
Jorge Loco

6 1811 FM 249
Taquerias
Mi Jalisco

7 2820 FM 249
Los Tacos
Locos

8 2820 FM 249
Taqueria
El Nuevo Sabor

9 11849 FM 249
Loz Locoz
Tacoz

10 13642 FM 24
El Taco
Mexicano

11 14234 FM 249
Taqueria
Campechanos

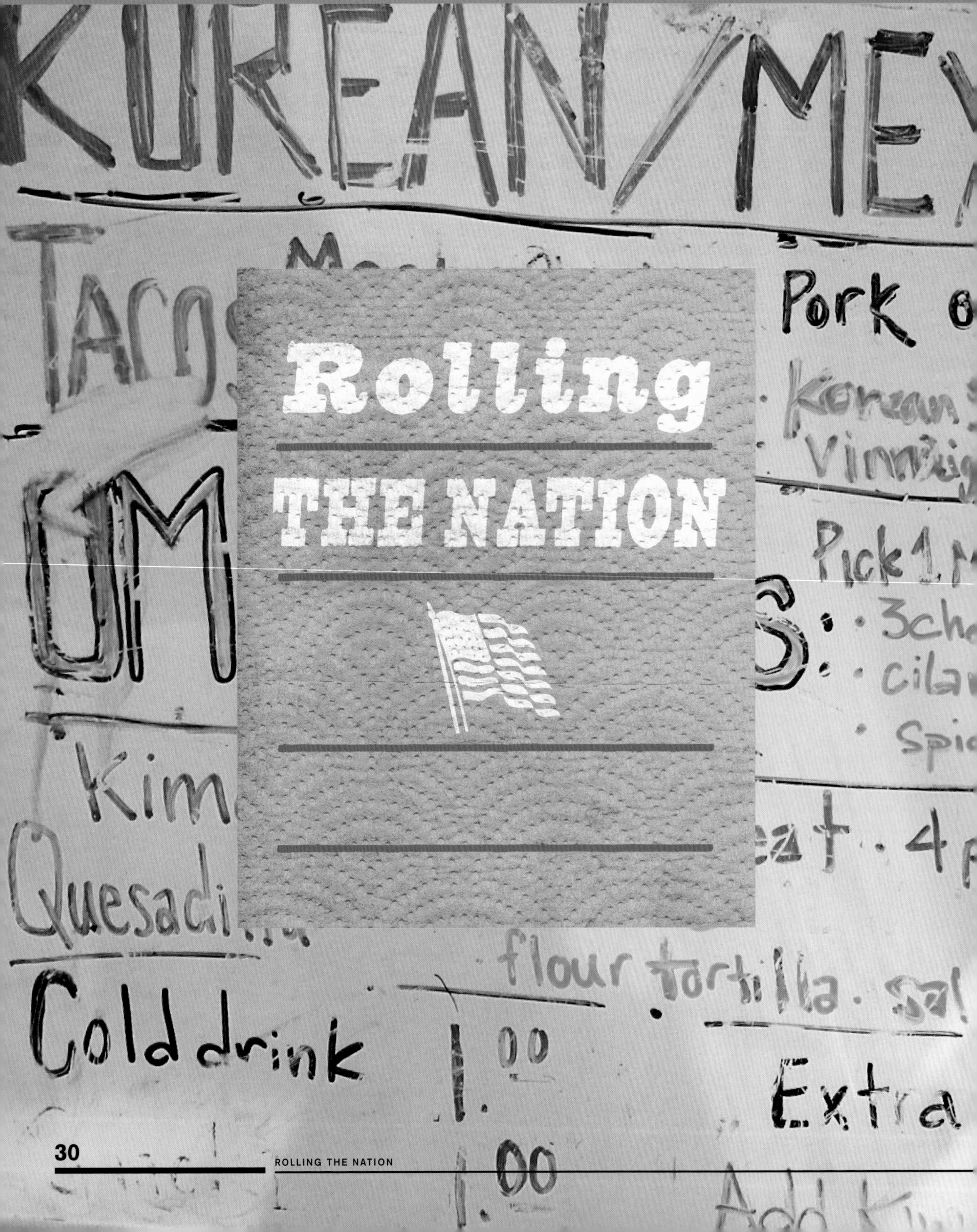

Rolling

THE NATION

Food trucks, street food, street eats, street grub, road food, mobile food units, mobile food trailers, mobile eateries, kitchens on wheels — whatever you call them, they're sweeping the nation.

The modern mobile food movement was born in Los Angeles, in November 2008, when Roy Choi opened his first Kogi Korean BBQ truck.

His business model was both pure genius and simplicity itself: the combination of fun, ambitious food with Twitter® and a truck. In Kogi's first year of operation, Choi racked up sales revenue of $2 million — without the cost of a brick-and-mortar restaurant. These days, he operates five Kogi trucks and has more than 100,000 Twitter followers and has branched out into two brick and mortar restaurants as well.

That kind of success begged to be imitated. First in L.A. and Manhattan, then all across the country, entrepreneurs took to the road to sell a dizzying array of food: *Crêpes*, cupcakes, *sushi, dim sum, dosas, tapas, schnitzel*.

Photo: Eric Shin

Even regular, land-based restaurants jumped into the game, using food trucks to extend their brands.

I estimate that between 20,000 and 30,000 food trucks roll regularly in the U.S. Nancy Kruse, President of

the Kruse Company and one of the foodservice industry's most-quoted analysts, believes that the American food truck industry now does $5 billion a year in business — almost 1 percent of the total foodservice industry sales, and growing fast. Food trucks, she says, are becoming "the little segment that could."

Technomic, a food-service consulting firm, found that in 2009, 13 percent of the U.S. population had visited a mobile food unit in the previous six months. That's about one in eight of us — an impressive figure. But when the same survey was conducted less than a year later, the percentage had doubled to 26 percent — an incredible rate of growth in any business. And there seems to be plenty of room to grow still more: A survey by the National Restaurant Association found that 47 percent of consumers say they'd be willing to patronize food trucks if their favorite restaurants opened them.

Kevin Higar, Technomic's Director of Research and Consulting, has a sweet job: He travels around the country examining trends in the food business. "Two kinds of groups are getting into food trucks," he told me. "For the millennials as well as some Gen X-ers, this is a great way for them to express themselves. Then there are those who are older and choosing a second career. They want to be their own boss."

Choi racked up sales revenue of $2 million — without the cost of a brick-and-mortar restaurant. These days, he operates five Kogi trucks and has more than 100,000 Twitter® followers and has branched out into two brick and mortar restaurants as well.

A number of cities, he notes, have burgeoning mobile food scenes. Austin "is very hip with its trailer parks" where food trucks congregate. Washington, D.C., Spokane and Seattle are strongholds. Orange County is still going strong, as is New York — though in New York, a limit on the total number of trucks is cramping growth.

Hudson Riehle, the Senior Vice President of Research for the National Restaurant Association, notes that "these days, consumers love convenience and aren't particularly tied to restaurants with waiters, tables and chairs. Two thirds of all restaurant traffic is what we call 'off-premises,'" he notes — meaning takeout, delivery, drive-through, curbside and mobile. In other words, two-thirds of all restaurant food is now eaten *outside* of restaurants.

"Convenience is the most important factor for today's consumer", Riehle notes, and the mobile food revolution both adds points of access and provides quick meal solutions for consumers. "We're seeing the trend in food trucks, from the chef-entrepreneur to the multi-unit national chains that are getting into mobile," he says.

He also cites figures from the Bureau of Labor Statistics: "From the third quarter of 2009 to the third quarter of 2010, mobile locations grew 6.7 percent — compared to 1.5 percent for other eating and drinking locations".

than a trend. "Consumer demand for food from food trucks is so high," he says, "that what's going on is a permanent industry awakening."

And finally, as a sign that food trucks have become ubiquitous, Costco now sells a box of Korean Street Tacos. The same food that is spurned by some when available on the side of the road is validated by being sold at a mainstream retailer. Street tacos are now chic.

"That trend is here to stay", says Kevin Higar. Food trucks "are where the consumers are, and they're interacting with consumers' lifestyles." And consumers, he says, "definitely feel that the dollars they spend at a food truck are appreciated."

And finally, as a sign that food trucks have become ubiquitous, Costco now sells a box of Korean Street Tacos.

Other experts agree. "It is a virtually unstoppable trend," said Suzy Badaracco, President of Culinary Tides, a trend-spotting company. "The consumer force behind this trend is very strong. It is very well supported by all kinds of consumers and is becoming ingrained in the fabric of society", she added.

Ray Villaman, President of Mobi Munch, Inc., sees food trucks as more

Food Truck
HISTORY

Mobile food has been around as long as human beings have moved from place to place. And certainly, the concept isn't new in Texas. In fact, two Texans, Charles Goodnight and Oliver Loving invented the chuck wagon in 1866. So important was the chuck wagon to Texas that in 2005, it was designated the official state vehicle of Texas.

In 1866, Goodnight embarked on a cattle drive, moving 2,000 longhorns, from Texas to what is now New Mexico. It was a journey which would take eight weeks. In order to provide provisions for his cowboys he modified an army surplus wagon known as a Studebaker. This became known as a chuck wagon after the slang term the cowboys called the food that was served from them.

THE CHUCK WAGON — THE COWBOYS KITCHEN

The caption on the back of this linen postcard, published by I.I.C., El Paso, Texas, circa 1930, says, "This kitchen-on-a-wagon follows the round-up and served plenty of frijoles, meat and potatoes before it gets back to the home ranch."

Tamales were one of the original street foods. In Los Angeles and in Texas, in the 1870s through the 1890s, *tamaleros* sold them on the street from horse drawn wagons, trolleys and push carts. At first, they were almost always made elsewhere and merely kept warm on the wagons. This, in turn, led to their being made on portable kitchens right there on the street. In cities like New York in the 1890s, night workers were often met by night lunch wagons known as Night Owls. During the 1890's, the first hot dog carts also took to the streets in major cities. Known as Dog Wagons, they were made of wood and heated by kerosene. Lunch wagons were the predecessors of the American Diner.

By the 1920s, *tamales* had been joined by other Mexican specialties such as *tacos, menudo* and *barbacoa*. Horse drawn wagons soon gave way to motorized transportation.

In 1920, Harry Burt of Youngtown, Ohio, invented the "Good Humor Bar". It was the first chocolate-covered ice cream bar on a stick. He sold them from a fleet of twelve trucks equipped with freezers.

Horse-pulled mobile canteens, or field kitchens, fed the troops in World War I. By World War II, they had become Canteen Trucks. Mobile Canteens, (AKA Mobile Kitchen Trailers, or MKTs, as many people know them) date back to the 1950s.

Good Humor Ice Cream started in 1920 in Youngstown, Ohio.   Photo courtesy Unilever

In 1920, Harry Burt of Youngtown, Ohio, invented the "Good Humor Bar". It was the first chocolate-covered ice cream bar on a stick. He sold them from a fleet of twelve trucks equipped with freezers.

In the 1950s, ice cream trucks were gaining favor, and food carts could be found at any amusement parks. And at least since the 1970s, we've had lunch wagons, *loncheras* or *loncherias*, serving the needs of construction workers at work sites. The word *lonchera* comes from the Spanglish word *lonche*, meaning lunch or any food brought from home.

In his book, <u>Taco USA</u> (Scribner, 2012), Gustavo Arellano identifies the earliest *taco* truck in the U.S. as Taco

Tico. It was run by two New York housewives in the Riverdale neighborhood of the Bronx in 1966. The earliest *taco* truck operating in Los Angeles was King Taco, which dates to 1974.

Plenty of those old-style *taco* trucks and BBQ trailers still roll Houston's streets. But these days, there's a distinctly different new generation — one that's worldly, upscale and tech-savvy. Some trucks are owned by chefs who use websites and social media to let their fans know their every move. Houston even has a site that lets you keep up with many such "Twitter trucks" with a single click: www.houstonfoodtrucks.com.

These days, in Houston, you're as likely to find a "*tikka* truck" serving Indian cuisine or a burger bus serving a great hamburger, as you are a coach serving cupcakes, a wagon serving wieners or a taco truck serving tripe *tacos*. There is another big difference in today's mobile food trucks and that is that many of the new ones have gone gourmet. In the words of Paul Lukas, who reviewed for the Wall Street Journal the book, <u>FOOD TRUCKS</u>, by Heather Shouse,

In the 1950s, ice cream trucks were gaining favor, and food carts could be found at any amusement parks.

"street food has become gentrified." Professionally-trained chefs now own many of the new units hitting Houston streets.

The prolonged economic recession that began in 2008 meant it was

harder to get credit and probably more feasible to start out small, especially if you were a new operator. For someone starting out in the hospitality industry, a food truck is an excellent way to get your feet wet while learning the trade and is not as daunting as opening a full-scale restaurant. Many of the owners of today's new trucks are young and entrepreneurial and may not be given the opportunity

Photo courtesy Unilever

they need by established operators to show what they can do, so the only way to start out is by doing it themselves. From the customer's standpoint, the economy also caused people to have to stretch their food dollars a whole lot more and since eating from a food truck is gener-

ally less expensive than eating at a sit-down restaurant and even eating fast-food, consumers were looking for ways to eat well yet inexpensively. At another level, the explosion of social media meant that owners of food trucks could stay close to their customers and could tweet their locations and specials at any time of the day or night. Lastly, we've become a nation of foodies and our culinary demands and curiosity are constantly increasing and we're always looking for something new and different to try. And what better way to try a new dish or cuisine than at a food truck?

One day, as I was driving north on Yale around Twelfth Street, I spotted this modern-day reproduction of a stagecoach. It turns out that these hand-built stagecoaches are imported from Mexico. This one can be yours for a mere $7,000. It is set up with gas burners and electrical wiring and would be terrific at a BBQ cook off. I would be concerned about cooking in it since it is all made of wood. It would also need to be transported to its location on some sort of trailer. Still, if drawn by some magnificent horses, wouldn't it be the ultimate Texas food truck?

EVERY KIND Of Food. EVERY KIND Of Vehicle.

BBQ PITS BY KLOSE

Dave Klose will make you a BBQ pit in any configuration you want. He is always looking for a new challenge but hasn't found one that he can't turn into a BBQ pit.

This is a BBQ pit made by BBQ Pits by Klose, right here in Houston. It was made for Continental Airlines and is a 1 to 10 scale model of a Continental 777 wide body jet. It is 30 feet long and weighs 38,000 pounds. The smoke stack is in the tail.

In 1991, Dave Klose built the World's Largest Mobile BBQ Pit. It weighed 34,350 pounds and had a capacity of 6,000 pounds of meat and was capable of feeding 12,000 people. It was 48 feet long and 60 inches in diameter. Klose builds his pits by hand, utilizing thick metal so that they retain the heat. This monster will cook for 24 hours on only ¼ cord of wood. The red smoke stack at the front is 35 feet tall.

Klose built this BBQ pit along with Orange County Chopper. Here, the smoker is in the side car.

Dave Klose will make you a BBQ pit in any configuration you want. He is always looking for a new challenge but hasn't found one that he can't turn into a BBQ pit.

These days, an astounding variety of wheeled contraptions sell an astounding variety of food. There are tiny, human-powered push carts, hot dog carts and bicycle carts; there are full-size school buses converted to "bustaurants"; there are 53-feet, 18-wheel tractor-trailers. And there's just about everything in between.

This 'smokehouse' used to be on Reed Road but has since moved to an undisclosed location.

Pushcarts selling *paletas* (popsicles) are very popular in Hispanic neighborhoods.

Modern-day ice cream carts were on display at the National Restaurant Show. The show, in Chicago's McCormick Center, occurs every year in May.

Bicycle carts selling snacks and fruit drinks are also popular in Hispanic neighborhoods.

NATIONAL RESTAURANT ASSOCIATION'S ANNUAL SHOW

The 2011 NRA show expanded the focus on food trucks devoting three educational seminars specifically to food trucks.

In 2010, for the first time, the National Restaurant Association's annual show in Chicago devoted a pavilion to food trucks. They not only showcased two trucks — Street-Za Pizza, which roams the streets of Milwaukee, and the Ludo Bites truck from Chef Ludovic Lefebvre in Los Angeles — but also featured companies that fabricate trucks and others that specialize in graphic wraps, point-of-sales systems and so on. Restaurateurs ate it all up: The 2011 NRA show expanded the focus on food trucks, featuring those same two trucks plus half a dozen more, and devoting three educational seminars specifically to food trucks.

This terrific-looking BBQ trailer can be found off Jensen at the 610 Loop, however, every time I visited it, it was never open.

Pink Logan, of Logan Farms Honey Ham, parks this truck outside his store at 10560 Westheimer.

Locally, Amy's Ice Cream caters ice cream parties out of its truck.

A Houston Chick Fil-A franchisee also deploys a catering truck.

Photo: Tavistock Freebird's, LLC.

Photo: Tavistock Freebird's, LLC.

The Austin-based chain Freebirds gives a peace-love-and-*burritos* vibe with its hippie-ish VW bus. The chain's trailer, which it uses for a rock-and-roll tour, has a harder edge.

THE HEB GROCERY CHAIN

HEB runs two food trucks. One is called Fork in the Road and operates out of the parking lot of the new Montrose Market.

The HEB grocery chain uses trailers as sampling vehicles for new store openings.

Their HEB Cola trailer is in the shape of a cola can, complete with pull top.

The new HEB Montrose Market on Alabama at Dunlavy hosts Food Truck Fridays once a month where up to eight trucks serve food. In addition, HEB also runs two food trucks. The first is called Fork in the Road and operates out of this location. They serve such goodies as gourmet burgers, andouille poboys, truffle fries, chili and pulled pork sandwiches.

The second truck is their Central Market food truck which operates out of the parking lot of the Central Market on Westheimer. It is known as the Roadie and the offerings are more upscale (as befits the Central Market clientele) and include such items as a Thai curry-braised pork sandwich, Ancho-braised beef short ribs and a veggie wrap made with *vindaloo*-roasted vegetables with curry yogurt.

BERRYHILL BAJA GRILL

It's certainly a step up from the cart used by Walter Berryhill when he first started selling his tamales in 1928.

Houston-based Berryhill Baja Grill, home of the Original Fish Taco, has a food truck that hit the road in the summer of 2012, which they call the "Bad Boy".

It's certainly a step up from the cart used by Walter Berryhill when he first started selling his tamales in 1928. The cart can still be found on Westheimer at Revere.

The Tailgaiting Sports Grille on FM 1960, took an old bus and cut half of it away and turned it into a stage.

Pusser's, the single malt rum made in the British Virgin islands, dispatches two trucks to boating venues around the U.S.

Jack in the Box™ recently launched its Munchie Mobile.

The Holmes Smokehouse sausage trailer attended the opening of a Whole Foods store in Houston.

Dairy Queen's Blizzard Mobile toured the U.S. in 2010, in celebration of the Blizzard's 25th anniversary. The truck was decommissioned shortly thereafter.

At grocery stores in Los Angeles, the Tostitos brand handed out samples and easy-to-make recipes during *Cinco de Mayo*.

DOS EQUIS-SPONSORED TRUCK "FEAST OF THE BRAVE".

The idea was to find some of the wildest things to put on a *taco*, then see who was brave enough to eat it.

A Dos Equis-sponsored truck roamed the streets of New York and other cities for *Cinco de Mayo* in 2011. Calling itself "Feast of the Brave," the truck served *tacos* filled with tongue, ostrich, veal brain and crickets.

In May, 2012, Dos Equis® came to Houston. They did a special promotion to celebrate the 150th anniversary of *Cinco de Mayo*, taking the H-town strEATs food truck and completely wrapping it with their "Feast of the Brave" theme.

Photo: Dos Equis. (Cuauhtémoc-Moctezuma Brewery)

The idea was to find some of the wildest things to put on a *taco*, then see who was brave enough to eat it. Leave it to two of Houston's most creative chefs to do just that. The

Photo: Dos Equis. (Cuauhtémoc-Moctezuma Brewery)

idea, which was tested in New York last year, rolled out to six cities in 2012: Houston, Austin, Dallas, Miami, Chicago and Los Angeles. Each city competed for bragging rights to see which city was the 'bravest'. The brave part comes in the form of the free mini *tacos* being served. Jason

Hill and Matt Opaleski of H-town strEATs came up with some terrific recipes highlighting four *tacos* you are unlikely to find anywhere else. You got to choose one of the following tacos: alligator, shark, crickets or the 'mystery' *taco*, which turned out to be scorpion. Each one had a different level of "bravery points" associated with it, with 10 for the entry level gator (yes, it tastes like chicken) .

"We wanted to give people a really interesting experience by bringing the food truck to the next level and have people try something they've never tried before", said Ryan Thompson, Brand Manager for Dos Equis. That they did.

Photo: Dos Equis. (Cuauhtémoc-Moctezuma Brewery)

Photo: Dos Equis. (Cuauhtémoc-Moctezuma Brewery)

Photo: Dos Equis. (Cuauhtémoc-Moctezuma Brewery)

Photo: Dos Equis. (Cuauhtémoc-Moctezuma Brewery)

Photo: Wienerschnitzel

Photo: Taco Bell Corp.

Wienerschnitzel has its own Wiener Wagon.

Taco Bell's truck also toured the U.S., handing out free items.

Photo: Pizza Hut, Inc.

Photo: Johnny Rockets

Pizza Hut just launched a 53-foot, 18-wheel tractor-trailer.

The Johnny Rockets chain operates a truck in Washington, D.C.

Photo: California Pizza Kitchen

Photo: Ben & Jerry's Homemade, Inc.

California Pizza Kitchen has a trailer in Los Angeles.

National chains dispatch mobile units too — including this one from Ben & Jerry's.

Photo: QIP Holder LLC

Community Coffee uses a trailer for special events.

Quizno's has a trailer.

JOHNSONVILLE BRATS' BIG TASTE GRILL

It is 65 feet long and weighs 53,000 pounds, and can knock out 2,500 brats per hour.

Johnsonville Brats' Big Taste Grill bills itself as the "World's Largest Grill, Period." Introduced in 1995, it is 65 feet long and weighs 53,000 pounds, and can knock out 2,500 brats per hour.

Hungry, anyone? The proceeds from the sales of their sausages go to charities.

Photo: Johnsonville Foods

CONNECTICUT PUBLIC SCHOOL

A solution to feed underprivileged kids for a free lunch during the summer holidays.

This food truck is the brainchild of Chef Tim Cipriano, Executive Director of Food Services for the New Haven, Connecticut Public School system. He came up with a solution to feed underprivileged kids that cannot get to a school for a free lunch during the summer holidays. Tim decided to bring the food to the kids via a food truck. During July and August he plans on serving 40,000 lunches.

Photo: Tim Cipriano

EVERY KIND OF FOOD. EVERY KIND OF VEHICLE

Burger chains Carl's Jr. and Hardee's also operate trucks.

The Arby's truck stopped in Houston to celebrate the grand opening of a new Pearland location.

A Houston Tasti D-Lite franchisee sells soft-serve cones out of this truck.

The Sprinkles Cupcakes chain has a cupcake mobile.

Austin-based Deep Eddy uses an old VW bus to promote its brand of sweet tea vodka.

The theme of Heinz Ketchup's summer road trip? "Dip, squeeze and go."

MACY'S "CHEFS A-GO-GO" TOUR
Donations go to Feeding America, the nation's largest domestic hunger-relief organization.

Macy's, the department store, operates a food truck that also donates money to charity. In the summer of 2011, it launched its "Chefs A-Go-Go" tour across the nation. Chefs including Cat Cora, Todd English, Marcus Samuelsson and Rick Bayless, all members of Macy's Culinary Council, cooked up side dishes to accompany burgers. (Unfortunately, Houston is not one of the scheduled stops.) While the food is free, voluntary donations go to Feeding America, the nation's largest domestic hunger-relief organization.

Photo: Macy's, Inc

KRISPY KREME "GLAZE THE NATION" TOUR
Krispy Kreme Doughnuts celebrated their 75th anniversary.

In 2012, Krispy Kreme Doughnuts celebrated their 75th anniversary. In order to mark this occasion, they completely restored a 1960 Flexible Starliner bus and rolled across the U.S. on their "Glaze the Nation" tour, covering 40 states and 50,000 miles.

Photo: Krispy Kreme doughnuts

EVERY KIND OF FOOD. EVERY KIND OF VEHICLE

Taco Cabana's trailer, normally kept in San Antonio, visits Houston for special events such as the annual Theater District's Open House.

In Portland, the Vancouver, Washington-based Burgerville chain recently debuted its Nomad truck.

The southern California chain Border Grill is the brainchild of chefs Mary Sue Milliken and Susan Feniger, of Food Network's *Too Hot Tamales*. They recently added a food truck to their line-up.

Founder Wing Lam in front of his California-based Wahoo Fish Tacos food truck.

Annie's Pizza brought a truck and trailer, which is touring the country on a 'Slice of Heaven Tour', a Whole Foods Market in Houston. In the bed of the truck, which they call their 'truck farm', they have a live garden, growing veggies like the ones on their pizza

THE SEINFELD "NO SOUP FOR YOU!" FOOD TRUCK.

This food truck toured eight cities across the nation serving such Soup Nazi classics as Mulligatawny Soup.

During the summer of 2012, the Seinfeld "No Soup For You!" food truck toured eight cities across the nation serving such Soup Nazi classics as Mulligatawny Soup, Junior Mints, muffin tops, black and white cookies, Twix™ and Snapple™.

DOGGIE ICE CREAM AT K99 AND THE HMS FLAKE 99.

In London, you'll find the world's first ice cream truck for dogs and the world's first amphibious ice cream van.

In London, the pet-crazy British get to treat their canine companions to doggie ice cream at K99, which promotes itself as "the world's first ice cream truck for dogs." It plays the theme tune to *Scooby-Doo* and serves such canine creations as Canine Cookie Crunch and Dog Eat Hog World.

Fortunately, Houston has its own version of these canine cones with the Snow Dog Ice Cream Truck. Snow Dog caters kids' birthday

parties, serving ice cream to the kids and homemade organic yogurt, honey and peanut butter treats to their canine guests.

Shannon Holliday and Miles of the Snow Dog Ice Cream Truck. Footnote: Sad to say but in the course of writing this book, Miles passed away. He will be missed.

Many grocery-store brands, including Pepsi™ and Oscar Mayer, use mobile units to promote their offerings.

This new Oscar Mayer™ Wienermobile launched on Memorial Day weekend in 2011 to celebrate the 75th anniversary of the Wienermobile.

The original Oscar Mayer™ Wienermobile was introduced in 1936.

The Hershey's™ Kissmobile appears at events and parades.

Planters™ says that its Nutmobile "is inspired by how peanuts naturally give back to the earth." It runs on biodiesel, and has solar panels and a wind turbine on the roof.

For its traveling taco truck, Familia Camarena Tequila hires local chefs in each city, asking that they prepare dishes with Camarena™ as an ingredient

Purina's Chef Michael's brand of dog food opened a food truck just for dogs in Boston to launch a new line of products. If you visit their Facebook page, you can sign a "PAW-tition" to show support for doggie trucks.

Ruiz Foods has a truck to promote its NASCAR sponsorship and its Tornados™ brand of snacks.

Pepperidge Farm has a Goldfish™ mobile.

THE VERTS KEBAP TRUCK

Austin, Texas has the world's smallest food truck in the form of a Smart™car serving a Turkish specialty found all over Germany.

Austin, Texas has the world's smallest food truck in the form of a Smart™ car. Launched towards the end of 2011, two young German entrepreneurs, Michael Heyne and Dominek Stein, launched the *Verts Kebap* truck because they missed this specialty, which is found all over Germany. Known to us as a *Donner Kebab*, in Germany it is known as *Doener Kebap*. It was introduced into Germany in the 1960s by the many Turks that were invited there as *Gastarbeiter*, or guest workers. Converted by the German company, Frenzel, the space where the front seat used to be now houses two large batteries which power a refrigerator and food warmer. There are two sinks squeezed in there as well. Food is prepared and served out of the back of the vehicle. While the whole concept of food trucks is mobility, this concept is *über*mobile and can quickly flit around town, stop, set up and start serving in minutes.

THE KOGI BBQ SCION XD MOBILE

MV Designz shop in Santa Ana custom built this for Roy Choy.

The MV Designz shop in Santa Ana custom built this Kogi BBQ Scion xD Mobile for Roy Choy with an aluminum BBQ grill in the trunk with controls behind the license plate, cooking utensils and room for sauces and seasonings in the taillights, a sink in one of the rear-passenger doors and a refrigerator in the other, all remote controlled.

Photo: Toyota Motor Cars USA, Inc.

Delverde™, an Italian manufacturer of premium pasta, launched its food bus, dubbed the Taste of Italy, on the East Coast to broaden its consumer reach. In addition to a professional kitchen, the bus also has a lounge area.

The Great American Cookie Company™ uses a truck at special events.

Mars, the makers of Dove™ ice cream bars, launched a truck in Chicago. Touted as a stress-buster, the truck offered not only free Dove Bars and chocolate, but also massages and manicures.

The Freschetta™ pizza truck accompanied the recent summer tour by pop/R&B singer Natasha Bedingfield. According to consulting company Brand Connections, the truck aimed "to harness the emotional power of music to authentically engage young women, the brand's target consumers."

James Coney Island's™ Coney Cruiser is a beast of a food truck. At thirty four feet long and thirteen high, it is the largest truck in Houston. It is purported to have cost some $300,000. It has a fully-equipped kitchen ready to serve 2000-3000 people per day. Note the walk-up soda fountain.

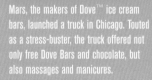

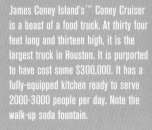

THE FAR-OUT FIVE

Five of the most unusual uses of mobile food units that I came across are from the Singapore Tourism Office, Air France, LinkedIn, DoubleTree hotels and The Gap.

Photo: S.P.I.C.E.

Photo: LinkedIn

Photo: S.P.I.C.E.

Photo: S.P.I.C.E.

The Singapore International Culinary Exchange (S.P.I.C.E.) built transport. containers and sent them around the world to promote Singaporean cuisine. The cities visited included Hong Kong, Shanghai, Moscow, London, Paris, New York, Sydney and Dubai.

The Air France mobile unit visited New York in March 2011 to increase the awareness of gourmet in-flight meal service in their Air France's first-class section. The tasting menu was designed by Joël Robuchon, the well-known chef responsible for the in-flight meals.

Photo: Andrew Federman Photography

Photo: Andrew Federman Photography

In the spring of 2011, LinkedIn used two trucks in New York City and San Francisco to launch LinkedIn Today, a social news product. Dubbed the Mobile News Café, it allowed people to get a taste of LinkedIn Today while sipping locally brewed premium coffee: Martha & Brothers in San Francisco, and Brooklyn Roasting Company in New York.

Gap 1969's four-truck fleet, known as Pico De Gap, was launched in August 2011 to celebrate the launch of Rosella Giuliani's new upscale line of jeans, the

1969 collection. Marcel Vigneron, a former *Top Chef* contestant, developed the menu, which included braised lamb neck with *chile negro* (dried *Pasilla* chile), *guajillo carnitas* (fried chunks of pork made with *guajillo* peppers), shrimp with *pimenton de la vera* (smoked paprika) and spicy tofu. The trucks will make appearances in Los Angeles, New York City, Chicago and the brand's hometown, San Francisco.

Finally, and perhaps the noblest use of a mobile food unit, goes to the Greater Houston Area Red Cross, which uses emergency response vehicles to feed people after an emergency.

Hilton's DoubleTree hotel chain launched its CAREavan on a 50-city tour in the summer of 2011 to celebrate the silver anniversary of their signature chocolate chip cookie. The truck gave away hundreds of thousands of cookies.

FOOD TRUCKS ON TV

These days, you don't just see food trucks on the street. You see them on TV.

On the Food Network's *Great Food Truck Race*, a reality show hosted by Tyler Florence, seven teams compete in a coast-to-coast culinary battle for a fat grand prize.

But *Eat Street*, also on the Food Network, may be more familiar to Houston food-truck fans. It describes itself as a "lip-smacking celebration of North America's tastiest, messiest and most irresistible street food.... Seeking out the very best curbside eats all over North America, *Eat Street* is your grease-stained roadmap to the ultimate street food experience." So far, those ultimate experiences have included Houston's own Fusion Taco (April 20,

2011) and Oh My Pocket Pies (June 22, 2011).

When Eat St. came to Houston the first time a couple of years ago, they were a little underwhelmed. Well, we sure fixed that, because in May 2012, when they returned to shoot another segment for season four, which will begin airing in 2013, they found a lot more trucks to talk about and a vibrant food truck scene. During their visit they filmed The Modular, Phamily Bites, The Waffle Bus, The Rice Box, Stick It and St. John's Fire.

ABC is developing a sitcom, *Family Owned*, in which a son takes over his family's food-truck business. "Food for Thought," a 2011 episode

FOOD TRUCKS ON TV...

Since food trucks are so much a part of the culture in Los Angeles, it's only natural that they figure in new TV sitcoms and movies.

of *CSI:NY*, involved a food truck that exploded right in front of investigator Sheldon Hawkes and his girlfriend; the young chef inside was killed. The ensuing investigation revealed that the truck had been a front for prostitution: Order the #5 Special and pay $500, and you'd get a styrofoam box with a hotel address and room number written inside. There a prostitute would be waiting.

Since food trucks are so much a part of the culture in Los Angeles, it's only natural that they figure in new TV sitcoms and movies. Two movies which opened in the Spring of 2012 feature food trucks in their plots. In *Think Like a Man*, the main male character wins back the girl of his dreams by opening his own food truck. In *The Five- Year Engagement*, another relationship is saved when the main male character buys an old ambulance and turns it into a "Taco-Mergency" food truck, which someone dubbed the 9-1-Yum truck. In the show, *Friends with Benefits*, the main character opens a food

truck called Rock A Roni and finally, in the ABC series, *Happy Endings*, the main male character gets over being dumped by opening a food truck called Steak Me Home Tonight.

The History Channel's Modern Marvels series aired a program devoted to Food Trucks on 11/14/2011.

An even more explicit connection between food trucks and sex came, naturally, in the first porn movie to feature a food truck. *The Flying Pig* starred the real Flying Pig food truck, owned by Joe Kim of Los Angeles. In the movie, the truck's gourmet offerings had aphrodisiacal qualities. It's food porn — with the emphasis on "porn."

DO YOU WANT TO RUN A FOOD TRUCK?

Why does mobile food attract so many would-be chefs and business owners?

In part, because it's cheaper to launch a food truck or cart than to open a brick-and-mortar restaurant: The cost of buying and operating a truck is far lower than most restaurant rents. And staffing costs? Usually, the owner is the staff: the driver, order-taker, chef, server, bus boy, cashier and mechanic all rolled into one.

How much cheaper? Roughly speaking, opening a food truck costs between 10 and 30 percent as much as opening a brick-and-mortar facility. Food truck owners in Houston told me that to get their trucks rolling, they spent anywhere from $20,000 to $300,000.

Trucks, too, are more flexible than brick-and-mortar restaurants. If a truck's concept flops, it's cheap and fast to re-tool. Often it requires nothing more than a new menu and (maybe) a new paint job.

Success, of course, is easy to handle: You can open spin-off trucks or even a brick-and-mortar location. (The thriving Frosted Betty cupcake truck, for instance, gave Nicola Mora and her father, Frederico, the confidence to open Frosted Betty Bake Shop

at 833 Studewood.) Same with the Eatsie Boys.

All that, of course, appeals to people already in the food business. Says Chris Tripoli, of A La Carte Foodservice Consulting Group: "It's an excellent way for a catering company to grow and to build a brand, since they're already used to working multiple units and managing a number of trucks."

But trucks appeal even to established brick-and-mortar restaurants. For instance, Sylvia Casares, owner of Sylvia's Enchiladas restaurants, saw adding a food truck as chance to expand her brand and presence in the market. And no, she doesn't think the Sylvia's truck steals sales from her restaurants: "If I'm going out for dinner, I'm going to be dressed up, so I probably am not going to eat at a food truck."

With so many players already in the game, is the trend played out? Consultant Tripoli doesn't think so — particularly when it comes to Houston. "There are still opportunities to fill needs," he says. "Houston is definitely lagging behind the national trend. We came to this trend later

than other cities, and we're heavily restricted in Houston.

"As for advice I'd give someone thinking about jumping in: First and foremost, have reasonable expectations. Food trucks work for a limited theme and limited product line.... If this is your first, it's very hard to build a new brand when you're going to the same places that other brands (trucks) are already going. Also, watch out for the legality issues. People think that they can drive anywhere, park anywhere at any time and just start selling — not so. You must plan ahead and understand all of the requirements, like getting a landlord's approval to park on his premise or ensuring that your truck is tied to a home base (commissary)."

If opening your own truck sounds appealing, it's easy to start gathering information at the U.S. Small Business Administration website. This page offers tips specifically for budding mobile-eats entrepreneurs: http://community.sba.gov/community/blogs/community-blogs/business-law-advisor/tips-starting-your-own-street-food-business.

DO YOU WANT TO RUN A FOOD TRUCK?...
And of course, you'll need to navigate all the regulations.

You should also check out the two websites that cover the industry. Mobile Cuisine Magazine (mobile-cuisine.com) claims to be "the nation's first magazine covering everything in the mobile food industry."

And Mobile Food News (www.mobilefoodnews.com) styles itself as "The Industry's Source for News and Information."

Want to know even more? Consider the University of Houston Small Business Development Center's class "Mobile Food — First Steps to Success," in which industry experts discuss what it takes to open your own truck.

To test your idea, you might consider a "pop-up" food truck, similar to the pop-up restaurants that open and disappear in as little as thirty days. Chef James Ashley of Pure Catering used The Kitchen Incubator, Lucrece Borego's support system for would-be food entrepreneurs, and found that the New Mexico Chile Company, another Kitchen Incubator client, had a truck that it used only for promotional

purposes. Ashley set up the truck one day, tested his concept, learned everything he could, videotaped it all and moved on. No commitment, low cost — and a great way to test an idea. He later went on to open his Bare Bowls Kitchen food truck, which, in the interest of full disclosure, I have share in.

Would you rather go with a proven concept? Consider running a franchised truck. At the 2011 National Restaurant Association show, Farhad Assari, developer and owner of the Sâuçá truck, which operates in Washington, D.C., was actively seeking franchisees. For a one-time franchise fee of $30,000,

Farhad Assari, and his Sâuçá truck

$75,000 for a fully equipped truck and 6 percent of sales, you can learn from someone else's mistakes and successes (www.saucafranchise.com).

But let's say that you want to outfit your own truck. Where do you start? Busi-

nesses that transform trailers, old trucks or school buses are quickly opening up in the city. At least four businesses in Houston build food trucks. The Rodriguez Brothers Custom Catering Trucks (832 721-7570), Taquerias Mobiles (832 298-9764), Taquerias El Gigante Verde (646 420-4147) and Mobile Partner Group (832 589-4044) are all turning out trucks as fast as they can. Old school buses are readily available in Houston for conversion into food trucks.

And of course, you'll need to navigate all the regulations that apply to your business. Houston, unfortunately, has a tangle of regulations — though it appears likely to join the tide of other cities that have already made city rules food-truck friendly. Why? First the revenues from taxes and fees. Second, and more importantly, consumers (read: voters) want food trucks.

Houston Mayor Annise Parker has appointed a special task force to study and improve current ordinances. Through her media liaison, Parker expressed her support of rolling cuisine:

"Food trucks add to the vibrancy of community and street life in Houston. They provide affordable, unique, inspired food that will add to Houston's already famous brick-and-mortar restaurants and our growing reputation as a food destination."

The Parker-launched City Hall Farmer's Market, on Wednesdays at lunchtime, in front of City Hall, has become a magnet for food trucks.

"As the City Hall Farmers Market (CHFM) grows and becomes more successful, I hope to add additional food trucks. We will either continue to add food trucks on Walker and McKinney Streets, surrounding the CHFM, or we may open up part of the library courtyard for food trucks, across the street from the CHFM, and create a mini-food truck court. Food trucks are one of the many reasons for the instant success of the CHFM."

The nitty-gritty, says Parker, is the city's responsibility to ensure that food trucks operate safely.

"I have asked my Sustainability Director to convene a Mobile Food Unit Stakeholder Committee made up of pertinent city departments (Fire, Health, etc.), the Restaurant Association, food truck owners, the Downtown Association and other interested parties.

"The Stakeholder Committee has been working for a few months to delineate the issues that make it difficult for food trucks to be more prolific in Houston and come up with a set of recommendations for me to review. Once I am comfortable with the changes, I will work with City Council on making the necessary code and ordinance changes. While we want to expand and grow the food truck culture in Houston, we also want to ensure they meet all safety standards and provide high-quality food for Houstonians. Health

and safety are key concerns. I believe we can expand the street food culture, create community, add to the vibrancy of Houston's street life, all while ensuring the health and safety of all involved in the food truck industry. It's an exciting time for food, and food trucks, in Houston!"

Perhaps the best sign that the food-truck movement has finally arrived in our city was Houston's first-ever Food Truck Festival, which took place on May 14-15, 2011, at the Southwest Campus of Houston Community College. Twenty-five trucks participated. In addition to the food, there was also beer and wine, live music and a "vendor village", where artisans plied their wares. According to the organizers, over 5,000 people attended the two-day event, which benefited the Houston Metropolitan Chamber and Houston Community College Foundation.

As soon as the gates opened, crowd-descended on the trucks, and the lines

grew quickly. On Saturday, the wait was up to two hours, with many of the trucks running out of food. Even on Sunday the wait time at most of the trucks was between 45 minutes to an hour. Obviously Houston has pent-up demand for serious street food.

"We learned a lot from that experience," said Debra Ford, of Food and Vine Productions, who organized the event. "This year, we've made some significant changes, all designed to make the event more enjoyable for visitors and food truck owners alike," added Debra.

DO YOU WANT TO RUN A FOOD TRUCK?...

Austin is extremely food-truck friendly with over 1,300.

Perhaps the most important change in the 2012 staging of Haute Wheels was that they limited the number of visitors to 2,500. In addition, 34 trucks participated. There was a lot more shade as well as tables and chairs in the Beer and Wine Garden, plus the food trucks pared down their menus to be able to serve more people more quickly. All of these changes made the event much more enjoyable for all.

One local Houston business, Noel Fine Furniture on the Southwest Freeway, hosted a preview of what that could be like in Houston. For its Food Truck Food Court on September 9, seven trucks showed up at lunchtime and fed around 300 people.

In the Spring of 2012, The Museum of Fine Arts, Houston started its Fine Art Food Trucks program. Every day, from 11:00 am-3:00 pm a different food

truck was serving food in the parking lot in front of the museum.

They offered a Lunch + Look loyalty card such that, when you presented your card and your receipt from the food truck, you received same-day general admission free between 12:00 noon and 2:00pm. Furthermore, when you collected ten stamps, you received half off your museum membership.

At the tail end of the summer of 2012, The Houston Press, along with Houston's own St. Arnold Brewing Company, sponsored Food Truck Fridays. On the first Friday of every month, four food trucks gathered in front of the House of Deréon Media Center, 2204 Crawford.

When the University of Houston decided to redo the University Center on the

Main Campus, they had to shut down five restaurants. What did they decide to do? Bring in food trucks to feed the students, faculty and staff during the eighteen month construction period.

There is talk about setting up a food truck court for up to eight food trucks on the Washington corridor, where many trucks already congregate in the evenings. Then there's Phul Court on the corner of Leeland and Austin that is already playing host to a number of food trucks. Austin, Dallas, Fort Worth and San Antonio already have such parks.

The Fort Worth Food Park opened December 2nd 2011 at 2509 Weisenberger near Montgomery Plaza. Six trucks will be stationed there.

Austin, Texas is extremely food-truck friendly. It has over 1,300 registered food trucks and has a number of areas of town where food trucks congregate. The first is the South Austin Trailer Park and Eatery on

First St. near Elizabeth St., where a collection of mobile food vendors gathers daily.

Then there is the area known as So-Co (for South Congress) which is also known for the hip zip: 78704, where they have not only a number of food

trucks but porta-potties and an ATM as well.

Now that's food-truck friendly.

There is also an area known as So-Fi (for South First street), where yet another collection of trucks can be found.

Downtown Austin is awash with food trucks. You can hardly go one block without seeing a food truck on almost every corner. On Third St., four to five trucks gather daily.

So popular are food trucks in Austin that when the new high-rise condominiums called South Shore on Riverside were completed, a spot was purposely left for three of four trucks to tether permanently.

In January 2011, San Antonio opened the city's first mobile food truck park, named the Boardwalk on Bulverde.

Many of these mobile food vendors can be hired to cater a special on-site event, birthday party, or fundraiser. Call them to set up something unique, different, fun and definitely memorable and let them worry about the cooking while you enjoy yourself. Some building managers hire trucks to spice up the lunch offerings available. When the truck pulls into the parking lot of a building, it creates something different and exciting for their tenants. Truck owners are also finding that companies are hiring them to add novelty to the good ol' holiday party. Some bars are begging today's new breed of truck to show up on or near their premises since it takes away the burden of having to provide food of any kind. This way, the bar can focus on selling booze and patrons can get some good, cheap nosh without having to go far before they return to what they do best – drink and have fun.

Enjoy the terrific food and adventure that awaits you. Good truck hunting.

NAME THAT TRUCK

Food trucks have very creative names. Tamara Palmer wrote a blog entitled "Pavement Cuisine" for the *San Francisco Weekly* in which she identified "Ten Awesomely Named Food Trucks"

Kim Jong Grillin' (Portland)

Chairman Bao (San Francisco)

India Jones (Los Angeles)

Buns On Wheels (Seattle)

The Mud Truck (New York)

The Rolling Stove (Del Ray Beach)

Rebel Heroes (Arlington)

Big Gay Ice Cream Truck (New York)

The Dump Truck (Portland) dumplings

Patty Wagon (Los Angeles)

As fun and creative as these are, I think she missed some of the best ones. I scoured the web for food trucks in the largest cities in the U.S. and came up with my own list of interesting and amusing truck names.

Atlanta: Yami Sushi

Austin: Chi'lantro (Korean/Mexican from kimchi and cilantro) Cutie Pie, Man Bites Dog, Takorea, mmmpanadas, Holy Cacao, Best Wurst, Coat and Thai, Tac Gos, The Pizza Box, Donut Wheel, Kebabalicious, Bar-B-Que-T, Pick Up Stix (Kabobs), Bread Basket, Pig Vicious

Baltimore: Juanna Burrito?

Baton Rouge: Taco De Paco

Boston: Campus Trolley, Jack & The Bean Bowl, Passage To India, Tealuxe,

Chicago: Happy Bodega, All Fired Up, Meaty Balls

Cleveland: Dim And Den Sum

D.C.: Curbside Cupcakes, Sidewalk Sweetsations, Founding Farmers, Chili Bowl, Food Chain, The Dairy Godmother

Detriot: Tongue Thai'd, Peaches & Greens

Honolulu: Jawaiian (Jamaican/Hawaiian)

Houston: Fez Express, Hit and Run, Oh My Gogi, Phamily Bites, H-Town Streats, Flaming Patties, Pi Pizza,

L'es-Car-Go, Stick It (skewers), Waffle Bus, Kurbside Eatz, Nola's Creole 2 Geaux, Boiling Bugs (crawfish), The Hunger Trap, The Meat Wagon, The Waffle Bus, Kurbside Eatz

Las Vegas: Fukuburger

Los Angeles: Crazy Creole Café, Papas Tapas, Franken Stand, Naan Stop, Fresh Fries, Great Balls on Tires (Meatballs), Coolhaus (Ice Cream), Dogzilla, Let's Be Frank, Manila

Machine, Big Swirl, The Brunch Box, Cupcakes a Go Go, King Kone, Get Shaved, El Flamin' Taco, The Munchie Machine, The Gastrobus, Shrimp Pimp, Street Hawker, The Greasy Wiener, Mariscos Jaliscos,

Tito's Tacos, Paco's Tacos, Wurst-küche, Sugar Babies, Road To Seoul, Pyongyang Express, Eatalian Café , El Flaco Taco, Noshi Sushi, Take a Bao, Church & State, Hurry Curry, Tommy Taco, Wokcano Café, Souplantation,

Oki Dog, Tiki's Taco, Taco Time, El Taco Naco, Happy Boba, Hot Pot, Sweet E's, Tu Tacos, Garden of Eating, Crabulous, Hollywood Bowl, Scoops, Torres Tacos, Kukees, Cait's Cakes, Snookies Cookies, The Price is Right, My Sweet Cupcake, Meet 'n Potatoes, Tacos Coco's, Grill 'Em All, India Jones Chow Truck, Taste My Taco, Oh For Sweets Sakes, Barbies Q, Crepe N' Around, Takosher (Kosher brisket tacos), Truck Norris, Get your Lardon, Fresh Fries, Get Shaved, Slapyomama, Meet n Potatoes

Miami: Dim Saam a Gogo, Sugar Rush, Gastropod, Wing Commander, The Filling Station, Pinchoman (a *pincho* is a snack or *tapa*), Coral Bagels, Arabian Nights, The Rolling Stove, Mi so hungry, Ms. Cheezious,

Milwaukee: Brat Stop, Street Za Pizza, Fast Foodie,

Minneapolis: Chef Shack

New York: Shake Shack, The Milk Truck, Cake & Shake, Treats Truck, Pizzamoto, Fish and Sip, Eata Pita, Ciao For Now, Street Sweets, Yorganic, The Munch Truck, Breadman , Rice to Riches, The Village Pourhouse, Frites n' Meats, Flacoz Tacoz, Sweet Revenge, Magic Fountain, Roasting Plant, Cheap Shots, Frying Dutchman, Grub Truck, Mexicue (Mexican and BBQ fusion)

Philadelphia: Coup De Taco, Noshery, Pita Pit, Viva Las Vegans, Guapo's Tacos

Phoenix: Truckin' Good Food

Portland: The Dump Truck (Dumplings), Tapas and Tinis, Fuel, Scoop Deck, Starchy & Husk,

St. Louis: Pi on the Spot,

San Diego: Chop Soo-Ey, Ms. Patty Melt

San Francisco: Curry Up Now, Curry Kart, Seoul on Wheels, Crepes a Go Go, Adobo Hobo, Chairman Bao, Suppenkuche, Tacos Pacos, Tacolicious, Pietisserie, All You Knead (pizza), Hall of Flame, Double Decker, Togo's, Coffee to the People, Curbside Coffee, The Pooch Coach (Dog treats)

Seattle: Halláva Falafel, Street Treats, Mee Sum Pastry, Mobile Chowdown, Po Dog Hot Dogs, Grateful Bread.

TIPS TO HELP YOU ENJOY YOUR FOOD TRUCK EXPERIENCE

Along this journey, I learned a lot about how best to approach eating at a Mobile Food Unit. Here are some tips to help you enjoy your mobile dining experience to its fullest.

Explore the city.

My journey to locate Houston's Top 100 Food Trucks took me to parts of the city I had never visited in the 34 years I have lived here. It was most definitely a fascinating and eye-opening experience and one worth sharing. The city we call home is large and diverse and filled with ethnic areas that just cry out for more exploration. I recommend you drive the city and discover for yourself just how really diverse it is.

Bring cash.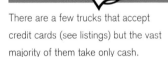

There are a few trucks that accept credit cards (see listings) but the vast majority of them take only cash.

Don't expect a receipt.

Since most of the transactions are in cash and since most of the transactions are also small, between $1-5, most truck owners don't give receipts. Some, however, do, if asked. Of course, if you do need one, there are many ways in which some kind of receipt can be generated. Most trucks will have a business card or advertising flyer, so ask the server to jot down the total amount on one of these and sign or stamp it.

Save your truck hunting for evenings and weekends.

Many owners of these mobile food units have other jobs during the week and open only at night or on weekends. The other consideration is that many of the customers of these trucks do not have the time to venture out except at night or on the weekends, so it makes sense that the trucks are there to greet them when they're ready to shop and eat.

Be prepared to eat with your hands.

This is street food. It's not white-table-cloth, fine-dining and besides, how else do you eat a *taco* or a *torta* except with your hands? Therefore, bring some moist wipes or hand sanitizer. You'll need them, since no quantity of napkins will ever remove the smell of curry or the stickiness of a cupcake or a sno-cone from your hands.

Don't wear your best clothes.

If you eat at mobile food trucks, face it, at some point, you will get some food on you. Whether it's the sauce from the *carne guisada taco* or the gooey, melted cheese from a Korean *Quesadilla*, it's probably going to drip all over you. Get used to it.

Try something new.

Eat something you've never eaten before and at a place you've never eaten before. It's easy just to eat the kind of food you've eaten your whole life. It's safe but it's also boring. The array of food available at mobile food trucks ranges from the unctuous *barbacoa* to sweetbreads and cow's stomach. From pig's ears to goat meat. If you're already an adventurous eater, you'll find these offerings exciting, if you're not, you may be trepidatious about eating something strange or different. Yet here is the perfect opportunity to do this. If you try a dish at a restaurant that you end up not liking, you're out a whole lot more than if you try it at a mobile food unit. Give it a try. There's no telling what you'll discover.

Meet someone new.

Nothing brings people together like food. There's something communal about eating at a mobile food unit that you generally don't experience at a brick and mortar restaurant. Stuffing a *taco al vapor* in your mouth and then moaning and rolling your eyes in delight somehow unites people as they wonder if what you're eating is better than what they're eating. It may even lead to your giving some of your food to complete strangers and letting them sample what you're raving about; and rave you will.

Have a back-up plan.

Since the nature of this industry is mobility, if you start out with the intention of visiting one specific unit and the unit is not where you thought it was supposed to be, you end up being hungry and maybe even settling for the next restaurant you see. Don't give up. Bring with you a listing of trucks in the general vicinity of the particular truck you're looking for and be persistent. It will pay off in great-tasting, inexpensive food, even if you waste a tankful of gas finding it. If you want to hit a bulls eye, head for any of the truck clusters or the listing of the best places to find trucks mentioned in the book and you are bound to find something that you'll enjoy. If you have a smart phone, use the TruxMap, Eat St or Roaming Hunger apps to locate trucks near where you are.

Be flexible.

Just because the truck listings in this book cite the operating hours, you should take this information with a grain of salt, since owners can change plans at the drop of a *taco*. Owners are also subject to the whims of nature. When it rains, it kinda puts a damper on business and when the truck breaks down, business stops until it's repaired. If the owner is sick, the truck may not leave the garage. Try a dose of understanding and find another truck.

Don't expect to be served alcohol from a truck.

Current laws prohibit mobile food units from serving any alcohol unless the unit is owned by a brick and mortar restaurant that already has a liquor license and that mobile unit is on private property and catering a party. However, since many of Houston's food trucks park near bars, you should have access to some form of alcoholic libation.

Prepare in advance for a call of nature.

Mobile food trucks do not have any kind of bathroom, although within Harris County they are required to be within 500 feet of one, so take this into consideration before you down that two-liter soda or six-pack just before venturing out for your favorite street food.

Brush up on your Spanish.

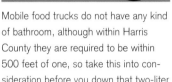

Since the vast majority of these mobile food trucks are owned or run by Mexicans, Guatemalans, Hondurans, Salvadorans, Venezuelans, Colombians and Puerto Ricans, if you are considerate enough to order in Spanish, the level of service you are likely to receive will be significantly enhanced and the smiles will be all the brighter. Use the Dictionary and Glossary at the back of this book to help you navigate the menus of some of these places. I have tried to include every foreign word on every menu along with descriptions. Any attempt you make at communicating in their language will be genuinely appreciated.

Be prepared to be hot. Or cold. Or wet.

The weather plays an important role in how much business a mobile food unit does on a given day. It's a well-known fact that when it rains, sleets, snows or is foggy, a lot of people just don't go out to eat.

Chances are, if you're eating at a mobile food truck in Houston, you're gonna be outside and, unless it's between November through March, you're gonna be hot, and eating hot food is likely to make you even hotter, so be prepared for this.

Ask the owner/server for a recommendation.

You may find yourself uncertain about what to order or unfamiliar with some of the dishes on the menu. I have always found it to be a great idea to ask the owner (or server) for a suggestion. After all, he knows what his customers like. It pays to take his advice.

Take Your Time.

Taking into account that your food is being made to order even as you watch it being made - which is a lot more than can be said for brick and mortar restaurants - you will have to accept that the from-scratch preparation used by many mobile food units takes time. So make sure you give yourself enough time and, more importantly, chill out. Perhaps spend the time talking to others, who may also be hanging around the truck waiting for their food, about other trucks they have visited and enjoyed.

this FIRM OUTER LAYER covers

a soft, chewy cake interior

LOCATION
Various

PHONE
832-347-4987

HOURS
Various

FOOD
Cake balls, cake pops, brownies

PRICES
$

OWNER
Angie Jackson

STARTED
2011

PAYMENT
All

SPECIAL SERVICES
Catering

TWITTER
angiescake

FACEBOOK
angiescake

WEBSITE
http://angiescake.com/

ANGIE'S CAKE

—

Angie Jackson started her **cake-ball business** in 2008, working out of a commercial kitchen.

It all began while she was marketing real estate. Angie received many a recipe from her co-workers, and one day, someone gave her a recipe for cake balls. Soon after that, she spotted another recipe for cake balls in the newspaper, but it wasn't until she became addicted to a baking blog that the idea of making them professionally began to set in. She spent the next two years juggling a fledgling business

They're the perfect cross between a cake and a piece of candy

with her full-time job. Then, as she puts it, "The fun part of my life took over." She and her husband, Marty, added the truck in 2011.

Angie's cake balls are slightly larger than ping-pong balls, and each has

a firm, exterior icing, usually made of chocolate; they're the perfect cross between a cake and a piece of candy. This firm outer layer covers a soft, chewy cake interior. They're incredibly tasty. Each one is also individually decorated with either sprinkles, pieces of nuts or coconut, or drizzles of icing. In addition to cake balls, Angie also makes cake pops, which are cake balls on a lollipop stick.

I tried a six-cake-ball sampler, which comes in an elegant box with each piece in its own paper holder: Ginger Beer, Vanilla, Birthday Cake, Lemon, Chocolate and German Chocolate. These are Angie's most popular cake balls from a list of 17 that appear on her website. But don't let 17 be your limit; if you have a favorite cake that is not listed, I'm betting that Angie can

17 FLAVORS OF CAKE BALLS // CAKE POPS
ROBUST CHOCOLATE FLAVOR BROWNIES //

figure out how to make it into a delectable cake ball.

It was hard to choose a favorite since each one tasted better than the last. But as I'm a sucker for anything with lemon in it, I'd choose it over the rest — but not by far.

The cake balls are the perfect size for a snack. I find cupcakes larger than I need when I just feel like something sweet. But the problem with Angie's cake balls is that it's hard to eat just one.

Angie also makes brownies. The one I tried was rich and had a robust chocolate flavor without being cloyingly sweet. It also had lots of nuts in it, adding to the texture and flavor.

Angie can be found at various events around the city, and says she will soon take her truck to the streets on a more regular basis. She also delivers in the Houston area.

the

STUFFING

CAN BE

only discovered

when you break off a piece

LOCATION
7121 Fondren

HOURS
Mon-Sun: 8:00am-10:00pm

FOOD
Honduran

PRICES
$$

STARTED
2009

PAYMENT
Cash only

ANTOJITOS HONDUREÑOS

—

There are **three trucks** with exactly the same name.

There is this one, another adjacent and parked in the same parking lot, and a third on Airline Drive. Since this one is an old school bus, the serving window is fairly high off the ground. Customers reach it by climbing steps.

Since this one is an old school bus, the serving window is fairly high off the ground.

We tried the *taco de pollo*, a large corn tortilla that has been fried until crispy.

It is smeared with mayonnaise, stuffed with shredded chicken and *curtido*, or shredded cabbage, along with pink, pickled onion slices and a good helping of a sweet tomato sauce on top.

Next was the *pastelito de carne*, or beef-stuffed pasty. The flat disk is similar to an *arepa* in size and consistency, color and shape. The stuffing can be discovered only when you break off a piece to eat it. The same *curtido* and pickled onions are also served on top of this snack.

TACO DE POLLO // PASTELITO DE CARNE
CHICHARRON CON YUCA // ASADA CON TAJADA

Next was the *chicharron con yuca*, for which they take large chunks of roasted pork with the crackling still attached and serve them with fried cassava. It is an excellent-tasting dish,

Large chunks of roasted pork with the crackling still attached and serve them with fried cassava

not unlike the Cuban *pernil*, which is also often served with cassava.

Finally, the carne *asada con tajadas*, stewed beef served on top of slices of unripe, fried plantains, along with refried black beans, a hunk of *queso fresco* and the ubiquitous *curtido* and pickled onions.

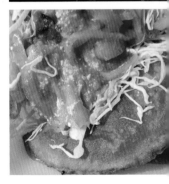

✤ a ✤

HOT DOG

CALLED

chevere

launched in guatemala

LOCATION
6371 Windswept

HOURS
Various

FOOD
Guatemalan

PRICES
$

STARTED
2008

PAYMENT
Cash only

ANTOJITOS SAN MIGUEL DE GUATEMALA

—

I'm not sure how a **simple hot dog** came to epitomize Guatemalan food nor how it got the name *"chevere."*

This is one of a handful of trucks that open early in the morning, close for lunch, then reopen in the evenings.

I'm not sure how a simple hot dog came to epitomize Guatemalan food nor how it got the name *"chevere,"* which normally means "cool." But when I asked the server what foods they most often served, this was the

Chiltepe is Guatemala's most widely used hot pepper. It is tiny, green and almost round.

first thing he mentioned, followed by *papas con pollo* and tacos. I tried the hot dog. Other than the addition of chopped cabbage, or *curtido*, as a topping, along with some *Picamas* sauce, a commercial Guatemalan

green hot sauce made from *chiltepes* peppers, the hot dog and bun were pretty much standard fare. *Chiltepe* is Guatemala's most widely used hot pepper. It is tiny, green and almost round, about the size of a very large caper.

It is interesting that the server referred to the "chicken with French fries" as "French fries with chicken." I do not know if this is common or just peculiar to this particular server. Two drumsticks with a well-seasoned batter are served with nondescript, somewhat limp fries. Just before being served, everything is doused with ketchup and mayo, whether you ask for it or not.

The dish that I almost passed up was the taco, since I had tried Guatemalan tacos previously and found them to

GUATEMALAN TACOS // HOT DOGS WITH CHOPPED CABBAGE AND *PICAMAS* SAUCE // FRENCH FRIES WITH CHICKEN //

be similar to Mexican *flautas*: stuffed, rolled up and fried. But the server said their tacos were different. So I ordered one, and was glad I did. He took two corn tortillas and dipped them in hot oil, then placed them on a griddle to warm them. He turned them a few times, then placed the shredded beef filling

The broth, absorbed by the cabbage and meat, made the taco pleasantly moist.

inside and topped it all with *curtido* and *salsa de tomate*, or thin tomato broth, which he ladled out of a covered bowl. The broth was soon absorbed by the cabbage and the meat, making the taco pleasantly moist.

After I got home, I researched the mystery of the hot dog's name. In the seventies or eighties, a brand of hot dogs called *Chevere* was launched in Guatemala and sold from hot dog carts all over the country. The name became eponymous with hot dogs. The carts have long since disappeared, but the name remains.

❋not just❋

SELLING

GREAT

mexican food

I am selling ambiance

LOCATION
Various

PHONE
713-520-1738

HOURS
Various

FOOD
Mexican

PRICES
$$$

OWNER
Armando Palacios

STARTED
2008

PAYMENT
All

SERVICES
Catering only

FACEBOOK
ARMANDOS/55526409546

WEBSITE
armandosrestaurant.com

ARMANDO'S

——

Because of the type of customer I serve, **everything** had to be first-class.

This is not your typical taco truck at all. It's a glorious, stainless-steel-and-chrome, fully equipped gourmet kitchen on wheels. Armando Palacios,

"I don't sell tacos," said Armando. "I sell an experience."

the owner of the very successful Armando's restaurant in River Oaks/Upper Kirby, is not out on the street soliciting business; he does only high-end catering. "I don't sell tacos," said Armando. "I sell an experience. If you come to my restaurant, you know I am not just selling great Mexican food. I am selling an ambiance. I get asked all the time to cater parties, and I wanted to do something different, so I designed and built this high-end truck. Because of the type of customer

I serve, everything had to be first-class, so we went with Wolf appliances and decked everything out in stainless steel."

Armando normally serves chicken and beef fajitas as well as his signature margaritas, but can also cater his full menu. He can do breakfast tacos. Events cost $3,000 and up for turnkey service, including servers.

Armando was kind enough to invite me to the Houston Polo Club, where every Sunday in the spring and the fall you will find his truck. He takes care of the concessions for the club and, since he has an off-premise license, serves beer, wine and champagne. (It is the Polo Club, after all.) I had the nachos, which he tops with *queso* and seasoned ground beef. They are made

CHICKEN AND BEEF FAJITAS // MARGARITAS
BREAKFAST TACOS // FAJITA BEEF TACOS
FISH TACOS // SALSA BAR

with thick, homemade tortilla chips. This was followed by fish tacos, which consisted of two well-seasoned tilapia

One thing you can always count on at Armando's restaurant is that the food is consistent

filets stuffed into homemade corn tortillas along with shredded cabbage, slices of avocado and *pico de gallo*. The fajita beef tacos, also served on homemade corn tortillas, are one of Armando's signature dishes. The salsa bar on the outside of the truck has a fiery orange-colored salsa and a milder green salsa along with *pico de gallo*, chopped onions and cilantro and lime wedges.

One thing you can always count on at Armando's restaurant is that the food is consistent. The same goes for the food served on his truck.

we
ASKED FOR
SPICY
and jay
willingly obliged

LOCATION
11200 S. Wilcrest

PHONE
713-624-2009

HOURS
Mon-Thur: 6:30pm-9:00pm,
Fri-Sat: 6:30pm-9:30pm

FOOD
Indian

PRICES
$$

OWNER
Jay Kapadia

STARTED
2008

PAYMENT
Cash only

SERVICES
100% vegetarian

WEBSITE
bansurifood.com

BANSURI INDIAN FOOD CORNER

—

I found that there was not an **Indian food truck** in town, so I decided to open the first one

Jay Kapadia moved to Houston from the western Indian state of Gujarat when he was 13 years old. When he finished school here, he worked in the family dry cleaning business for twenty years. "After twenty years, I became

Jay brought the taste of Indian street food to Houston. Jay and his wife serve Indian *chaat*, or street snacks

fed up with it, so I looked for something else to do" said Jay. "I started to see all the taco trucks around town and when I looked into it, I found that there was no Indian food truck, so I decided to open the first one," Jay added. Jay brought the taste of Indian street food to Houston. Jay and his wife serve Indian *chaat*, or street snacks, in a variety of forms. *Chaat* means to lick. "People love what I do and every day, people say to me 'thank you for being open'", said Jay. He is only open at night and the scene is a hectic one since the parking lot he occupies is small and people tend to linger and talk, way after they have consumed their snacks. To say that there is always a crowd here would be an understatement. This truck is open for only a few hours at night

One nice thing about the food served here is that it is 100% vegetarian.

and is one of the busiest I visited. In addition to the *chaat*, maybe the blare

CHAAT // VADA PAV CONSISTING OF TWO POTATO PANCAKES // FALUDAH // DAHI PURI RAGDA, A STEW-LIKE MIXTURE

of traditional Indian music coming from the truck is another draw.

A *bansuri* is a transverse flute used in Indian music. As I looked at the name written on this truck, I wondered if the transverse lines that were placed on top of each word (see photos of logo on truck, below) symbolized this instrument. When we placed our order the first evening we visited him, Jay gave us a number and told us we'd have to

They are served on a soft bun which Jay has custom made for him. They're sort of like vegetarian sliders.

wait about fifteen minutes for our food. He wasn't kidding. We waited along with lots of other people who were crowding the parking lot. One nice thing about the food served here is that it is 100% vegetarian. The *chaat* we sampled were all very different. We asked for them spicy and Jay willingly obliged. First was the *Dahi Puri*. Jay takes six, tiny pastry shells, then fills them with a white pea mixture which he covers in yogurt and tops with strips of cilantro. They are small and bite-sized and are so light that they feel like mere wisps as they quickly disappear.

Next was the *Vada Pav* consisting of two potato pancakes which Jay cooks on the griddle. They are served on a soft bun which Jay has custom made for him. They're sort of like vegetarian sliders. On one side of the bun is a garlic chutney and on the other, one made of coriander and mint. Finally, the *Ragda*, a stew-like mixture of potatoes, vegetables with Indian spices.

Jay had recently expanded his menu to include popular Indian drinks like Mango *Lassi*, made with yogurt and fresh mango as *Faludah*, a milk-based drink with rose and cardamom flavors as well as basil seeds, almonds and tiny strands of sago starch not unlike vermicelli only much, much thinner. The basil seeds Jay uses have a similar consistency to tiny tapioca balls. The pink, rose syrup on the bottom of the plastic cup must be stirred into the rest of the drink for maximum effect. A big dollop of vanilla ice cream sits on top of the dessert drink and once it melts, adds a wonderful creaminess to the drink. The almonds scattered throughout also add a welcomed crunch. He also offers popular Indian soft drinks like Limca and Thumbs Up.

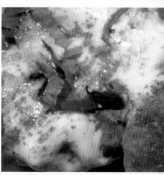

a

REMARKABLE

SMOKE

flavor

as well as a firm texture

LOCATION
6501 Laura Koppe

HOURS
Tue-Sun: 12:00pm-2:00am

FOOD
Barbecue

PRICES
$$

STARTED
2000

PAYMENT
Cash only

PHONE
832-731-2940

OWNER
Gregory Carter

SPECIAL SERVICES
Catering

BAR-B-QUE DONE RIGHT

—

I'm superstitious, I use only **red oak or post oak**, and only from East Texas.

The first thing you will notice about Greg Carter is that he likes to talk to everyone. "I probably talk too much," he says. But I don't agree. I think he is just a happy, gregarious guy.

After being a territory manager for Blue Bell Ice Cream for 17 years and doing barbecue events on the weekends, Greg decided he "had a passion for this" and started cooking terrific barbecue full-time. He won't sell you any brisket unless he deems it ready for

His fanaticism translates into damn good barbecue, not to mention great sides, like a creamy potato salad and two types of beans.

consumption, which is only after a full twelve hours of slow cooking. While I was waiting for my food, he discouraged two other people from buying the brisket because it wasn't ready. And

when my buddy an fellow food writer Robb Walsh visited him to write a piece about him, he, too, was turned away because it wasn't ready. The man has the courage of his convictions.

Greg is fussy about the wood he uses to smoke his meats. "I grew up in the country," he said, "and maybe I'm superstitious, but I use only red oak or post oak, and only from East Texas. Earlier today, I had a guy come by wanting to sell me a trailer of wood for 50 bucks. I turned him down because I just prefer the wood from East Texas." His fanaticism translates into damn good barbecue, not to mention great sides, like a creamy potato salad and two types of beans. He makes *charro* beans but was out of them the day I visited because he hadn't stopped serving until 3 a.m. the night before and was still trying to get caught up when I showed up at 1 p.m. the next

TENDER BRISKET // RIBS // SAUSAGE
CREAMY POTATO SALAD // TWO TYPES OF BEANS

day. The beans he served me were his pinto beans, which contained quite a lot of bacon pieces and were very tasty. The ribs were firm and did not fall off the bone, indicating that they had been painstakingly slow-cooked with indirect heat, not boiled beforehand. The brisket had a remarkable smoke flavor as well as a firm texture. The sausage was outstanding. Its texture was coarse, and it had a nice heat to it - not so much as to be intrusive, but sufficient to get your attention.

I knew I had to return to try his brisket.

"Looks like this is your lucky day", was the answer I received when I called Greg one Friday afternoon inquiring whether or not he had any brisket and

He cooks the brisket for seventeen hours at no more than 250 degrees.

charro beans. It was indeed my lucky day. Greg reached into the vertical pit, whose interior was completely black and dark brown in color, indicative of the many hours of slow smoking he has used it for over the nine years he's been cooking out of this trailer. As he pulled out a slab of brisket, wafts of smoke emerged. He removed the silver foil from around the brisket and proceeded to slice the meat. "Do you want me to lean it?" asked Greg. When

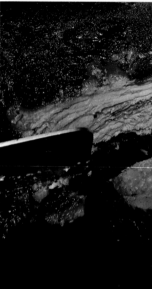

I said "Yes", he removed most of the fat from the top of the brisket, leaving thin streaks of fat that were in the middle of the meat. That's what makes it so tender. "I used to have a customer that came here and ordered just the fat. That's all he wanted,' said Greg. He cooks the brisket for seventeen hours at no more than 250 degrees. This ultra-slow cooking method yields a smoky brisket so tender and moist that it pulls apart with just a few tugs. There are, however, crispier parts on the outside.

"I used to be on a cooking team. Each of us had one job. Mine was to cook the brisket. I learned how to make the *charro* beans from the guy who cooked them on the team, but I adapted them to my own recipe," said Greg. Nothing is rushed at Greg's trailer. The beans take five hours. Onions, garlic, yellow and red bell peppers, tiny pieces of pork belly and cilantro all go into his version, which is plenty tasty.

I also very much enjoyed his potato salad. The potatoes were still firm and it had visible pieces of hard-boiled egg and pimiento, with salad dressing and mustard being the only other additions.

Greg has been perfecting his barbecuing skills for many years and it definitely shows in the quality of his food. This is some of the best 'que available in city.

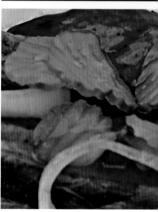

the mix
OF SWEET
SPICY
and salty
is fabulous

LOCATION
9431 Highway 6 South

PHONE
832-665-9688

HOURS
Tue-Thur, Sun: 12:00pm-7:00pm,
Fri-Sat: 12:00pm-8:00pm

FOOD
Chicago hot dogs,
Italian beef sandwiches

PRICES
$

OWNER
Charles Rivers

STARTED
2011

PAYMENT
All

SPECIAL SERVICES
Catering

FACEBOOK
BBS-BEEF-and-Hot-
dog/150422524979318

WEBSITE
bbsbeefandhotdog.com

BB'S BEEF & HOT DOG

—

A good dousing of celery salt are all that is needed to finish this dog to **Windy City perfection**.

Charles Rivers is from the West Side of Chicago. He moved his family to Houston three years ago "to change things up a bit," he says. He and his wife, Brenda, first opened a restaurant with the same name as his truck at 11611 W. Airport. Other expat Chicagoans have already found him and flock to his place to satisfy a craving for a real Chicago-style hot dog, an Italian beef sandwich or a Maxwell Street Polish.

What makes a Chicago-style hot dog different? "Mustard and no ketchup, some celery salt and an all-beef, Vienna hot dog," said Charles. "Ketchup will ruin a hot dog." There are no ketchup bottles or containers anywhere on his truck, and you'd better not bring your own, either. Brenda runs the restaurant, and Charles decided to open a food truck in early 2011 with his son, Charles Junior.

"All the ingredients are imported from Chicago," commented Charles. "That way I know what I'm dealing with." The hot dog bun is studded with poppy seeds. The bun, hot dog and kosher pickle are all from the Vienna Beef

"All the ingredients are imported from Chicago, that way I know what I'm dealing with."

Company. Onions, a bright green relish, a slice of tomato, a couple of sport peppers (small green peppers about an inch and a half long with not a lot of heat), and a good dousing of celery salt are all that is needed to finish this dog to Windy City perfection. The mix of sweet, spicy and salty is fabulous.

The Maxwell Street Polish sausage is synonymous with Chicago. It all started at the open air Maxwell Street Market,

90 TRUCK REVIEWS BB'S BEEF & HOT DOGS

ITALIAN BEEF SANDWICHS POTATO // CHICAGO-STYLE HOT DOGS // MAXWELL STREET POLISH

colloquially known as Jew Town, on Chicago's Near West Side. This area is one of the city's oldest residential districts, and is also known as the birthplace of Chicago blues.

For his take on the Maxwell Street Polish sausage, Charles uses a plain bun smeared with mustard. He tops a grilled Vienna beef sausage with sweet marinated grilled onions and a couple of sport peppers. The recipe for the onions, developed by Charles's wife, is a closely guarded secret. One taste and I clearly understood why.

Now to the Chicago Italian Beef sandwich. Charles takes a French roll, which comes from the Connella Bakery in Chicago, and first dips it in *jus*, which softens it as it absorbs the great-tasting gravy. He fills it with thinly sliced, seasoned beef, which has been generously coated with even more *jus*. He tops that with a *giardiniera*

The Maxwell Street Polish sausage is synonymous with Chicago.

mixture, which includes hot cherry peppers, celery and green peppers. The result is a messy creation that is hard to put down lest it fall apart. Taking a

bite is sure to make the sandwich ooze its *jus* all over you, so watch out. But the combination of the perfect bread, beef and topping make the terrific-tasting sandwich worth the trouble.

the

FRIED EGG

ON TOP

makes this

an A-plus burger

LOCATION
Various

 HOURS
Various

 FOOD
Hamburgers

 PRICES
$$

 STARTED
2010

 PAYMENT
All

 PHONE
281-386-2447

 OWNER
Justin Turner

 TWITTER:
berniesburgers

 FACEBOOK
Catering

 WEBSITE
berniesburgerbuss.com

BERNIE'S BURGER BUS

—

Justin likes everything **homemade**, so he even makes his own ketchup.

Owner Justin Turner told me about the place where he purchased his 1986 International school bus: "It's way out on 290 at Telge. I paid $3,000 for the bus, but then I spent $45,000 getting it ready." (The Rodriguez Brothers, on the east side of downtown, gave it a fully operational kitchen.)

The name Bernie is in honor of his grandfather, Bernie Schubert. Justin is originally from Chicago. He went to culinary school in Memphis and ended up in Houston, following Shane Battier, who used to play for the Houston Rockets and was later transferred to the Memphis Grizzlies. Justin was Battier's personal chef for many years but decided to stay in Houston instead of following his employer back to Memphis. He tried his hand at various chef jobs in the city but couldn't find one that paid the kind of salary he was looking for, so he decided to open his own food truck. We're glad he did.

All of his menu items have some clever reference to school. For example, his burgers are named The Principal, The Bully, The Substitute, Detention, Fall Break and so on. I noticed he was missing some Discipline and a Teacher's Pet. He seemed to like these additions.

Justin likes everything homemade, so he makes his own ketchup, as well as a *chipotle*-enhanced version with a little more kick. The mayo, mustard and pickles are also homemade, and you can quickly tell the difference. One of Justin's Electives is what he

the Cheddar cheese he uses is from Texas, and the buns are from Houston's Slow Dough Bakery.

calls "tipsy onions": he slow-cooks the onions until they caramelize, then deglazes the pan with Jack Daniels. The result is wonderful. He hand-forms the patties from grass-fed, organic Black

BLUE CHEESE BURGERS // HOMEMADE OREOS
FRIED EGG-TOPPED BURGERS // TIPSY ONIONS

Angus beef. He is also using as many local ingredients as he can find, so the Cheddar cheese he uses is from Texas, and the buns are from Houston's Slow Dough Bakery.

I tried The Substitute, which is a burger topped with blue cheese, some wonderful, thick-sliced, applewood-smoked bacon and some of those tipsy onions. It was outstanding. It was, however, The Extra Curricular Activities Blue Cheese Fries that stole

Justin also offers superb hand-cut sweet potato fries, which should not be missed.

the show. These hand-cut, skin-on fries are topped with even more blue cheese, the same applewood-smoked bacon as on the burger and green onions. Dipping them in both kinds of ketchup made for quite an experience. As I placed my order, Jason reminded me that that was an awful lot of blue cheese. I smiled. He understood.

On my next visit, Justin suggested I try The Homeroom, one of his best sellers. It is topped with a fried egg, and Justin asked me if I wanted the egg runny. I said yes. When I first I tried a hamburger with an egg on top a number of years ago, I was so impressed with how it tasted, I always look forward to ordering it anywhere I can find it.

Here, Justin uses the same applewood-smoked bacon and tipsy onions with Texas Cheddar cheese and *chipotle aioli*, which he smears on each side of the bun. The *aioli* provides a nice spice level, and the egg on top makes this an A-plus burger. Justin also offers superb hand-cut sweet potato fries, which should not be missed.

For dessert, he serves homemade "Oreos," which are made by Sarah Crowl, also known as Little Miss Bakewell. They are larger in diameter and thicker than the commercial kind, although she nailed the color and consistency. The creamy filling has a pleasant cinnamon flavor.

Jason has been so successful that he has opened two more trucks and is now scheduled to open a brick and mortar place.

his

RIBS REMAIN

FIRM

and are

extremely tasty

LOCATION
3416 Airport

PHONE
832-343-8798

HOURS
Thur-Sat: 10:00am-10:00pm

FOOD
Barbecue

PRICES
$

OWNER
Joseph Hickman

STARTED
2002

PAYMENT
Cash only

SPECIAL SERVICES
Catering, delivery

BEST BAR-B-QUE

—

The trailer dates to the 1990s, which makes it **one of the oldest** in Houston.

"I bought this trailer for my dad when he retired from the railroad," said Joe Hickman, "but after a couple of weeks, he had some different ideas." So here Joe is. The trailer dates to the 1990s, which makes it one of the oldest in Houston.

Joe uses a dry rub that includes meat tenderizer without any MSG. "You know, a lot of us suffer when we use MSG," said Joe. He lets it sit overnight. As for his wood, "I use red oak or live oak. If you use pecan, it gives the meat a bitter taste and also darkens the meat." After searing the brisket, he cooks it fat side down at 350 degrees. After three or four hours, he flips it and lets it cook the rest of the eight or nine hours it takes to render the meat perfectly smoked. He adjusts the temperature by moving the meat to a cooler part of his large oven.

Joe makes his own sauce using ketchup, red wine, brown sugar, honey-Dijon mustard, smoke mesquite

His ribs remain firm and do not fall off the bone. They are extremely tasty.

seasoning and Worcestershire sauce. The sauce is both sweet and tangy and complements the meat without getting in its way. He also makes his owns beans using Old Bay seasoning, onions and cilantro. I found the beans to be okay, but much preferred the potato salad. He cuts the potatoes into large chunks and adds onions, green pepper, hard-boiled egg, pickles and not a lot of mayonnaise; so that the taste of the potatoes comes through.

His ribs remain firm and do not fall off the bone. They are extremely tasty. Joe also insisted I try his chicken. I

BARBECUED CHICKEN // BRISKET
RIBS // CRAWFISH // SAUSAGE // BOUDIN

am not the biggest fan of barbecued chicken — I normally find it to be dry — but his is exceptional. I removed the dark, outer skin, which contained most

The brisket — some of the best I've found — was moist, juicy and smoky.

of the smoke flavor. What was left was a gently smoke-flavored, moist piece of chicken. It was very good indeed.

Now for the brisket. The brisket — some of the best I've found — was moist, juicy and smoky. The red smoke ring was clearly evident in every slice, and the dry rub imparted lots of flavor. I particularly enjoyed the dark, almost burnt end cuts, since they had the most flavor of all.

By the time I reached Joe around noon on a Saturday, he had already run out of his sausage and his boudin. So I planned a return trip to sample these as well.

By the time I got back, crawfish season had started. I followed Joe to the back of his trailer, where he had a rig set up with two burners running full blast, one with a huge pot of crawfish, the other with a large pot of corn, potatoes and turkey necks. Since these were still in the cooking stage, he reached

into the cooler he uses to keep the cooked food warm and scooped out a huge mound of crawfish, a couple of potatoes and pieces of corn as well as some pieces of turkey neck. Joe's crawfish were perfect; spicy but not too spicy: My fingers didn't burn unpleasantly all the way through the meal. The well-seasoned turkey necks were also excellent. It's surprising just how much meat is on one. Eating them reminded me of eating oxtails: The only way to approach the task is with your hands, and getting the meat off the bone is a challenge worthy of the reward.

❋ the ❋

DARK BROWN

TANGY

sauce

is served on the side

LOCATION
9431 Highway 6 South

PHONE
713-530-8268

HOURS
Wed-Sat: 10:00am-8:00pm,
Sun: 11:00am-7:00pm

FOOD
BBQ

PRICES
$

OWNER
Lejon and Latasha Stewart

STARTED
2009

PAYMENT
All

FACEBOOK
Big6-Bar-B-Que/126946267359567

WEBSITE
big6barbque.com

BIG 6 BAR-B-QUE

—

Lejon will proudly let you sample **everything** he makes.

Lejon started out by catering barbecue in 2006. Last year he bought this trailer, which he parks on Highway 6 South, just north of Bissonnet. Everything here

Lejon uses a combination of pecan and oak wood in the smoke box at the trailer's rear.

is homemade, including the barbecue sauce, deer sausage, potato salad, chili beans, boudin (you have to ask for it, since it's not on the menu) and peach cobbler. As I arrived at the trailer, the sweet smell of smoke filled the air, and smoke rings wafted from the smoke stacks at the rear of the trailer.

Lejon asks if you want your brisket fatty or lean. I prefer the marbled, fatty version, since the fat adds flavor and

makes the meat even more tender. If you're not sure what to get, Lejon will let you sample everything he makes. The brisket had the traditional ring of fire indicating a nice slow cook. Lejon uses a combination of pecan and oak wood in the smoke box at the rear of the trailer. The dark brown, tangy sauce is served on the side, so that you can add as much as you like. The ribs undergo a dry rub before cooking and are marvelous by themselves, without the sauce.

The sides are excellent. In the potato salad, finely cut potatoes mingle with pickles, onions, peppers and lots of mayo. The pinto beans have a chili flavoring that adds to their overall spiciness. The corn on the cob is also

smoked, but not so much that the flavor overpowers the delicate flavor of the corn. Perhaps the best find of all, however, is the deer sausage, which uses coarsely ground meat along with some gristle. It, too, is quite spicy and not in the least bit dry; Lejon adds enough fat to make it moist through-

Perhaps the best find of all, however, is the deer sausage.

out. The smoked boudin is another story. The twelve-inch long, thick sausage is very smoky in flavor but is quite dry. Opening the casing, drizzling the BBQ sauce over the rice and meat mixture helps moisten it and adds an even more distinctive flavor.

✤he✤

COOKS HIS

MEAT

fat-down

for the first 2 hours

LOCATION
5719 Brittmoore, Unit 30

PHONE
713-896-3903

HOURS
Mon-Fri: 11:00am-5:00pm,
Sat: 11:00am-3:00pm

FOOD
BBQ

PRICES
$

OWNER
Bill Blaylock

STARTED
1982

PAYMENT
All

BLAZIN' BILL'S BBQ

—

He's been selling cooking wood and making BBQ out of this trailer since 1982, making it one of the **oldest mobile food units** in Houston.

The first thing you notice at Blazin' Bill's is the wood — lots of it piled high in all directions. This is a good sign. "I've been selling cooking wood and making BBQ out of this trailer

We don't have any knives here, so the meat'd better be tender.

since 1982," said Bill Blaylock. That makes Blazin' Bill's one of the oldest mobile food units in Houston. To be in business that long, Bill must be doing something right. Your first taste of his barbecue will convince you that he is.

He uses only oak and pecan, and cooks his meat fat-down for two hours, then fat-up for the rest, at 200

degrees for 10 to 14 hours. Like most other pitmen, he uses his own dry rub. "Of course, I've been doing this for so long, I don't time anything anymore," said Bill. "I just look at the meat and I know when it's done. This is real, old-fashioned pit BBQ. We don't have any knives here, so the meat'd better be tender."

I always ask about whether the sides are homemade before I decide to order them. In Bill's case, the potato salad is commercial, but his beans, those are another story. "My mother, who is in her seventies, makes the beans for me every week. They take about three days to make. She soaks them for at least one day, then adds garlic, onions,

PORK RIBS // BRISKET // POTATO SALAD
OUTSTANDING BEANS // SAUSAGE

chicken broth, ham hocks, some Rotel™ tomatoes and some other things that I can't tell you." Needless to say, the beans were outstanding.

Bill's sauce is also homemade and is thin, not thick like other sauces. There is a slight vinegary taste, which Bill acknowledged by telling me, "but not too much, otherwise it gets too sharp." The sausage had a nice smoky taste, although the standard commercial links themselves could have done with more

My mother, who is in her seventies, makes the beans for me every week.

flavor. Bill's pork ribs are the small kind and were properly firm; as they should be, they did not come away from the bone without a little help. Bill's brisket had the red smoke ring indicative of the very slow smoking it undergoes. It was superbly tender and with enough smoke flavor to let you know its presence, yet not so much as to overpower the other flavors.

It'll MAKE YOU SIT UP and slap yo mama.

LOCATION
900 FM 359, Richmond

PHONE
281-342-2645

HOURS
Various

FOOD
Cajun

PRICES
$$

OWNERS
Billy and Misty Sonnier,
Carlene Singletary

STARTED
2011

PAYMENT
All

SPECIAL SERVICES
Catering

FACEBOOK
Cajun-Way-Craw-
fish/160401800680455

WEBSITE
cajunwaycrawfish.com

CAJUN WAY CRAWFISH

—

The lengths they go to in order to serve the **very best** possible are almost unheard of.

Billy Sonnier is originally from Lake Arthur, Louisiana. He moved here 17 years ago. His wife, Misty, is from Houston, and they recently opened this trailer in Richmond, Texas, along with Misty's mother, Carlene Singletary, and Jennifer Fox, a friend of Misty's, who was "adopted" by the family many years ago.

How did they get into the business? "We were coming home from a trip and arrived late at night craving some Cajun food," said Billy. "I turned to Misty and said, 'You know what I'd really like? I'd like to be able to pick up some Cajun food at a drive-through.'" Alas, there was nothing like that nearby. So they decided then and there to open the next best thing: a Cajun food truck.

When you do something you love, the money is secondary. This is definitely the case with this family. The lengths they go to in order to serve the very best possible are almost unheard of. For example, Billy's crawfish is driven to his Richmond location every day by a friend of his who happens to be a high

Billy's crawfish is driven to his Richmond location every day by a friend of his.

school coach in Katy, who makes the daily trip to Louisiana starting at 4:30 a.m. Billy's shrimp are fresh and never frozen. They come from a supplier in Denton, in east Texas. Billy makes the two-hour round-trip drive every time he needs some. The bread for the po-boys and the *pistollettes* is also from Louisiana. Nothing, absolutely nothing is second-rate. Everything is made by hand, except for the imported bread, and the boudin, which comes from

— you guessed it — Louisiana. Lake Charles, to be precise.

This attention to detail makes the food unforgettable. Billy's gumbo is dark brown and completely opaque, with a flavor that shouts "homemade." Carlene told me that Billy takes all day to make it. This does not surprise me. Unlike many a roux that I have had over the years, it does not taste the least bit burnt, which means that the flavors of the seafood he uses in it, shrimp and lump crab meat, can be easily distinguished. "I always cook my shrimp in the gumbo. I don't just add cooked shrimp at the end," said Billy. I might have guessed.

Billy's red beans and rice are good but lack some of the smoky ham-hock flavor I always associate with this dish. Since I prefer the sauce in my red beans to be thick, I found his to be a little on the thin side. However, I am being extremely picky here.

The *pistolettes* were simply amazing. A specialty of Louisiana dating to the 1920s, *pistolettes* were originally made from small French rolls. The inside of the bread is removed and replaced with a crawfish and crabmeat stuffing made with lots of cheese to hold everything together, then fried.

The name comes from the shape of the rolls, which supposedly resembled little pistols. The bread itself is also very interesting in that the exterior has the taste and consistency of a donut. The sauce used as part of the filling is so good that, as they say in Louisiana:

attention to detail makes the food unforgettable. Billy's gumbo is dark brown and completely opaque,

"It will make you sit up and slap yo mama."

Normally sides are an afterthought. Not here. They are astonishingly good, and could easily take center stage. The potato salad has the perfect mix of potato chunks and smooth mashed potatoes. Mixed with mayo, hardboiled eggs and pickles, it is something to return to often. The same is true of Billy's coleslaw, to which he adds pieces of shrimp. In Louisiana, this is known as a *lagniappe* — a little something extra. I had never had coleslaw this way, but you can bet I'm going to add shrimp to the next batch I make. The onion rings are sliced ultra-thin and coated with a seasoned batter: very crispy and very tasty.

Like everything served here, the

crabcakes are made fresh daily. Billy uses only lump crabmeat and, looking at the ratio of crab to filling, it's easy to see that he does not scrimp on the

He simply pan fries the crabcakes and serves them with a homemade whipped garlic butter sauce to which he adds some wine.

crabmeat. He simply pan fries them and serves them with a homemade whipped garlic butter sauce to which he adds some wine. If he sold this sauce by the jar, he could live off its proceeds — it's that good. (Note to self: Next time, ask for extra sauce.)

Billy also makes his *remoulade* and tartar sauces from scratch. When I tell you he leaves nothing to chance, I mean it. The difference in the taste of a homemade sauce versus a commercial one is stunning.

The boudin was perfect. Billy barely smokes it — enough to impart just a hint of flavor. I've had it elsewhere where it was so smoky that it turned completely black and smoke was all you taste. Also, the filling is not all rice. There's a lot of meat in this sausage.

Misty asked me what kind of fish I would like on my fish platter and how I would like it prepared. I told her to make it as she would for herself. I ended up with a filet of blackened tilapia and one of battered and fried catfish. I was glad I placed my trust in her. The batter on the catfish formed

a hard, crunchy crust around the filet and, true to their Louisiana roots, the batter was well seasoned and the catfish delightful. The tilapia was also well seasoned, but in none of the dishes did I feel that they had gone over the top with their spices.

The fried shrimp were also exceptionally good. They hand-batter each order as it is placed. They use the same batter that they use on the fish, and it makes the shrimp hold their texture. I also ordered a grilled shrimp po-boy, since they had told me they brought the bread with them from Louisiana. They season the shrimp with the same seasoning used to blacken the fish, then finish it off with strips of lettuce, pieces of tomato and red onion and a slathering of a special sauce that they kept a secret. Needless to say, it, too, was great.

And finally, the crawfish. Cooking crawfish is how Billy got started in this business, so you'd think he'd know a thing or two about cooking them. He does. Sometimes I've had crawfish so spicy they're unbearable to eat; even your fingers start to hurt after a short while. Not so here. We made it through two pounds in no time and with no pain — a tribute to how well Billy knows his *métier*.

IT'S

very

MESSY

to eat

but worth every napkin

LOCATION
130 Heights Blvd.

PHONE
713-894-0057 / 713-384-0067

HOURS
Mon-Fri: 5:00pm-1:00am,
Sat-Sun: 9:00am-12:00am

FOOD
Mexican

PRICES
$

OWNER
Enrique Vasquez,
Rafael Ramirez Cariño

STARTED
2010

PAYMENT
Cash only

SPECIAL SERVICES
Catering

FACEBOOK
Carino/119248981453486

WEBSITE
carinotacotruck.com/

CARIÑO TACO TRUCK

—

It is obvious from the **spotless nature** of the truck that both take great pride in their work.

Enrique Vasquez, the long-time bartender at Armandos, and Rafael Ramirez Cariño, the chef, had worked at the restaurant for more than two decades. Like other entrepreneurs I met, they decided to go into business for themselves after seeing the opportunity first-hand: Enrique coordinated the food truck that Armando takes to all his catering events.

They bought themselves an old school bus and had a local firm convert it for them. The bus is painted bright

The *quesadilla* was stuffed with ground meat and melted cheese and was delightful.

orange, similar to the team color for the Dynamos.

They have a cute slogan: *"Viva La Tacovolucion."* Rafael is from Puebla, Mexico, and Enrique from Mexico City.

It is obvious from the spotless nature of the truck that both take great pride in their work. The food was excellent. The *quesadilla* was stuffed with ground meat and melted cheese and was delightful. It was served with lettuce and a slice of tomato on the side. The *taco al pastor*, made with finely diced seasoned pork, was equally good. The best in show, however, was the Mexican hot dog. They wrap a standard hot dog sausage in bacon before cooking it on the griddle. Then they top it with cubed onions and tomatoes and slices of jalapeños and completely cover it with thin drizzles

QUESADILLA // TACO AL PASTOR //
MEXICAN HOT DOG // PAPAS FRITAS TOPPED
WITH CHEESE //

of ketchup, mustard and mayonnaise, which form stripes on top of the dog. Messy to eat, it is worth every napkin

The best in show, however, was the Mexican hot dog. They wrap a standard hot dog sausage in bacon before cooking it on the griddle.

it takes to wipe the condiments off your face and hands. The *papas fritas* (french fries) are also noteworthy: Topped with cheese and a delicious, seasoned beef, they make a meal unto themselves.

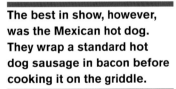

the
CATFISH
IS
wonderful
as are the hush puppies

LOCATION
6110 FM-1969 East

HOURS
Mon-Thur: 11:00am-8:00pm,
Fri-Sat: 11:00am-9:00pm

FOOD
Barbecue and catfish

PRICES
$

STARTED
2010

PAYMENT
All

PHONE
713-416-1733

OWNER
Stephan Perry

SPECIAL SERVICES
Catering

CATFISH COVE

—

He decided to open a food truck that specialized in **just two things:** fried catfish and barbecue brisket.

Stephan Perry grew up in Dayton, Texas, where he worked for a small, local seafood restaurant. After seeing how much business it did, he decided to open a food truck that specialized in just two things: fried catfish and barbecue brisket. He bought a brand-new

Stephan dips the catfish filets in cornmeal, to which he has simply added salt and pepper. A quick dip in the golden hot oil of his deep fryer, and the filets are close to being ready.

trailer, and he and his wife, Sarah, did all the work themselves to convert it to a food truck.

You may not be able to tell this from the pictures, but this place is spotless, inside and out. His first intent was to run the truck in Dayton, but a city ordinance there prohibits food trailers from parking in the same spot for more than 90 days in any one year. Since that's fewer than there are weekend days, Stephan scrambled to find another location. He is now parked on 1960E, just outside Atascocita, and has many happy customers. He is already working on a second truck just for catering. This way he can always be at this current location for the loyal customers he has developed in the few short months he has been in business.

Stephan dips the catfish filets in cornmeal, to which he has simply added salt and pepper. A quick dip in the

FRIED CATFISH // BARBECUE BRISKET // HOMEMADE COLESLAW // HUSH PUPPIES

golden hot oil of his deep fryer, and the filets are close to being ready. Stephan ensures that not a drop of grease remains on the catfish when he serves it. Add some crinkle-cut French fries, which he seasons well with salt and pepper, and you're ready to go. While the tartar sauce is not homemade, the coleslaw is. It contains both green and red cabbage as well as carrot pieces. The slight sweetness is a delight to the senses. The catfish is wonderful, as are the hush puppies, which are crispy on the outside with firm centers.

Unfortunately, Stephan is still trying to get the hang of the electric smoker he uses to make his barbecue brisket. The slices of brisket I tried were too

The coleslaw contains both green and red cabbage as well as carrot pieces.

firm and dry, and the commercial sauce he uses needs a little TLC and person-alization. I am convinced, however, that someone who can make catfish this good will tinker with the brisket and sauce until he eventually gets it right. In the meantime, order the catfish. You won't be disappointed.

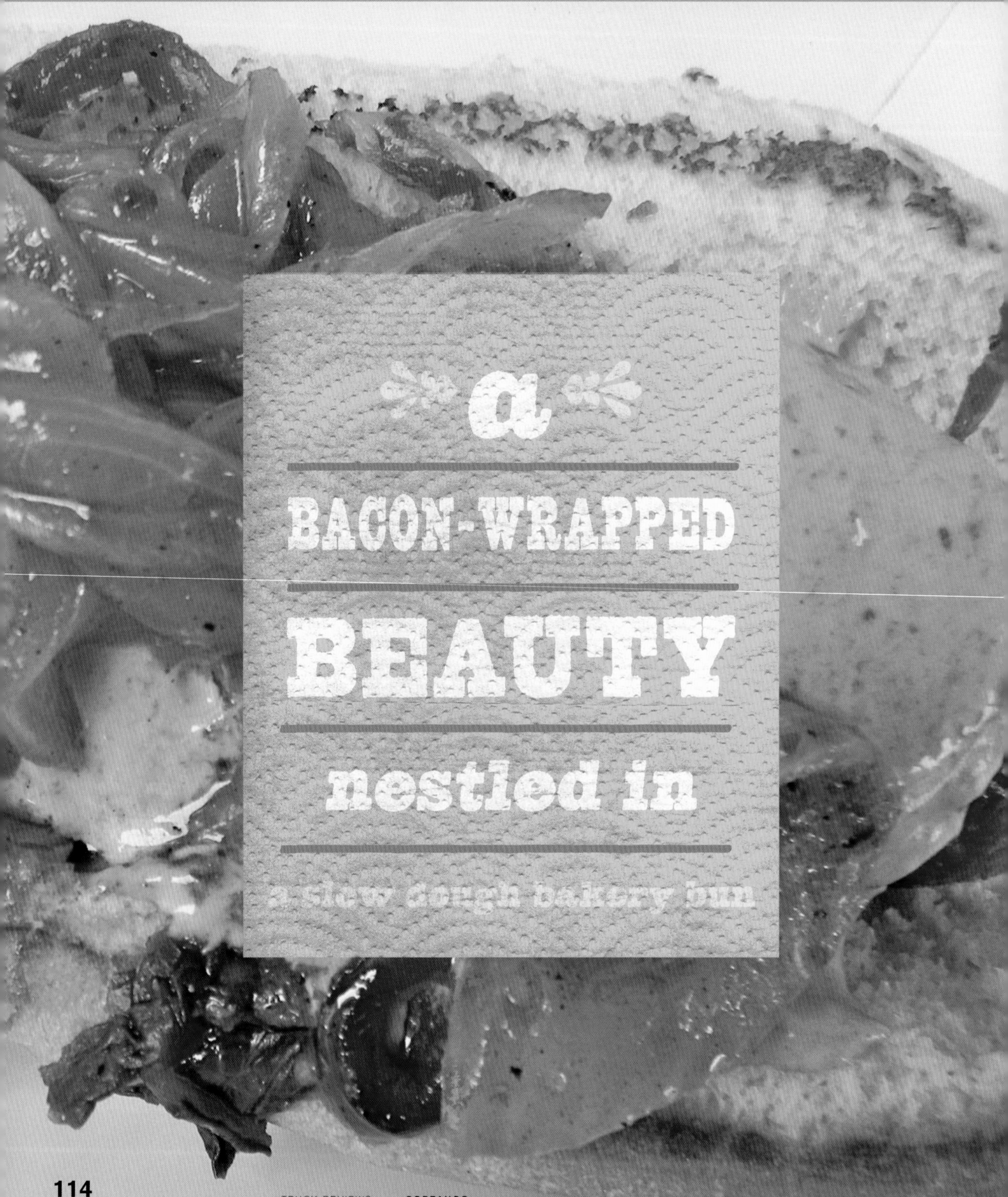

a BACON-WRAPPED BEAUTY nestled in a slow dough bakery bun

LOCATION
Various

HOURS
Various

FOOD
Korean/Mexican fusion

PRICES
$

STARTED
2012

PAYMENT
All

FACEBOOK
/coreanoshtx

OWNER
Louis Cantu

WEBSITE
http://houston.coreanostx.com/

TWITTER
/coreanoshtx

COREANOS

The Austin truck made the **Smithsonian's list** of the top 20 food trucks in the nation!

Louis Cantu grew up in Houston and moved to Austin in 2003, where he worked in a number of restaurants, including Second Bar Kitchen, Congress and the Peached Tortilla food truck. He recently returned to Houston with more than he left with: A food truck. And not just any 'ole food truck, but the Coreanos food truck that opened in Austin in 2010 and recently made it to the Smithsonian's list of the top 20 food trucks in the nation! In case that isn't enough to impress you, Yelp tells us Coreanos was one of the top 10 eateries in Austin in 2011 – not just food trucks but restaurants as well!

"The guys who opened it didn't really understand everything that was involved in running a food establishment. They didn't have their heart and soul in it," said Louis. Louis and his partner, Tom Morris, bought the truck from the original owners and plan on running two Coreanos trucks, one in Austin, the other in Houston. "I decided I wanted to return to Houston, to come back home," said Louis. "I think

this is Houston's time as a foodie town. 2012 will be a good year in food and wine in Houston," Louis predicted.

"I plan on simply enhancing the recipes and flavors developed by the original owners.

Coreanos means Koreans in Spanish and the food they serve is a fusion of Mexican and Korean cuisines The Korean cuisine comes in the form of the marinades and spices they use as well as meats like beef short ribs. The Mexican influence is in the form of the salsas, grilled onions, cilantro, tacos and burritos. The result is a very tasty mix of these two wonderful cuisines. The logo for the truck has an Asian wearing a sombrero and smoking a pipe.

"I plan on simply enhancing the recipes and flavors that were developed by the original owners by using better ingredients and bigger, bolder flavors," Louis said.

I first tried the OG Burrito, which they make with beef short ribs that they have

marinated in a Korean spice mixture. I asked Louis the meaning of the name OG. "OG is a street term for top dog or leader," Louis informed me. Not understanding how this term could have that meaning, I searched the Urban Dictionary and discovered that OG is an abbreviation of the term: Original Gangster and refers to someone in a gang who has been around a while, an old school gangster who has paid his dues.

Louis takes a large flour tortilla and warms it on the grill, then fills it with the beef short ribs, some French fries, Korean slaw, some caramelized *kimchi*, which has an interesting char on it, a sesame oil vinaigrette and some roasted garlic spread mixed with Korean *Gochujang* (hot pepper paste). Onions and cilantro are added at the very end. It's hard to get your mouth around this whopper of a burrito but well worth the effort. The beef is so tender and the fries so crispy that the textural differences make for a fascinating experience. The caramelized *kimchi* is also a very different way to serve this condiment with its deep-rooted, almost sweet flavor.

I also ordered the Three Wise Fries, where they take an order of French fries and top them with grilled onions and all three of the meats they have available: spicy marinated chicken, some of the beef from the soy-marinated short ribs, and some spicy,

twice-cooked pork belly, which has been slow-braised until it falls apart. On top of the meat and fries combination Louis adds cheese and some sauce that he has dubbed '*el scorcho*', which is a pink, creamy chipotle sauce with a really nice kick. Eating these fries is like eating any dish that is entitled 'the kitchen sink', a sort of hodge-podge of everything they have available at the time. The collection of flavors works remarkably well.

On my next trip I tried the Mexican Hot Dog. It's an all-beef Vienna frank topped with grilled onions. It's also a bacon-wrapped beauty, nestled in a slow Dough Bakery bun.

Next was the Beef Short Rib Taco with red and white cabbage slaw and a topping of sesame seeds, which add a really nice Asian flavor to this taco.

The Quesozilla was also a fascinating mélange of flavors. For this dish, Louis uses two kinds of cheese, Monterrey Jack and mild Cheddar, which are sandwiched between a large flour tortilla that has been folded in half and grilled long enough to melt the cheese and hold the rest of the ingredients together. Louis fills it with spicy chunks of twice-cooked pork belly. He also adds some caramelized *kimchi*, some *pico de gallo* and a dollop of *el scorcho* sauce, which announces itself with every bite.

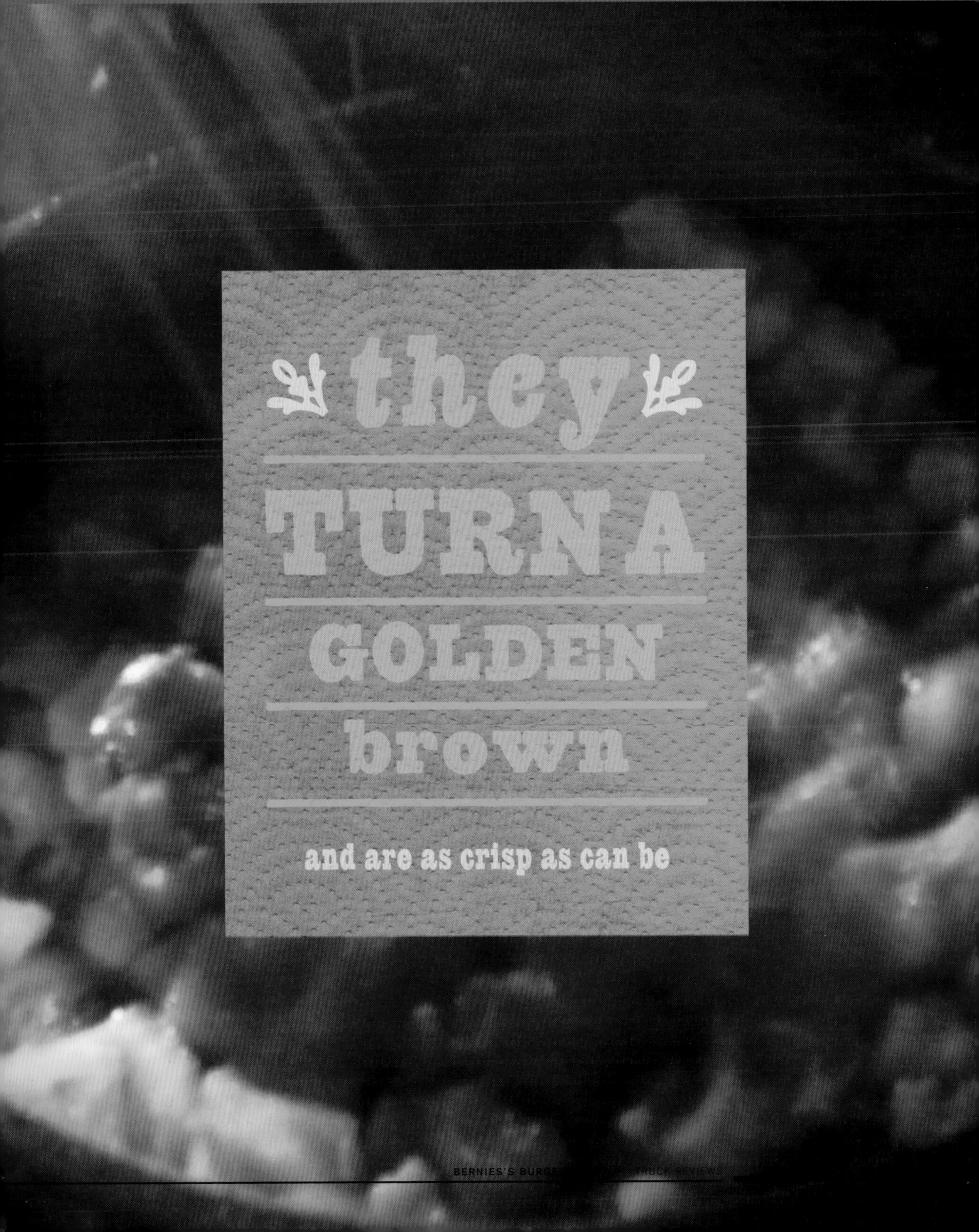

they

TURN A

GOLDEN

brown

and are as crisp as can be

LOCATION
3500 Zephyr

HOURS
Mon-Sun: 4:00pm-2:00am

FOOD
Pork Cracklings, BBQ

PRICES
$ $

OWNER
Wayland Carroll

STARTED
2009

PAYMENT
Cash only

CRACKLIN' HUT

—

Simply packaged in zip-lock bags, nothing fancy, but easy to grab hold of and **easy to eat** right there on the street

"Fresh 'n hot, straight out tha pot, cooked on tha spot" that's the sign on the side of the trailer that tells you what to expect from this trailer that sells Louisiana pork cracklings in either a mild version or a spicy one, which has lots of Tony Chachere's™ seasoning on it.

They are simply packaged in zip-lock bags, nothing fancy, but easy to grab

Wayland starts out with large pieces of pork skin which he cuts into small cubes about one-inch in size

hold of and easy to eat right there on the street or in your car. The spicy

version definitely lives up to its name. Wayland starts out with large pieces of pork skin, which he cuts into small cubes about one-inch in size. "It takes about an hour of cooking in the hot oil before they're ready," said Wayland. Finding some that still have some meat attached is like hitting the jackpot. When they're still warm, they are truly incredible.

Wayland and his brother make the pork cracklings and BBQ right outside a local night club. Club patrons who have developed a hunger at 2:00am can step outside and grab a quick snack before returning to the club. Wayland

LOUISIANA PORK CRACKLINGS // SPICY PORK CRACKLINGS // HICKORY SMOKED BAR-B-Q

and his brother also cook BBQ out of this trailer, however, every time I visited them, it was never quite ready.

Club patrons who have developed a hunger at 2:00 am can step outside and grab a quick snack before returning to the club

When you first stumble upon this trailer, you will notice the steady flumes of smoke emanating from a smokestack on the top of the trailer and then more smoke rising from behind the trailer, where Wayland cooks the pork skins until they turn a golden brown.

a BEAUTIFUL ROSE COLOR

and the icing

an intense strawberry flavor

LOCATION
Various

 HOURS
Various

 FOOD
Cupcakes

 PRICES
$

 STARTED
2011

 PAYMENT
All

 OWNERS
Janell Stringham,
Crystal Schultea

 SPECIAL SERVICES
Catering

 TWITTER
cupcakesagogotx

 FACEBOOK
CupcakesaGoGoTruck

 WEBSITE
http://cupcakesagogo.net/

CUPCAKES A GOGO

—

All the **cupcakes** are made from scratch with organic and all-natural ingredients.

I don't know if it's because they're small indulgences or because they enable a nostalgic return to childhood, but cupcakes are just hitting their stride in Houston, especially with the addition of this latest truck. It's big, with pink and white stripes, and has sparkling sequined cupcake on the rear. You can't miss it.

"It's a huge truck," said Janell. "We wish we could have found a smaller

The strawberry version is loaded with real strawberries and the icing had an intense strawberry flavor

one, but this is what we've got. It was an old Snap-on™ Tools truck."

Janell and her partner, Crystal, are originally from Houston but moved to Los Angeles in 2009 in search of careers in the movie industry. When that didn't work out, they decided to open their Cupcakes A Gogo truck. They did so well with the first one, they opened a second. "The competition in LA is fierce, so we decided to sell one truck, keep the other and move back to Houston," said Janell.

All the cupcakes are made from scratch with organic and all-natural ingredients. The strawberry version is loaded with real strawberries; they give the cupcake a beautiful rose color and the icing an intense strawberry flavor. The banana-and-peanut butter

VANILLA-MILK CHOCOLATE // RED VELVET CAKE COOKIES AND CREAM // LEMON // CARROT CAKE

combination — one of my favorite pairings — played as well together as I expected. And with a touch of chocolate to boot: Its smooth icing was topped with a Hershey's® kiss.

"We do very traditional flavors, but we also offer sugar-free and gluten-free

The banana-and-peanut butter combination's smooth icing was topped with a Hershey's® kiss

versions of our cupcakes," Janell said. They also sell mini versions, in addition to the full-sized kind. And they're thinking about adding ice cream or gelato.

Other flavors include vanilla-milk chocolate, classic vanilla, red velvet cake, carrot, double chocolate, cookies and cream, lemon, and mint chocolate chip.

the

RIBS ARE

FIRM AND VERY

tasty

an excellent smoke flavor

LOCATION
6371 Windswept

PHONE
713-447-4319

HOURS
Fri: 12:00pm-10:00pm,
Sat: 12:00am-11:00pm

FOOD
Barbecue

PRICES
$ $

OWNERS
David and Terrie Chartain

STARTED
2005

PAYMENT
Cash only

SPECIAL SERVICES
Catering, custom smoking

DC
BARBECUE

—

Most beans are either sweet like baked or tangy like ranch-style, but here, the beans **are the best** I've ever tasted.

David and his wife, Terrie, have been smoking ribs, links, brisket, chicken, turkey legs and, as David says, "anything you can smoke" for many years. Terrie makes all the sides from scratch, and David cooks the meats. They also built their trailer from scratch. Hanging around both of them, even for a little while, you can quickly tell that they enjoy working together.

David's ribs undergo his dry-rub treatment and then hours on the smoker.

Let's talk sides first. The potato salad is thick and hearty. It contains lots of pickles and thick-cut potatoes. Normally, it's hard to rave about the beans at any barbecue place — they're either sweet like baked beans or tangy like ranch-style, but here, the beans are the best I've ever tasted. Terrie adds chili and ground beef to them, and they're almost a meal in themselves.

David's ribs undergo his dry-rub treatment and then hours on the smoker. When cooked, the meat comes away from the bone at the end of the ribs, and the bone gets a nice char on it. He uses only oak, which he says helps him control the cooking. The ribs are firm and very tasty. I tried to get the recipe for his rub as well as his BBQ sauce, but all he would tell me was that they're both "family recipes that go back to my father." David also makes his own sausage, using a blend of coarsely ground beef and pork. It had an excellent smoke flavor.

BARBECUE RIBS // SAUSAGE // BRISKET
POTATO SALAD // BBQ BEANS // LEMON CAKE

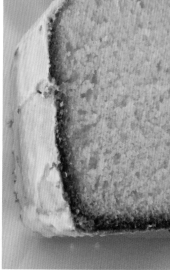

David uses a three-step process on his brisket. First he administers his dry rub, followed by searing it on the fatty side. This is followed by five hours at 350 degrees with the fat up, so that the juices flow into the meat. The brisket had a nice red ring of fire, but I found the meat to be somewhat dry. The homemade sauce helped a lot.

Whatever you order here, you will not go home hungry. The plates are that full. If you order a three-meat platter, it is highly unlikely you'll be able consume it all in one sitting.

A lemon cake that was as moist as can be and, lucky for me, still warm.

There's one more surprise waiting for those who order any plate: a slice of Terrie's homemade cake. The day I showed up, Terrie had made a lemon cake. It was as moist as can be and, lucky for me, still warm. Needless to say, this little addition made everything just perfect.

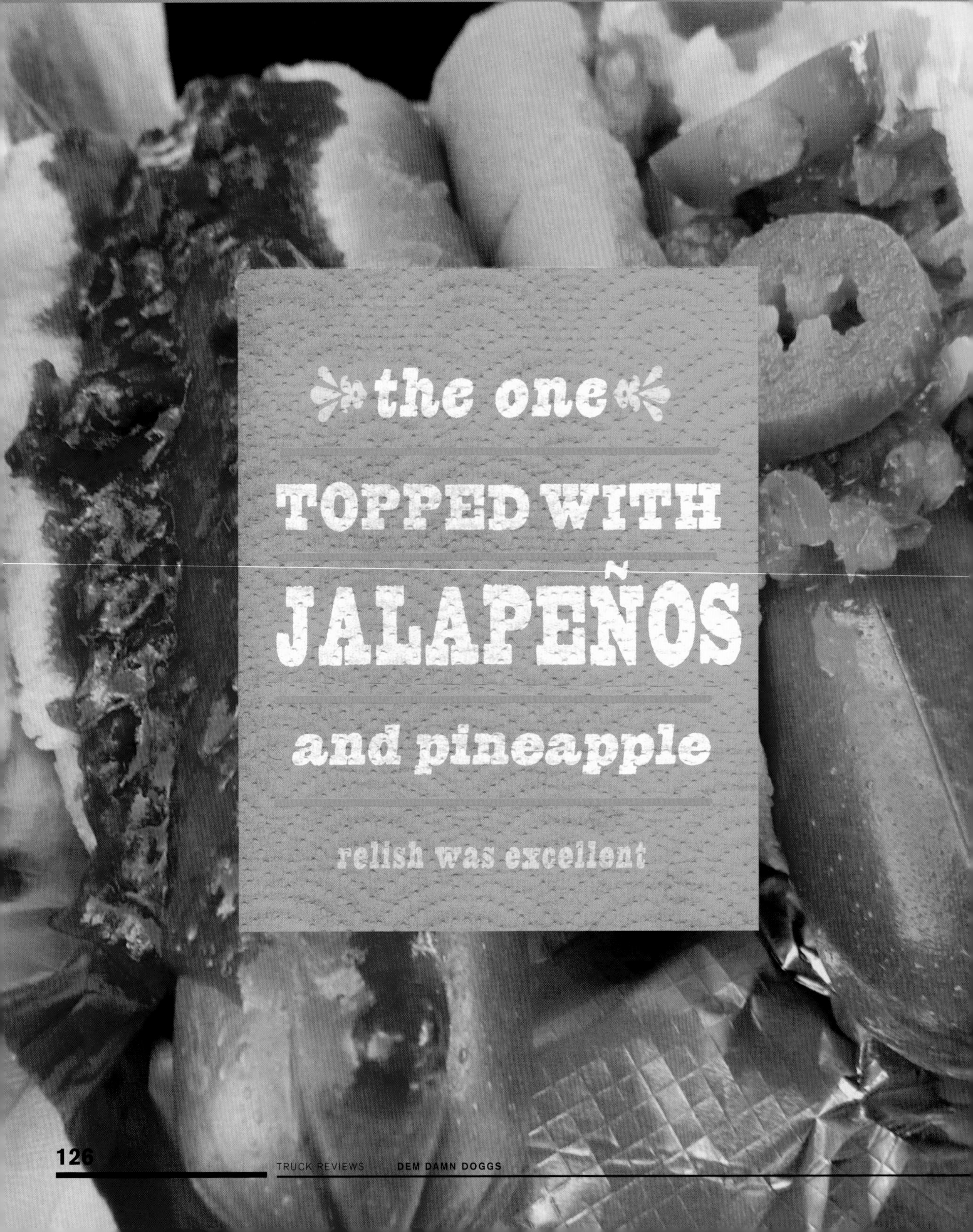

❋the one❋

TOPPED WITH

JALAPEÑOS

and pineapple

relish was excellent

LOCATION
4001 Tierwester

PHONE
832-794-0417

HOURS
Mon, Wed, Fri: 10:00am-6:00pm

FOOD
Hot dogs

PRICES
$

OWNER
Juniper Tyler

STARTED
2010

PAYMENT
All

SERVICES
Some Kosher

WEBSITE
http://www.demdamndoggs.com/

DEM DAMN DOGGS

—

Juniper retired from the teaching profession and decided to pursue a dream that she and her brother had: to open an **old-fashioned hot dog stand**.

While technically this is not a truck or a trailer, it is Houston's first hot dog stand. Juniper retired from the teaching profession and decided to pursue a

She currently offers 100 percent all-beef Kosher franks, turkey franks, veggie hot dogs and Italian sausage

dream that she and her brother had: to open an old-fashioned hot dog stand. After trying a few locations downtown

without much success, they settled on a parking lot opposite the campus of TSU. She seems to have found the right spot.

She currently offers 100 percent all-beef Kosher franks, turkey franks, veggie hot dogs and Italian sausages on a poppy seed bun, as well as nachos and Frito pie. She plans to expand her offerings to include Doggs Damn Desserts and Dem Damn Daquiris.

CHICKEN AND BEEF FAJITAS // MARGARITAS
BREAKFAST TACOS // FAJITA BEEF TACOS
FISH TACOS // SALSA BAR

I tried a Bigg Juicy chili dog with onions and cheese, as well as one with *jalapeños*, pineapple relish and spicy mustard. The chili version was good;

The chili version was good; but the one topped with *jalapeños* and pineapple relish was excellent. The combination of sweet and hot blew me away

but the one topped with *jalapeños* and pineapple relish was excellent. The combination of sweet and hot is irresistible.

the

CHICKEN

WAS THE TRADITIONAL

orange-red

color on the outside

LOCATION
12672 Veteran's Memorial Drive

PHONE
832-798-8196

HOURS
Mon-Sun: 5:00pm-12:00am

FOOD
Indian, Pakistani

PRICES
$$

OWNER
Vinod Bhai

STARTED
2006

PAYMENT
Cash only

SERVICES
Halal

DESI GRILL AND MORE

—

After we placed our order, the first thing Vinod did was pat out the bread dough for the *naan* and place it inside the **makeshift *tandoor*** to cook.

Vinod has been running this Indian *dhaba*, a small roadside stand that serves food, since 2006. Vinod moved to Houston in 1982. He is an experienced chef and restaurant owner, having owned Bombay Delights and an-

The sheikh kabab had a wonderful char flavor to it. Juice from the meat dripped onto the rice

other restaurant on Hillcroft. His father moved to the U.S. from Delhi in 1972, when he opened the first Gaylord Indian restaurant in New York. This was followed by a second one in Chicago. The Gaylord chain of upscale Indian restaurants was one of the first attempts to build an empire based on Indian cuisine

by following the Indian diaspora.

I asked Vinod if the Indian population in the northwest part of Houston was large enough to warrant an Indian food truck. I commented that his son, who runs the Tandoori Night truck on Highway 6, was better situated, since the population of Indians and Pakistanis had to be larger there. Vinod told me that his customers come from all around to buy his food. After tasting it for the first time, I understood why.

After we placed our order, the first thing Vinod did was pat out the bread dough for the *naan* and place it inside the makeshift *tandoor* to cook. The *tandoor* oven is made from an old 55-gallon oil drum but serves its purpose well.

PANEER MASALA // SHEIKH KABAB
CHANNA MASALA // BOTI // NAAN //
DELICIOUS CHUTNEY

Then Vidal turned his attention to the *sheikh kabab*. He formed the pre-seasoned ground lamb by hand around the flat metal skewer. He took his time with this, ensuring the shape was perfect, so that it would cook evenly. This was followed by a similar process for the chicken *boti*, only this time he placed large chunks of chicken, green pepper and onion on the skewer before placing both skewers in the *tandoor*. After a few minutes of cooking on one side, Vinod turned the skewers to cook the other side.

Next was the preparation of the rice. He first tossed some basmati rice, which was already cooked, into a skillet along with some onions, green peppers and chickpeas, as well as pieces of lamb and spices such as cloves and coriander. The rice was outstanding, and watching it being prepared gave me ideas of how to do something similar with leftover rice.

The *sheikh kabab* had a wonderful char flavor to it. Juice from the meat dripped onto the rice, adding flavor. The chicken was the traditional orange-red color on the outside. It also had a nice char flavor, along with lots of ginger and garlic.

For vegetables, we ordered the *channa masala* and the paneer

masala. The chickpeas in the *channa masala* came with a thick, spicy sauce. The heat should not have come as a surprise to us, since when Vinod asked how spicy we wanted it, we had told him to treat us as he would Indians. He immediately took a whole *jalapeño* and chopped it up into the chickpeas.

The *paneer*, or chunks of cheese, came with a similarly thick sauce, but the dish was not as spicy as the chickpeas. The garlic *naan*, a flat bread fresh out of the oven, was piping hot, with steam escaping as we tore into it. It was finished with some *ghee* and garlic. It was some of the best *naan* I've ever had: thick in some parts, thin in others, doughy and stretchy with holes here and blister marks there. It was perfect for sopping up the sauces. Vinod's dishes also come with a delicious chutney made from mint, onions, cilantro, garlic, ginger and *jalapeño*. It is quite spicy and should be approached with caution.

Inside the city limits, regulations prohibit food trucks from being located near places to sit. But since Vinod is outside the city limits, he's been able to set up a comfortable, covered, communal seating area behind his truck. Indian music plays from a small boom box.

*long RIBBED FRIED PIECES of dough

popular in latin america

HOURS
Mon-Fri: 7:00am-9:00pm,
Sat: 8:00am-8:00pm

FOOD
Mexican, churros, hot dogs,
funnel cakes

PRICES
$

STARTED
2009

PAYMENT
Cash only

PHONE
832-387-0760

OWNERS
Marisol and Raul Estrada

SPECIAL SERVICES
Catering

DON CHURRO

—

The array of flavors here is the **largest** I have ever come across. The 13 listed on the menu included flavors I'd never tried before

The name of this truck suggests that it produces *churros* — long, ribbed fried pieces of dough popular in Mexico and much of the rest of Latin America — which indeed it does. But it also produces everything else you would find on a typical taco truck, such as tacos, *tortas* (rolls), *quesadillas*, hot

His fanaticism translates into damn good barbecue, not to mention great sides, like a creamy potato salad and two types of beans.

dogs, burritos, *gorditas* (stuffed corn cakes) and *aguas frescas* (fruit drinks or punches).

You can order *churros* either plain or stuffed. "Plain" means rolled in sugar

and cinnamon. "Stuffed" means rolled in sugar and cinnamon, then cut in the middle and augmented with the sort of filling that you find in doughnuts. The array of flavors here is the largest I have ever come across. The 13 listed on on the menu included flavors I'd never tried before, like *coco* (coconut), *piña colada* and *fresa* (strawberry). The *piña colada*, made by combining the *coco* with the *piña* flavors, is amazingly true to the flavor of the drink of the same name. The *churro* dough and the flavorings are all made from old family recipes from Guanajato, Mexico. Marisol and her husband, Raul, are incredibly nice people and want nothing more than to ensure that you enjoy their food.

CHURROS // TACOS // TORTAS // HOT DOGS
BURRITOS // QUESADILLAS // AGUAS FRESCAS
GORDITAS // STUFFED CHURROS // FUNNEL CAKES

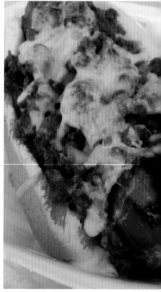

I also sampled one of their Mexican hot dogs, called the Shorty. Given its name, I expected a smallish sausage. It wasn't. The large all-beef dog is

The large all-beef dog is wrapped in bacon, then topped with mozzarella cheese and diced pork, which has been well-seasoned and marinated before cooking.

wrapped in bacon, then topped with mozzarella cheese and diced pork, which has been well-seasoned and marinated before cooking. It was one of the tastiest dogs I have ever tried. After eating a number of Mexican hot dogs and enjoying every one of them, I wondered if I would ever again be able to consume a hot dog not wrapped in bacon. The bacon not only adds a lot of flavor but fat, which keeps the dog nice and moist.

♦ **4 slices** ♦

OF THICK

BACON

maple-smoked

was outstanding

LOCATION
Various

PHONE
845-430-8479

HOURS
Various

FOOD
American, chef-inspired

PRICES
$$

OWNERS
Matt Marcus, Alex Vassilakidis, Ryan Soroka

STARTED
2010

PAYMENT
Cash only

SPECIAL SERVICES
Catering

TWITTER
eatsieboys

FACEBOOK
Eatsie-Boys/161003190598767

WEBSITE
http://www.eatsieboys.com

EATSIE BOYS

—

Matt Marcus, the chef behind this truck, was trained at the **Culinary Institute of America** in New York and California.

The truck's name is a riff on the Beastie Boys, a 1990s rap group. Matt Marcus, the chef behind this truck, was trained at the Culinary Institute of America in New York and California. His work experience includes stints at Fat Duck in London and Cyrus in Sonoma. He also happens to be the son of Al Marcus, who owns Grateful Bread, purveyor of charcuterie, mustards, smoked cheeses and sauces to many of Houston's restaurants, and a regular at farmers' markets around town. Matt is joined in this venture by Ryan, who runs the front of the house, and Alex, who runs the back of the house. Matt and Ryan are the business brains behind the venture, but it is Matt's talent in the kitchen that makes this truck a don't-miss.

All the bread they use is from Hous-ton's own Slow Dough Bread Co. The first thing we tried was Frank the Pretzel. A homemade chicken *poblano* sausage with a heavy influence of thyme sat on a pretzel hoagie. The bread was coated with homemade

All the bread they use is from Houston's own Slow Dough Bread Co.

whole grain mustard, and the sausage was topped with Worcestershire-infused onions. One bite was all it took to fall in love with this "haute dog."

The Eggman was an egg sandwich with four slices of thick-cut, maple-smoked bacon. It came with a Hatterman's Poultry Farm free-range egg, which I asked to be cooked over easy, and a slice of American cheese, served on a challah roll.

FRANK THE PRETZEL // THE EGGMAN // PORK SNUGGIES // SABOTAGE

Biting into the sandwich made the egg ooze , revealing the yolk's true color — bright orange, which can only come from well-raised and well-fed chickens. The bacon was outstanding, and together, they made this breakfast sandwich memorable.

Lunch at the Eatsie Boys is just as exciting. To make Pork Snuggies, Matt brines and cures his own pork bellies.

Matt gives the sandwich a good dousing of the pork drippings just before serving.

Then he simply fries the thick slices on the griddle, places them on the steamed Vietnamese-style *bao* buns that he also makes, along with green onions, a drizzle of *hoisin* sauce and a slice of homemade pickle. He was inspired to make these after trying the steamed pork buns at Momofuko, in New York, where they are the specialty of chef David Chang. One bite and I could tell that Matt had nailed it. I was sad that only two came to an order.

The last thing I tried was Sabotage. (Like all the truck's offerings, it's named after the Beastie Boys song.) A crispy French roll is filled with shaved slices of oven-roasted pork, braised mustard greens and two slices of sharp

Provolone. Matt gives the sandwich a good dousing of the pork drippings just before serving. It is a terrific-tasting sandwich, with the pork offset by the bitter greens and the cheese helping to keep everything held together.

The success of this truck has led them to a brick and mortar place which they opened in the old KraftsMen bakery on Montrose.

>**they're**<

STUFFED

with

PULLED

chicken

and easily eaten by hand

LOCATION
6250 Bissonnet

HOURS
Mon-Sun: 9:00am-9:00pm

FOOD
Honduran

PRICES
$$

STARTED
2010

PAYMENT
Cash

PHONE
713-305-2835

OWNER
Lester Martinez

EL CARACOL COMIDA TIPICA HONDUREÑA

The interesting thing about this bus is that at the back, accessed through a separate door, he has **a small dining area**, complete with kids' chairs.

Owner Lester Martinez is from Honduras (El Progreso, in the Department of Yoro, to be precise). For many of the seven years that he's been in Houston, he worked as a sous chef. Now, as an entrepreneur, he enjoys a growing business. Earlier this year, he sold his first small truck and bought this large converted school bus, paying around $38,000 to get it rolling. The interesting thing about this bus is that, at the back, accessed through a separate door, he has a small dining area, complete with kids' chairs.

He makes his own home-made flour tortillas and uses them in the traditional *baleadas* (the Honduran version of tacos).

"*Caracol*" is Spanish for "conch." Because of the truck's name, I was eager to try the sopa *caracol*, or traditional

BALEADAS // HOMEMADE FLOUR TORTILLAS
FRIED CHICKEN // TROPICAL BANANA SODA

conch soup, but Lester advised me that he hasn't been making it for some time. Conch is not easy to find in Houston.

He makes his own homemade flour tortillas and uses them in the traditional *baleadas* (the Honduran version of

Fried chicken consisted of two pieces of crispy chicken in a crunchy, well-seasoned batter, served with shredded cabbage on a base of *tequenos*, crispy, fried plantains.

tacos). I tried the chicken tacos, which are rolled up like taquitos and fried to a crisp. They are stuffed with pulled chicken and are easily eaten with your hands. Two of them come to an order, and they are topped with shredded cabbage, red pickled onions, crumbled cheese and a sauce made from mayonnaise and ketchup. When I asked Lester what made the onions red, he told me what he always tells customers who ask that question: "I cut my finger while chopping the onions."

Fried chicken consisted of two pieces of crispy chicken in a crunchy, well-

seasoned batter, served with shredded cabbage on a base of *tequenos*, crispy, fried plantains. Lester recommended a tropical banana-flavored soda to wash it all down. The rich, golden yellow color makes it really inviting, and it tastes like liquid candy.

these

ARE VERY

DOUGHY

wide

yet not too thick

LOCATION
10910 Airline

HOURS
Various

FOOD
Churros

PRICES
$

OWNER
Guadalupe Camarena

STARTED
2010

PAYMENT
Cash only

EL GORGOJO CHURROS

—

These are very doughy, wide and yet not too thick. The **plain sugared version** has a texture and taste close to American donuts.

Guadalupe is from Arandas, in the state of Jalisco. The particular *churros* he makes, using a family recipe, are known as *churros gordos*, or fat *churros*. They are not the dense, ribbed versions that are dropped into hot fat from a funnel — the kind that you have probably seen many times in Houston. These are very doughy, wide and yet not too thick. The plain sugared version has a texture and taste close to American donuts.

Guadalupe first works the dough into a thick, long strip, then places it into the hot oil, careful not to splatter the oil everywhere. He uses two thin metal rods to form the dough into a circle. After a minute or so, when the dough

They are not the dense, ribbed versions that are dropped into hot fat from a funnel — the kind that you have probably seen many times in Houston.

is cooked on one side, he then turns it to cook on the other. A minute or two later, he removes it from the oil with the rods and lets it hang. Gravity removes the excess oil.

CHURROS GORDOS // PLAIN SUGAR TOPPED
CAJETA TOPPED // STRAWBERRY JAM TOPPED
HOT CHOCOLATE ATOLE

Toppings include plain sugar, *lechera* (condensed milk), *cajeta* (caramel) and

He also serves a delicious hot chocolate atole, which is also a family recipe.

strawberry jam. He also serves a delicious hot chocolate *atole*, which is also a family recipe. Eating these *churros* hot, right after they are cooked, is a wonderful experience.

it

ALSO COMES

WITH A

small arepa

the Venezuelan corn cake

LOCATION
14601 Beechnut

PHONE
409-717-2368

HOURS
Mon-Wed: 8:00am-6:00pm,
Thur: 9:30am-6:00pm, Fri: 8:00am-
9:00pm, Sat: 9:00am-9:00pm

FOOD
Venezuelan, Colombian, Mexican

PRICES
$

OWNER
Mireya McDonald

STARTED
2010

PAYMENT
Cash only

SPECIAL SERVICES
Catering

EL PUNTO CRIOLLO

—

Mireya's trailer may be tiny, but it has everything she needs to turn out **excellent food.**

Owner Mireya has an infectious smile, and when she talks about the food she prepares, she flashes it constantly. Her trailer may be tiny, but it has everything

This sweet corn fritter is folded over *queso fresco*, which easily melts under the heat of the corn fritter.

she needs to turn out excellent food. She even has room to sell some packaged goods to homesick Venezuelans. She is married to a man from Mexico, and even though she specializes in Venezuelan food, she has added tacos to the menu. As her husband told me, "It's good for business." The minute they put up a sign advertising tacos, their breakfast trade picked up.

Mireya makes a mean *cachapa*. This sweet corn fritter is folded over *queso fresco*, which easily melts under the heat of the corn fritter. *Pabellon criollo* is the national dish of Venezuela, and the one she makes is a large dish consisting of shredded beef served with white rice, some delicious black beans, and *maduros*, or fried sweet plantains. It also comes with a small *arepa*, the Venezuelan corn cake.

I also sampled a Colombian *empanada*. The *empanadas* in Colombia are larger than their counterparts in other countries, and they're baked, not fried. Consequently, the dry pastry becomes very flaky as you open the little package. The chicken version that we sampled was excellent.

EL PUNTO CRIOLLO   TRUCK REVIEWS   **145**

CACHAPA // PABELLON CRIOLLO // MADUROS
AREPA // EMPANADAS // HALLACA

El Punto Criollo

ayunos (Breakfast)
mble Eggs & Omelette
os Revueltos $3.00
mon y Queso $4.00
on Arepitas, Pan o Tortillas

Almuerzos (Lunch)
Pabellon Criollo $6.50
Sopa de Pollo $3.00

adas (Filled Pastries)
irne, Cazon,
, Queso

anadas Chilenas
Pollo o Carne
$2.75

Pastelitos
, Carne o Queso
$1.75

rinks (Bebidas)
escolita $1.35
ta Polar $1.25
ombiana $1.25

Arepas (Filled Corn (
Pollo, Carne, Atun,
Queso, Ensalada de
Huevos Revueltos, P
$4.00

Cachapas (Sweet Cor
Queso de M
Jamon y Qu

Tequeños (Cheese Sti
$0.60 Cada uno (Eac

Patacones (3 uni
Carne o Pollo $3

Tacos $:
ollo, Carne

Gordita $3.00
Pollo o Carne

Quesadillas $.
Pollo o Carn
Tortas $4.

During the holiday period, Mireya also makes a traditional holiday dish called *hallaca*, which resembles a tamale, only better. It is large, fairly flat and rectangular, and is filled with stewed beef and chicken, raisins, olives, carrots,

The *empanadas* in Colombia are larger than their counterparts in other countries, and they're also baked, not fried.

red peppers and capers. Its interior is extremely colorful. Unlike the Mexican tamale, where most of the flavor comes from the corn, the *hallaca's* flavor is in the filling, and it is delicious. You can also order these specialties to go.

it

BECOMES

EXTREMELY

crisp

to carry a large amount
of toppings

LOCATION
8705 Airline

HOURS
Sat-Sun: 10:00am-5:00pm

FOOD
Mexican

PRICES
$

EL REY DEL CHICHARRON

—

He imports the **chicharrones**, which he also calls **duro**, from Mexico. Made by a group of people in the small pueblo of San Luis Potosi.

Until I found this truck, I was under the impression that the word *"chicharron"* referred only to fried pork skin, which is also known as crackling. I was soon

When a raw chicharron hits the 350-degree oil, it puffs up to three or four times its previous size

corrected by the owner. He specializes in *chicharrones preparados*. He imports the *chicharrones*, which he also calls *duro*, from Mexico. Made by a group of people in the small pueblo of San Luis Potosi, they are completely flat rectangles, about six to eight inches in size, made of wheat

and corn flour.

When a raw *chicharron* hits the 350-degree oil, it puffs up to three or four times its previous size. The owner moves it around in the oil and turns it once it is cooked on one side. Once the *chicharron* is fully cooked, a process that takes only a couple of minutes, it becomes extremely crisp, sufficiently so as to carry a large amount of toppings without sagging or breaking.

The final stage of assembly is quite elaborate, and the toppings go on in a specific order. Shredded cabbage, pickled *cueritos* (pig skins, which remain

CHICHARRONES PREPARADOS // CURLY FRIES
FUNNEL CAKES // NACHOS CON QUESO

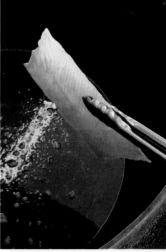

chewy until the end), *queso fresco*, sour cream, tiny cubes of tomato, slices of avocado, hot sauce and slices of lime all go on top of the crispy base.

Shredded cabbage, pickled *cueritos*, *queso fresco*, sour cream, tiny cubes of tomato, slices of avocado, hot sauce and slices of lime all go on top of the crispy base.

Eating it is a challenge: You're not sure whether you should pick up the whole thing and bite into it (not recommended), break off a small portion, or try to cut through it with a fork. Whichever approach you take, the incredibly satisfying snack will be worth the trouble.

Taking advantage his vat of hot oil, the owner also makes funnel cakes — though not at the same time.

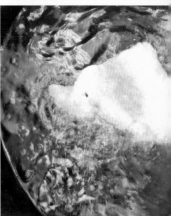

a
FOOT LONG
RIDGED
donut

with your favorite topping

LOCATION
800 S. Wayside

HOURS
Mon-Sun: 6:00am-9:00pm

FOOD
Churros, hot chocolate

PRICES
$$

PAYMENT
Cash only

EL REY DEL CHURRO

—

Without a doubt, the *cajeta* was the tastiest. It was, however, the ***Champurrado*** which blew me away.

This colorful truck was in the parking lot of the Fiesta supermarket on Fulton. As I approached, the lady was placing three large trays of *churros* on a shopping cart and about to wheel them inside Fiesta, where, I assume she also sold them. She sells hot chocolate and *churros*. *Churros* are a foot long,

Churros are a foot long, ridged donuts which come *regulares* or *preparado*, which means topped with your favorite topping.

ridged donuts which come *regulares* (plain, covered in sugar) or *preparado*, which means topped with your favorite topping. The toppings include *cajeta* or caramel, *lechera*, or condensed milk

and chocolate sauce, which, in this case, happens to be Hershey's®. 'Lechera' is an interesting word because it is actually the trademarked brand name for the Nestle® condensed milk. It has obviously become the generic term for condensed milk. Without a doubt, the *cajeta* was the tastiest. It was, however, the *Champurrado* which blew me away. It was just the thing for dipping those *churros* in. It was thick, creamy, sweet and piping hot. A chocolate *atole* drink is known as a *champurrado* in Mexico. It is made with Mexican chocolate, *piloncillo*, a hard, pyramid of brown sugar and cinnamon. It is also usually made with vanilla and anise although I detected neither of these in the one I tried here. The *Champurrado*

CAJETA CHURROS // LECHERA CHURROS // CHAMPURRADO, A CHOCOLATE ATOLE DRINK

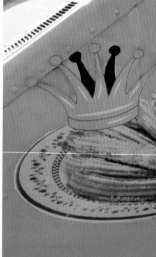

is traditionally served with *churros* for breakfast or for a mid-afternoon snack. Its thickness comes from the corn *masa* used to make it. *Atoles* are drinks made with a traditional *molinillo* or wooden whisk. The whisk is placed into the liquid

Atoles are drinks made with a traditional *molinillo* or wooden whisk.

and held between the hands, which are rubbed together to cause the liquid to froth, although the *champurrada* here was not in the least bit frothy.

As I was leaving, I noticed that the server was discarding some of the *churros* that had been left out. I asked the server why. He held up two *churros*, one which he was about to discard, the other, a freshly fried one and asked me which one I would pick. I chose the correct one. "You see this one?" he said, "It's all dry and hard. No good." Obviously, his customers can tell the difference and he won't settle for anything less than the best quality.

✦ with ✦

CHOCOLATE

AND PEANUT

pieces

stuffed with vanilla ice-cream

LOCATION
Various

PHONE
713-252-5551

HOURS
Various

FOOD
Ice cream, popsicles,
Mexican sweets and candy

PRICES
$

OWNERS
Ricardo Salazar

STARTED
2009

PAYMENT
Cash only

SPECIAL SERVICES
Catering

FANTASTIC ICE CREAM TRUCK

—

You can often find **Ricardo** at Discovery Green, where he puts smiles on the faces of hundreds of children.

Perhaps some of our fondest memories of childhood are about summer

Seeing the delight in the eyes of these kids and the long lines at the truck, you can understand that Ricardo is meeting a real need in the community as well as becoming self-sufficient.

vacations and the ice cream truck that roamed the neighborhood. The ice cream truck dates to 1920 when Harry Burt of Youngstown, Ohio invented the "Good Humor Bar, which was the first chocolate-covered ice cream on a stick. He was the first to sell ice cream from a fleet of trucks equipped with freezers.

Ricardo and his sister Elizabeth came to the U.S. from Colombia in 2007. Ricardo is hearing-impaired, and although he knew sign language, it was Colombian Sign Language; he had to learn the American kind. To put himself through school, he started an ice-cream truck business.

You can often find Ricardo at Discovery Green, where he puts smiles on the faces of hundreds of children. Seeing the delight in the eyes of these kids

75 KINDS OF ICE CREAM TREATS //
MANY DIFFERENT CANDIES // POPSICLES

and the long lines at the truck, you can understand that Ricardo is meeting a real need in the community as well as becoming self-sufficient.

The ice cream I tried fit perfectly with the overall premise of this book. It was a Klondike® Choco Taco®. The waffle-cone taco is folded in two and stuffed with vanilla and chocolate-fudge ice cream. It is then topped with more chocolate and peanut pieces. Fortunately for me, the ice-cream was reduced fat, but you could not tell this

Ricardo offers 75 kinds of ice cream treats, as well as many different candies.

by the mouth-feel. Ricardo offers 75 kinds of ice cream treats, as well as many different candies.

the TORTILLAS ARE LARGE and they fill them to capacity

LOCATION
Various

HOURS
Various

FOOD
Mexican

PRICES
$

STARTED
2012

PAYMENT
All

PHONE
713 819-6281

OWNERS
Homero Ponce-Lopez

TWITTER
/FirehouseTaco

FACEBOOK
/FirehouseTacos

WEBSITE
http://firehousetacos.com

FIRE HOUSE TACOS

—

"I learned to cook when I was a rookie at the **fire department**. 'The rookie cooks' was what I was told and since I was born in Mexico, I cooked Mexican food," said Homero.

What do you do after you served for thirty-one years in the Houston Fire Department? Open a fire house taco truck. That's what Homero Ponce-Lopez did when he retired from the HFD as Captain last year.

The truck is hard to miss, since it looks like a fire truck. With his experience,

The bright orange-colored meat next to the yellow minced pineapple was a feast for the eyes as well as the palate.

you might expect he'd get the details right, from the red paint job and the ladder and fire axe affixed to the side of the truck to the flashing blue light on top. Then there's the fireman's uniform and boots hanging from the side of the

truck. Oh, and don't forget the smoke alarm at the ordering window, which you're supposed to set off if you're not served immediately upon your arrival. However, with four guys manning this truck (Romero, his two sons and one of his nephews), I doubt that this ever goes off. When your order is ready, they announce it by ringing - what else? - a fire bell. They have thought of pretty much everything.

"I learned to cook when I was a rookie at the fire department. 'The rookie cooks' was what I was told and since I was born in Mexico, I cooked Mexican food," said Homero.

On my first visit, I tried all three of the tacos they had available. First was the Sizzling Chicken Taco. Like all the

SIZZLING CHICKEN TACO // *CHARRO* BEANS // BUFFALO CHICKEN *QUESADILLA* // PINEAPPLE PORK TACO // FAJITA TACO

tacos they serve, they come on a flour tortilla that is finished on the truck. The tortillas are large and they fill them to capacity, meaning that each one contains a lot of meat. Of all the tacos I tried, I found this one to be lacking in flavor. I mentioned this to Homero. My guess is that he fixed it the next time out. Next was the Fajita Taco, which was full of terrific-tasting fajita strips. Lastly, and my absolute favorite, was the Pineapple Pork Taco, whose bright red color was indicative of the use of *achiote* as coloring. The bright orange-colored meat next to the yellow minced

It is quite spicy and the vinegar-based sauce almost fooled me into believing that I was eating Buffalo wings.

pineapple was a feast for the eyes as well as the palate. Each taco comes with *pico de gallo*, onions and cilantro to order, so you get to customize your taco just as you like it. I also ordered a side of their *charro* beans. They were full of onions, tomatoes and, of course, bacon, which made them very tasty.

On my next visit I spotted the Buffalo Chicken *Quesadilla* on the menu. They first warm a large flour tortilla on the griddle, then they cook the chicken

in spicy Buffalo wing sauce and top it with Mozzarella cheese, which melts almost by the time it is served to you. Then they fold the tortilla in half. I asked for mine with onions and cilantro. It is quite spicy and the vinegar-based sauce almost fooled me into believing that I was eating Buffalo wings.

There are many wonderful things to rave about at this truck, not least of which is the fact that they accept donations at the truck for the Houston Fire Museum. Yet another reason to visit them is that Homero plans to offer his food free of charge to the brave souls fighting any 4 alarm or more fire, where the firefighters will have been battling a blaze for upwards of twelve hours. Once a firefighter, always a firefighter.

§ all §

THE SPICY

FLAVORS

work

remarkably well together

LOCATION
Various

PHONE
832-603-1971

HOURS
Various

FOOD
Gourmet hamburgers, sandwiches

PRICES
$

OWNER
Stiles Smith

STARTED
2011

PAYMENT
All

SPECIAL SERVICES
Catering

TWITTER
flamingpatties

FACEBOOK
flamingpatties

FLAMING PATTIES

—

It's hard to miss his **flaming red truck**. And not surprisingly, flames are the theme that runs through his menu.

Stiles Smith ought to know a thing or two about cooking a good burger. After all, he's been flipping them for the past 35 years, first running The Stables, a restaurant popular in Houston for four decades, until it closed in 2006; then as the operations manager for Prince's Burgers; and finally as owner of the Roadster Grill in Bellaire, which also made a mean burger. Since he has so much room in his truck, he calls it the Burger Beast. He is also about to give

Stiles uses only certified Angus beef, never frozen, at an 80/20 blend of lean and fat

the same name to a burger, which will be filled with either two or three patties; he hasn't decided yet.

It's hard to miss his flaming red truck. And not surprisingly, flames are the theme that runs through his menu. To any burger you can add "Extra Flame" in the guise of bacon, avocado, etc., including a Nasty *Jalapeño* Relish. He also offers "Flame Killers" (drinks).

First, let's talk meat. Stiles uses only certified Angus beef, never frozen, at an 80/20 blend of lean and fat, which makes the burgers plenty juicy. He forms every patty by hand, making it large enough to hang over the edge of the bun after being cooked. He uses three different buns: a regular white, a whole wheat and a *jalapeño* cheese, which adds additional flavor to any of the burgers. My first burger was the Blue Betty. Rather than just top a

FLAME KILLERS // BLUE BETTY BURGER //
SPICY NASTI BURGER // SWEET POTATO FRIES
SMITTY'S TWINS SLIDERS

patty with blue cheese, Stiles actually stuffs the blue cheese into the center of the burger so that it melts from within, allowing the flavor of the blue cheese to permeate the whole burger. A slice of Gruyere melts on top of the patty, which is topped with slowly caramelized onions, spicy chipotle mayo and just enough arugula to add a soft hint of pepper. It is a terrific burger.

Next was an order of his sliders, which he calls "Smitty's Twins." These mini burgers are also topped with the same caramelized onions and the standard accoutrements of mustard,

He uses three different buns: a regular white, a whole wheat and a *jalapeño* cheese

ketchup and pickles. They, too, are excellent burgers, nice and juicy. They disappear after only three mouthfuls.

The third burger was one called the "Nasti Burger." If you like spicy food, you're going to love this one. It is ar six-ounce patty, which reaches out over the edge of the *jalapeño* bun. It is topped with caramelized onions, a slice of pepper jack cheese and homemade pickled *jalapeño* relish. The bun is covered with a spicy chi-

potle mayo. All the spicy flavors work remarkably well together, and astonishingly, the flavor of the meat still clamors through. Like all the burgers here, this one is exceedingly juicy.

We tried his regular and sweet potato fries, both of which he also hand cuts. The regular fries were nice and crispy, but the sweet potato fries were a little soft and limp. Since we found him on opening week, we suspect that he will have corrected the problem by the time you read this.

❋ **they** ❋

TOP THEM
WITH
icing

only when you order them

FROSTED BETTY MOBILE BAKE SHOP

—

Cupcakes seem to take adults back to their childhood, and perhaps the small indulgences are more easily justified than big slices of cake.

This is one of half a dozen or so mobile cupcake trucks in Houston.

The problem is that it's hard to eat just one cupcake, especially since so many sound so good.

That's a lot, but each seems to be eking out a profit, and judging by the looks of their customers, they're making a lot of people happy in the process. Cupcakes seem to take adults back to their childhood, and perhaps the small indulgences are more easily justified than big slices of cake. The problem is that it's hard to eat just one cupcake, especially since so many sound so good.

Federico Mora, originally from Costa Rica, has lived in Houston since the eighties. He was in the marine transportation business before starting this business with his daughter, Nicole. Nicole, who wanted a name that epitomized retro, came up with "Betty." She was also responsible for the design of

MARGARITA CUPCAKES // COSMO CUPCAKES // WHITE RUSSIAN CUPCAKES // STRAWBERRY DAIQUIRI CUPCAKES // CAKE BALLS // COOKIES

the logo, truck and truck interior, as well as researching the many different flavors they make.

In addition to regular-size cup cakes, they make mini cupcakes as well as cookies and cake balls. They bake the cakes at their bakery and top them with icing only when you order them so they remain as fresh as possible. They vary the flavors daily and change out the magnetic signs on the truck that describe the flavors accordingly. The thing that distinguishes Frosted Betty from its cupcake competitors is its line

In addition to regular-size cup cakes, they also make mini cupcakes as well as cookies and cake balls.

of adult offerings, "Cocktail Cupcakes" with flavors like "Margarita," "Cosmo," "White Russian" and "Strawberry Daiquiri" — all made with real liquor.

The four we purchased were: a red velvet cupcake with a cream cheese topping; a raspberry cupcake with almond ricotta topping; a cardamom-flavored cupcake with pistachio topping; and a plain cupcake topped with salted caramel. It's hard to pick a favorite,

but the salted caramel's combination of sweetness and salt was particularly appealing.

more than a GALVESTON institution
it's the real deal

LOCATION
Various

PHONE
409-762-9625

HOURS
Various

FOOD
Seafood

PRICES
$ $

OWNERS
Casey and Nick Gaido

STARTED
2009

PAYMENT
All

SPECIAL SERVICES
Catering,

FACEBOOK
Gaidos/165355970149750

WEBSITE
gaidos.com

GAIDO'S

—

The impressive menu for the evening showed what a food truck can offer when it has a **restaurant's worth** of staff and equipment.

If a restaurant lasts 100 years, it must be doing something right. Gaido's was started in 1911, and it took them just 98 years to decide to open their first mobile kitchen, which is a real beauty. This 24-foot mobile kitchen is used to cater special events on the beach and anywhere else. It comes

The crew included maitre d's, waiters, bartenders, chefs, deejays, lighting techs and a host of hangers-on.

with four friers, two massive refrigerators, a six-top range and two griddles. It was the brainchild of Mr. Gaido Senior, who oversaw its construction in

Austin. I asked Nick Gaido how much it would cost, and he thought it was around $150,000. But an unnamed staffer said he thought it was closer to $250,000, since a lot of the equipment they had on the truck had to be custom-made.

I heard about this truck from Mike Riccetti, the author of Houston *Dining on the Cheap*, when we met at a dinner one night and I was describing my book. He asked if I had included the Gaido's truck, which I hadn't known existed. Immediately after that encounter I set about trying to find it. I contacted Casey Gaido,

PARMESAN-ENCRUSTED MAHI-MAHI // PECAN PIE
SEAFOOD-STUFFED MUSHROOMS // SHRIMP PUFFS
SHRIMP PIGGIES // BLUE CHEESE GRITS

who told me that their next event was one on Porretto Beach, a private beach on the east side of the island sometime in mid-April. I made plans to meet him there.

They started setting up the tents at 9 a.m. the morning of the event, and by the time I arrived around 6 p.m., the crew was in full swing, finalizing the details of the dinner for 100 that night. The crew included maitre d's, waiters, bartenders, chefs, deejays, lighting techs and a host of hangers-on. The star of the show, however, was the truck. While the truck runs on propane, it also uses electricity powered by three 15,000-watt generators, two in use at all times and one a spare...just in case.

The impressive menu for the evening showed what a food truck can offer

It comes with four friers, two massive refrigerators, a six-top range and two griddles.

when it has a restaurant's worth of staff and equipment. The offerings included seafood-stuffed mushrooms, oysters brochette, shrimp piggies (bacon-wrapped), chicken marsala, Parmesan-encrusted Mahi-Mahi, shrimp puffs, blue cheese grits, fried shrimp and stuffed shrimp, with pecan pie as dessert.

When the food was ready, it was transferred to chafing dishes for serving. "It costs a minimum of $5,000 for an event," Casey told me, "and that's just to get the truck out the door!" Obviously, this particular event cost considerably more than that, but when you consider the amount of set-up and tear-down, all the food and liquor and all the staff, you certainly have a lot of costs involved.

it WASN'T JUST A good dog

it was a great one

GOOD DOG HOT DOGS

—

Attention to detail, along with the dogs themselves **make the difference** between a ho-hum hot dog and an OMG hot dog.

With a dachshund as a mascot and frequent appearances at Boneyards Drinkery, a bar with a dog park attached, it should not surprise anyone that the gourmet hot dogs served here are definitely haute dogs.

Amalia Pherd studied at the Culinary Institute LeNôtre here in Houston. Daniel Caballero grew up in a family that owned restaurants and bars.

They even make all their own pickled *jalapeños*.

The buns, from the Slow Dough Bread Company, have a slightly sweet taste.

They are coated with butter before being warmed on the griddle. The hot dogs are a blend of beef and pork, although all-beef versions are also available. All the condiments are made in house — the whole-grain mustard, the *Srichacha* ketchup, the mayo, the relishes, all of them. They even make all their own pickled *jalapeños*.

This sort of attention to detail, along with the dogs themselves (all-natural, no preservatives or fillers), make the difference between a ho-hum hot dog and an OMG hot dog. The first thing we tried was the Corny Dog, which is served with ketchup and mustard. The

TACO *DE POLLO* // *PASTELITO DE CARNE*
CHICHARRON CON YUCA // *ASADA CON TAJADA*

meat was excellent, as was the thick coating of corn meal , crispy on the outsideoutside and softer on the inside. I had to agree with another customer, who had just finished hers as I was about to place my order; she said, "That was the best corn dog I ever had."

I asked the team what I should have next. Amalia recommended the Sunshine Dog; Daniel recommended the Ol' Zapata Dog. I stuck with Amalia's recommendation and was happy that I did. The Sunshine Dog consists of a dog covered with pickled red onion, dill relish, cream cheese and mayo. Biting through the natural casing of the dog quickly makes you realize that hot dogs are supposed to have a casing; many of the dogs you buy in the grocery store do not. Homemade mayo

Amalia also makes amazing potato chips by hand.

has an entirely different texture than the store-bought kind. It is thicker and has a much richer taste. This added to the appeal. It wasn't just a good dog; it was a great one. Amalia also makes amazing potato chips by hand. They're so thin you can see through them — so thin that when they hit the hot oil, they crinkle up rather than hold their shape.

✱ a ✱

VEGGIE

PATTY WITH

buckwheat

& celery, carrots, herbs and spices

LOCATION
2305 Wheeler

HOURS
Mon-Fri: 11:00am-7:00pm

FOOD
Vegan

PRICES
$$

STARTED
2011

PAYMENT
Cash only

PHONE
713-487-8346

SPECIAL SERVICES
Catering

TWITTER
greenseedvegan

FACEBOOK
greenseedvegan

WEBSITE
greenseedvegan.com

GREEN SEED VEGAN

—

They use **locally grown produce** from farmers who sell them whatever is fresh.

Both Rodney and Mattie are committed vegans. They serve an all plant-based cuisine for those who are trying to "eat clean," as they state on their website, or for those who "simply want to grant their digestive organs a long overdue vacation." Rodney trained at the Houston Community College Culinary Program, then did stints at various restaurants around town before opening Houston's first vegan truck. The pale-green exterior is reminiscent of wheat grass, which they sell at their fresh-pressed juice bar. They use

The pale-green exterior is reminiscent of wheat grass, which they sell at their fresh-pressed juice bar.

locally grown produce from farmers who come by and sell them whatever is fresh that day. Consequently, their menu changes, depending on what's available. They also do not serve any

soy products; the tempeh is made with garbanzo beans, allowed to ferment for a couple of days. These folks take their food and preparation very seriously.

The truck is normally parked near the campuses of TSU and UH, so they get a lot of student traffic. Vegans have a limited choice of eating establishments. So when they find a place that shares their world views, they tend to be very loyal to it.

The first thing I tried was the Illy Cheesesteak Sandwich. "We call it Illy since we don't serve any meat in it, and therefore, can't call it Philly Chees-esteak," said Mattie. Rodney uses portobello mushrooms, which he tops with wonderfully caramelized onions and melted "Cheddar cheese." Real Cheddar is an animal product, but this version, from Daiya in Canada, is completely dairy-free and made from only plant ingredients. It has a wonderfully bright yellow color and melts superbly,

ILLY CHEESESTEAK SANDWICH // KALE CHIPS
SWEET POTATO FRIES // FRESH-PRESSED JUICE BAR

binding everything together. I'm betting you will not be able to tell it's not made from dairy products. Rodney told me he tried a lot of different cheeses before settling on this one. He serves this on a mini-French baguette.

Next was the Dirty Burque. "'Burque' stands for Albuquerque, which is where Rodney is from, and because we use New Mexico green chiles in it," said Mattie. They make a veggie patty with buckwheat, to which they add celery, carrots, herbs and spices. They sauté the patty in a little coconut oil before assembling the sandwich on a whole wheat bun with arugula, avocado, New Mexico green chilies and "Cheddar" cheese.

I once tried a vegetable patty made by Morning Star and did not find it at all palatable. This, however, was moist, light and really delicious. When I told Rodney what I had tried, he quipped: "Then you never tasted a veggie patty."

A side of sweet potato fries seasoned with dill was crispy and delicious. Maggie insisted I try their kale chips. Since I had never had these before, I did not know what to expect. They make them by seasoning raw kale with sea salt and garlic, then dehydrating it for a couple of days. The result is a crispy chip with lots of flavor that you don't have to feel guilty about.

At their fresh-pressed juice bar, they make some terrific concoctions. The Pina Verde I had was the first time I had ever tried wheat grass, and Maggie warned that it might have a bitter taste. Not when they mixed it with pineapple juice and mint, it didn't!

The truck has been so successful that they transitioned to a brick and mortar place on Almeda.

❋ **he takes** ❋

OVEN-ROASTED

CHICKEN

breast

with fresh basil and slices of
red onion and green pepper

LOCATION
Various

PHONE
713-683-3866

HOURS
Various

FOOD
Panini, gelati, espresso, chocolates

PRICES
$

OWNER
Mark Caffey

STARTED
2011

PAYMENT
All

TWITTER
grillmarksho

FACEBOOK
Grill-Marks/216423981713056

GRILL MARKS

—

It's fun meeting people and fun **bringing food to the people**, as opposed to having the people come to you.

Mark has owned Chocolates By Mark in La Porte for the past 18 years and brings that knowledge of chocolate to his truck. "It's fun meeting people

He has developed an interesting menu of Italian sandwiches, each named after a classical artist.

and fun bringing food to the people, as opposed to having the people come to you," he said. Grill Marks is the first Houston truck with an Italian theme, with *panini, gelato* and espresso. He bought his vehicle from the City of Arlington, where it was a transit bus.

Mark uses only Boar's Head meats and cheeses, and he has developed an interesting menu of Italian sandwiches,

each named after a classical artist. The bread he uses is custom-made by a bakery in Clear Lake. Before he presses it on the *panini* grill, he brushes the bread with olive oil.

The first sandwich I tried was the Bellini, where he takes thin slices of oven-roasted chicken breast, fresh basil and slices of red onion and green pepper, then marries these ingredients with a Thai ginger-curry sauce. A few minutes under the *panini* press and the hot sandwich emerges, ready to eat. The taste definitely says Thai, but in a very subtle, not overpowering way. Mark makes all his own sauces, and this is what really makes the *panini* taste great.

THE BELLINI SANDWICH // ESPRESSO // THE GRECO GRILLED CHEESE SANDWICH // CHOCOLATE-COVERED BACON

Next was the Greco, a classic grilled cheese sandwich transformed with smoked gouda, a sharp cheddar and fontina. The result is a gooey mass of melted cheeses — an adult version of classic comfort food.

I also tried Mark's chocolate-covered bacon. Yes, you read that right. He takes four small pieces of bacon, then dips one end of each slice into rich milk chocolate. The juxtaposition

I also tried Mark's chocolate-covered bacon. Yes, you read that right.

of sweet and salty is a taste that you will not soon forget. An award should definitely be given to the person who first did this.

I sampled two different *gelati*. The first was a brown-butter flavor that tasted just like....brown butter. It was sensational, with a slightly salty flavor along with the sweet. The second was the Nutella® flavor, which tasted a whole lot more like chocolate than hazelnut. But I'm certainly not complaining.

nice

AND JUICY

WITH GOOD

smoke flavor

the brisket is superb

LOCATION
1515 FM 249

HOURS
Fri-Sat: 8:00am-6:30pm

PHONE
713-824-7112

FOOD
BBQ

PRICES
$$

OWNERS
Henry and Vanessa Scott

STARTED
1995

PAYMENT
Cash only

SERVICES
Catering

WEBSITE
bansurifood.com

H&V BBQ

——

I like to **mix up my wood** a bit, you know, make it a little different each time, so I use oak, pecan, hickory and mesquite.

"I started cooking BBQ in my trailer about sixteen years ago, then, when my trailer burned down a couple of years ago, I had this new one built," said Henry Scott. When I found Henry's trailer on Tomball Parkway one

The dry rub that Henry uses and the ingredients of the thin, vinegary BBQ are secrets Henry won't reveal.

Saturday, I was not looking for him. I was in search of another BBQ truck that had apparently gone out of business. As I approached Tomball Parkway from Antoine, I noticed the unmistakable sign of a BBQ truck - the smoke gently emerging from the stack on the back of his trailer. After driving up and

parking, I noticed his pickup truck full of wood – another good sign. "I like to mix up my wood a bit, you know, make it a little different each time, so I use oak, pecan, hickory and mesquite," said Henry. The dry rub that Henry uses and the ingredients of the thin, vinegary BBQ are secrets Henry won't reveal. He did tell me he cooks his brisket at 380 degrees for four to five hours. When I mentioned that seemed awfully fast compared to many other pit masters, he told me his pits were

Henry's sausage had a spicy kick to it and remained nice and juicy with good smoke flavor.

vertical, not horizontal and that they were commercial grade, which meant

SAUSAGE // BRISKET // POTATO SALAD // BBQ BEANS // BOUDAIN

they cooked faster, since the metal was thicker and retained more heat.

Henry's sausage had a spicy kick to it and remained nice and juicy with good smoke flavor. While the beans came out of a can, Vanessa, Henry's wife, added her own special touches to turn them into some excellent-tasting beans. The potato salad was very different, in that the potatoes were mashed with very few lumps. It also

Henry's brisket is superb. I do not believe that I had ever had brisket that was literally dripping with juice.

contained some pimientos and pickles and was very tasty. Henry's brisket is superb. It is so moist that I had to ask him if he keeps it in some of the juices; he said he didn't. I do not believe that I had ever had brisket that was literally dripping with juice. The red ring of fire was very evident. "It"s the fat in the meat that makes it that way", added Henry. Whatever it was, I knew I immediately wanted more.

Sliced Brisket $5.7
Smoked Ribs...............$5.7
Beef Sausage..............$5.5
Potato Salad............$1.5
BBQ Beans................$1.5
Boudain.....................$5.0
PLATES
One Meat....................$ 8.7

filled

WITH A VERY

TASTY

beef

carrot and garlic mixture

LOCATION
Various

HOURS
Various

FOOD
Filipino/Asian fusion

PRICES
$

STARTED
2011

PAYMENT
All

PHONE
713-456-0803

OWNER
Ryan Javier/Emily NG

SPECIAL SERVICES
Catering

FACEBOOK
HappyEndingsHTX

HAPPY ENDINGS

—

Emily and Ryan Javier are serving some fascinating **Asian Fusion** cuisine.

"This was my wife's idea," said Ryan Javier, who, along with his wife, Emily Ng, started the Happy Endings food truck. You can't miss the bright blue truck, which is decorated with different Asian themes. Ryan is Filipino while Emily has a Chinese background. Together they're serving some fascinating Asian Fusion cuisine.

"I used to sell mortgages, now I'm selling Geishas," added Ryan. The "Geisha" he is referring to is one of his top

The soft Hawaiian roll, which he slaps on the grill just long enough to warm it and give it some toast marks, has a sweet note to it.

selling sandwiches. "We serve all our sandwiches on Hawaiian bread, which we bake fresh every day," added Ryan. The soft Hawaiian roll, which he slaps on the grill just long enough to warm

it and give it some toast marks, has a sweet note to it. Ryan also makes the spicy wasabi mayo, which he lathers on each side of the roll before placing an all-beef, Japanese sausage in the middle. For those fearful of wasabi and its effects: Worry not. The color of the mayo is pale green and any heat is barely discernible. A dollop of *katsu* sauce, which is normally made with applesauce, onion, tomato paste, carrots and soy sauce, and the dog is ready for eating. What makes this a really fascinating hot dog is what Ryan puts on top of the sausage. Bonito flakes. These come from dried, fermented, and smoked skipjack tuna pieces. They are so whispery thin that they move around by themselves under the mere hint of air or any kind and melt almost the moment they hit your tongue. They have quite an intense taste of smoked fish, not unlike smoked salmon. It was

SHANGHAI EGGROLLS // *LONGANIZA* DOG
TERIYAKI LOLLIPOPS // BBQ PORK BUN

a taste experience unlike any other I can remember.

Ryan insisted I try the Shanghai Eggrolls. I'm glad he did so, especially since these are also homemade. Six crispy eggrolls come to an order. They are filled with a very tasty beef, carrot and garlic mixture and wound so tight that two mouthfuls is all it takes to finish one. They are accompanied by a homemade sweet chili sauce that is so good, it could easily be used on any dishes they serve here.

The Teriyaki Lollipops are chicken thighs that have had their meat pushed off the lower end of the bone in a technique known as 'Frenching', to form a lollipop of sorts, albeit a savory

The Teriyaki Lollipops are chicken thighs that have had their meat pushed off the lower end of the bone.

one. Two come to an order and they are served with a delicious homemade teriyaki sauce.

I caught up with them a second time at a fundraiser for the survivors of Typhoon Sendong that devastated the Philippines in late 2011. This time I tried the steamed BBQ pork bun, which is filled with a dark, rich *asado* made of pork that was superb. Eating the

sticky steamed bun is hard to do since the bun tends to stick to everything it comes in contact with, but it is well worth it just to get to the filling. I also tried the *Longaniza* Dog. Ryan takes three small *longaniza* sausage links and browns them on the griddle before stuffing them into a roll. There are many different kinds of *longaniza* available in the Philippines, but the slightly sweet version that Ryan serves is known as *longaniza hamonado*. It is coarsely-ground sausage that has a somewhat sweet taste and when combined with the slightly sweet roll, makes for a fascinating hot dog. *Hamonado* generally refers to meat cooked liked ham and sweetened with fruit juice.

Ryan and Emily are going through a considerable amount of trouble to make everything from scratch and it shows in the quality of the food they are serving. I only hope that that the enthusiasm they have at the beginning of their venture holds out and they don't decide to cut any corners.

the

TAMALES SERVED

HERE

have the

perfect consistency

LOCATION
4103 FM 2351

PHONE
(713) 498 4486

HOURS
Daily 11:00am-7:00pm.

FOOD
Tamales

PRICES
$

OWNER
Rick Elder

STARTED
1976

PAYMENT
All

FACEBOOK
/pages/HOT-TAMA-
LES/135181006505489

HOT TAMALES

—

"At **holiday times**, there are four of us working the truck, handing out tamales as fast as we can," said Allen.

When your father is Rick Elder and he's known as The Tamale Man and he's been selling tamales out of a truck since 1976, and he turns the business over to his sons, you know the pressure is on. Operating since 1976 makes this one of the oldest mobile food units in Houston. Rick's sons, Allen, Eric and Jay have been running the truck since 2009 and seem to be doing just fine. "We all used to help out growing up," said Allen, "so we pretty much knew what to do."

The truck has been parked in virtually the same location, give or take a mile or so, on FM 2351 in Friendswood, just west of Beemer, for over 35 years. They have raised a whole generation of tamale lovers. Online reviews tell us this. They also tell us about people who move away from the neighborhood but who return whenever they can to get their tamale fix.

It's hard to miss the truck with large signs on both sides of the truck proclaiming "Hot Tamales". No fancy graphics, no Twitter feeds, no advertis-

ing, just good, hot tamales. Oh, and you'll normally find a line waiting to be served. "At holiday times, there are four of us working the truck, handing out tamales as fast as we can," said Allen.

When they say 'Hot Tamales', they ain't kidding. When they hand them to you, they are almost too hot to handle. "People often ask me, 'How do I keep them warm until dinnertime?' and I tell them, 'Don't do anything to them until you're ready to eat them. They'll be plenty hot", says Allen Elder. The tamales,

They tell us about people who move away from the neighborhood but who return whenever they can to get their tamale fix.

which come six to a packet, are very well insulated. The first layer is two natural corn husks, which surround each tamale. Next, some wax paper, which does an excellent job of holding in the moisture and retaining the heat. This is followed

PORK, SPICY PORK AND CHICKEN TAMALES //
CHILE CON QUESO // NACHOS // GUACAMOLE

by a sheet of silver foil and finally, each packet of tamales is put into a brown paper bag, ensuring an added level of insulation. I tested out Allen's claim after I purchased my order. I bought them at lunch time and checked them again at 5:00 in the afternoon. They were still warm and perfectly edible.

Perhaps my favorite filling is the spicy pork because not only can you taste the meat but you get the added benefit of a little spice, which proclaims its presence.

The Elders sell only three types of tamales: Pork, Spicy Pork and Chicken. "All this time, we've been having the same family make the tamales," said Allen. Over the years, they have tried new things, including opening a brick and mortar place, which did not work out. There is a certain art in a tamale that sets one apart from another. When you unwrap them from their husks, if they're too soft and limp, they won't stand up on their own, making them hard to eat. When they're too firm, they stand up by themselves but are generally quite dry. The tamales served here have the perfect consistency and even when re-heated, never dry out. Then there is the ratio of filling to masa. Too much filling and the thing falls apart, too little

and all you taste is the masa. It takes an experienced hand to judge the ratio just right and it is evident that that hand of experience is making these tamales. Perhaps my favorite filling is the spicy pork because not only can you taste the meat but you get the added benefit of a little spice, which proclaims its presence.

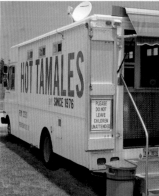

They have been slow to add to the menu. However, they now serve *Chile Con Queso*, nachos, guacamole and red and green salsas, the latter of which Allen warned me was fiery. It was, but in a very good way. "We keep a lot of these salsas in stock, because we have some people that come from far away that buy 30 at a time to take back with them," said Allen. Both salsas are quite smooth and not chunky. The green salsa is made from *tomatillos* and *jalapeños* and packs quite a punch while the red salsa packs slightly less heat.

The family is working on a second tamale truck, which will soon hit the street. "We want to ensure our customers, though," said Allen, "that we're not gonna move the original truck, or change anything on it, we're just gonna build a second one to bring to Houston. We are thinking about expanding the offerings on the second truck to include bean tamales and spinach tamales, since we get a lot of requests for these."

the

BATTER

MADE THE

catfish

light and crispy

LOCATION
14090 Bellaire

HOURS
Mon-Sat: 11:00am-9:00pm,
Sun: 11:00am-8:00pm

FOOD
Cajun, seafood

PRICES
$

STARTED
2004

PAYMENT
All

PHONE
281-988-5009

OWNER
Mai Diec

HOUSTON CATFISH STATION 1322

Gregory is from Mississippi and knows how to make **a mean piece** of catfish.

You'll find this truck just in front of the New Orleans Style Sno-Ball on Bellaire near Eldridge. Even though they say they open at 11:00, and even while the flashing neon sign said 'open', when I wandered over at around 2:00 pm one Saturday, there was no one around. Across the parking lot there is a permanent structure, from which crawfish are sold and an Asian gentleman popped his head out of the walk-up window and asked if he could help me. I told him that I wanted to order from the truck. He said he could provide the same food. I thanked him but asked if he knew when it might open. "Soon" was his reply. At that time I did not know that the man and his wife were the owners of the truck. Mai Diec is from Vietnam and the connection with the shrimping business is probably the reason they decided to open a place where seafood is king. When I asked Mai about the number 1322 at the end

of the name of their place, she told me that was her lucky number.

The cook and server, Gregory Turner, is from Mississippi and knows how to make a mean piece of catfish, not to mention a terrific gumbo and some homemade tartar sauce that will have you asking for more. It did not take him long to fire up the fryer and turn out some wonderful food. I started with a small bowl of gumbo, which had a deep brown, murky color and was thick and not thin. The shrimp, crawfish, sausage, rice and other ingredients all sank to the

I started with a small bowl of gumbo, which had a deep brown, murky color and was thick and not thin.

bottom when it was served but a quick stir brought everything to the surface.

I asked Gregory what breading he used on the catfish and he explained that it

BUTTERMILK HUSHPUPPIES // THE CATFISH BASKET // HOMEMADE TARTAR SAUCE //

• •

was called creamed meal. Since I was unfamiliar with the name, he dipped a small cup into the bag and showed me. My nose told me that breadcrumbs were in there in addition to cornmeal.

I immediately noticed the tartar sauce was different from the commercial, bottled kind.

The batter made the fish light and crispy and did not add any flavor to the catfish. The Catfish Basket contains five large filets and also includes some crinkle-cut French fries, which are fairly standard, and some buttermilk hushpuppies, which are superb.

I took one look at the tartar sauce and immediately noticed it was different from the commercial, bottled kind. It was darker in color and full, and I mean full of green pickles and tiny red peppers, which added a whole lot of color and taste to the sauce. There is only one other tartar sauce I've ever had that even comes close to this and it is Robb Walsh's remarkable duplication of the tartar sauce from the King's Inn in Baffin Bay. His recipe can be found in his latest book, Legends of Texas Barbecue.

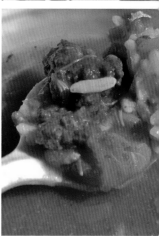

❖ *his* ❖

DEEP-FRIED

AVOCADO

is served

inside a corn tortilla

LOCATION
Various

PHONE
713-806-9267

HOURS
Various

FOOD
Chef-driven, globally inspired

PRICES
$

OWNER
Jason Gould, Jason Hill,
Matt Opaleski

STARTED
2010

PAYMENT
Cash only

SPECIAL SERVICES
Catering

FACEBOOK
htownstreatsston

TWITTER
htownstreats

H-TOWN STREATS

—

This truck offers some of the tastiest, most creative street food available in the city.

What happens when two trained chefs come together and open a gourmet food truck? Magic. This truck offers some of the tastiest, most creative street food available in the city. Jason Hill is originally from Ft. Lauderdale but studied at the Texas Culinary Academy in Austin before moving to Houston and working for Café Brasil, Aries, Gravitas, Voice and The Grove. He is an extremely talented and creative chef, and I predict that whatever you eat here will not disappoint.

Matt Opaleski is from Houston and worked at the Omni and Houston Country Club before becoming the pastry chef at Aries. Matt is responsible for the unbelievably good taro chips, which he makes fresh every day. He sprinkles them with hot pepper and lime zest, the flavor of which explodes in your mouth the minute your tongue comes into contact with it.

His pastry-chef training also helped him make a terrific *tres leches* cake for *Cinco de Mayo*. He infused the cake with Malibu and Myers's rums, which gave it a tropical taste of coconut. The meringue topping he used also made this a little different and decadent. On another occasion I tried his Choco-Peanut Butter Chip Pretzel cookie, and enjoyed the soft texture and the excellent combination of chocolate with PB.

Jason's *Banh Mi* Sliders are exquisite. He uses a homemade mayo that contains lots of yolks; it's not the pale yellow color associated with a commercial version but a rich, deep yellow and with a taste that makes you want to lick the spoon. He marinates the beef in fermented black beans before cooking it on the griddle, so it retains a rich, profound flavor. Add slices of pickled daikon and carrot and slices of fresh *jalapeño*, and you have a mean-tasting slider that quickly disappears. Another popular slider is the Blue Cheese Pimiento, to which he adds a slice of roasted tomato, then douses it with a green-onion *aioli*. As with everything else I had here, it, too, was extremely tasty.

I could not get enough of the Thai Short Ribs. Jason marinates pork ribs

FRIED PICKLES // *CUBANO* SANDWICH // THAI SHORT RIBS // FRIED AVOCADO // MONTE CRISTO BALLS

in a ginger-garlic sauce to which he adds fresh cilantro and fish sauce, then coats them in egg and flour and flash-fries them so that the exterior has a nice crispness. He recommends eating them with Lingham's chili sauce from Malaysia, one of the many sauces available on the shelf outside the truck. Take his advice. The only problem with these ribs is that they're so tasty, one order may not suffice.

Jason has developed a following for his Monte Cristo Balls. He takes sliced white bread, removes the crust and presses it almost flat and rolling it into a ball. He stuffs it with ham and Swiss cheese before dipping into French toast batter and dropping it into the fryer. The biggest twist of all is a finish with powdered sugar and a dollop of fresh, locally-grown strawberry jam. The juxtaposition of the savory filling with the sweetness of the jam and sugar make it another one of those dishes that I wished would never end.

A totally simple but delicious dish is the fried pickles. Jason rolls pickles in breadcrumbs and dill and deep-fries them. The crunchy coating and crisp pickles make an interesting combination, especially when dipped in his homemade ranch dressing.

Sometimes all you want is a grilled cheese sandwich. Jason's version is

as comforting as they come, though it won't resemble any cheese sandwich you ate as a child. He uses a Cajun Cheddar with a slight heat to it. His chipotle sauce, which covers the bread, adds to the overall spiciness. But it's his *caponata* that makes this a heck of a grilled cheese: The salad, made with raisins, capers, tomato, bell pepper and eggplant, adds a spectacular flavor to the filling. Don't miss it.

Another simple yet delicious sandwich is the *Cubano*. They take two slices of bread and spread a honey-mustard over them, then fill them with ham, Swiss cheese and with homemade pickles before placing the sandwich on the griddle until the cheese melts. It is satisfying and comforting.

For the fried avocado, Jason rolls a slice of avocado in cornflakes and crushed almonds, along with some *chile arbo*l, flax seeds and sesame seeds. He deep-fries it and serves it inside a corn tortilla with a creamy cilantro slaw. The coating stays exceptionally crispy all the way to the last bite — which isn't saying much, though, since it's gone in three bites.

This is one of the new breed of chef-driven trucks that, once you've tried the food, you'll want to follow around town, wherever it goes.

the

FISH IS

EXCEPTIONALLY

crisp

as are the fries

LOCATION
3801 Lockwood

PHONE
713-775-5101

HOURS
Fri: 3:00pm-10:00pm,
Sat: 12:00-10:00pm

FOOD
Fried seafood

PRICES
$$

OWNER
Inez Tates Varner

STARTED
2005

PAYMENT
Cash only

INEZ'S SEAFOOD TRUCK

—

In addition to catfish and shrimp, Inez also fries **whatever fish is fresh** that day.

Inez runs her trucks only on the weekends. During the week, she teaches school. She knows a lot about fish since she used to own Tates's Fish Market on MLK, then a "You Buy We Fry" restaurant until the overhead became too much. Now she does what she wants.

In addition to catfish and shrimp, Inez also fries whatever fish is fresh that day. The day I found her, she had fresh whole drum. The day before, she had speckled trout. Not feeling like digging bones out of my mouth, I decided on the Mixed Dinner plate, which consisted of two filets of catfish and five large butterflied shrimp.

Inez uses farm-raised catfish for two reasons. "People have got used to the taste," she says, "and secondly, this is the only kind that has any taste." She

uses a simple cornmeal breading, to which she adds her own secret spices. A quick dip into the breading, and it's straight into the fryer for a few minutes. Once the catfish and shrimp are

I decided on the Mixed Dinner plate, which consisted of two filets of catfish and five large butterflied shrimp.

completely without grease, she serves them with Texas toast, a small salad of iceberg lettuce with tomato, and fries sprinkled with seasoned salt. Inez cuts her potatoes by hand, and the extra effort is definitely worth it. Her catfish is dark brown, not the light golden color to which some other seafood trucks cook their fish. The extra moments in the fryer mean that the fish is exceptionally crisp, as are the fries.

Inez lists three desserts on the menu: peach cobbler, sweet potato pie and lemon pie. I was eager to try any of them, since they are all homemade. No

Inez lists three desserts on the menu: peach cobbler, sweet potato pie and lemon pie.

such luck. "I had my truck inspected last week," she explained, "and they told me I couldn't sell the desserts out of my truck because I make them at home. I would have to install an oven in my truck and make them here. They were good, too! Every week, I'd sell everything I could make."

She was one of the many who were trapped by the Texas food laws that used to prohibit the manufacture of baked goods and other homemade items unless they were made in a commercial kitchen. She would also have needed certain permits, licenses and insurance, incurring costs that would have far outweighed the sales she would have made. As of September 11, 2011, the so-called cottage industry laws were changed, and people like Inez can now make baked goods and other items at home and sell them to the public. If you're interested, visit www.texascottagefoodlaw.com for details and advice.

FRIED SHRIMP DINNERS	
SHRIMP	$8.
SHRIMP	$9.
SHRIMP	$10

MIXED DINNERS

CATFISH	AND 5 SHRIMP	
TROUT	AND 5 SHRIMP	

(All Orders Served with French Fries, Salad,

5 CHICKEN WINGS	$6.5
HAMBURGERS	$4.2
CHEESEBURGERS	$4.
HAMBURGER BASKET	$6.2
CHEESEBURGER BASKET	$6.4
FISH SANDWICH	$5.0
SMALL FRIES	$1.7
LARGE FRIES	$2.7
SODA	$0.6
WATER	$1.0

DESSERTS

EACH COBBLER	$3.0
TATO PIE	$3.0
MON PIE	$3.0

with

CHUNKS OF

CHICKEN

marinated

in jerk seasonings

LOCATION
Various

PHONE
713-307-5403

HOURS
Various

FOOD
Wraps, mac and cheese,
Indian fusion

PRICES
$ $

OWNER
Guli Essa

STARTED
2011

PAYMENT
All

SPECIAL SERVICES
Catering

TWITTER
tsawraptruck

FACEBOOK
itsawraptruck

WEBSITE
itsawraptruck.com

IT'S A WRAP MOBILE BISTRO

—

It's A Wrap's **film theme** is carried through in the film-strip décor that wraps the truck, as well as in the food she serves, namely wraps, and finally in the names of menu items.

After working in retail clothing for 23 years, in January 2011, Guli Essa went in to her job as manager of a store in the Galleria and found a notice announcing that in three days, the store would be closing... for good. Right there and then, she decided to follow her dream.

Guli's parents had owned snack shops in office buildings, and ever since

The theme for her truck struck her after many years of living in Hollywood.

she was a kid, she says, she "always wanted to own some sort of café." She felt that the best way to do that was through a food truck. The theme for her truck struck her after many years of living in Hollywood.

It's A Wrap's film theme is carried through in the film-strip décor that *wraps* the truck, as well as in the food she serves (namely, *wraps*), and finally in the names of menu items like the Bollywood. Even though Guli did not learn how to cook from her Indian parents, her heritage shines through in many of her world-fusion offerings.

Though she specializes in wraps, or stuffed tortillas, an unexpected winner from her menu is the mac-and-cheese balls. She takes traditional mac and cheese, which she makes with American cheese, and "wraps" balls of it in a

BOLLYWOOD WRAP // THE JERK WRAP //
THE CASABLANCA WRAP // THE FINDING NEMO

mixture of panko and Italian bread-crumbs before deep-frying them. The result is an extra-crispy exterior, which gives way to a rich and super-creamy filling. Guli is working on developing just the right dipping sauce for the dish. She tried a simple marinara sauce but didn't like it that much, so stay tuned.

We also tried two of her wraps. The Jerk Wrap is on a flour tortilla, which she coats with spicy cream cheese before stuffing it with chunks of chicken marinated in jerk seasonings, plus strips of lettuce and a delicious mango salsa. The Bollywood Wrap is served on *naan*, the traditional Indian flatbread, and consists of chunks of chicken cooked in Indian spices along with sautéed onions and tomatoes, topped with a cool cucumber *raita*, or yogurt salad, and a cilantro chutney. It is a superb wrap.

Guli also makes a selection of other wraps, including the Casablanca, a vegetarian Moroccan version with couscous, feta, hummus and grilled vegetables. Another is the Finding Nemo, for which she turns Cajun-seasoned tilapia into a fish taco. As I was leaving the truck, I heard one of Guli's customers say, "That was the best fish taco ever." To me, that's a good reason to return.

I use A BLEND OF BEEF & pork

with more pork because beef dries it out

LOCATION
7441 Calhoun

PHONE
281-702-1431

HOURS
Tuesday-Sunday: 11:00am-6:00pm

FOOD
Barbecue

PRICES
$

OWNER
Jake Mathews

STARTED
1994

PAYMENT
Cash only

JAKE'S OLD FASHION BBQ

—

I asked Robert which burger sells best. "The *jalapeño*-ranch burger," he said without hesitation.

According to the records kept at the Houston Health Department, this is one of the oldest trucks in the City of Houston. Jake originally started this truck

Jake's sauce is thicker than most yet not gloppy.

in 1988 after he retired from the post office. He bought the K&H Meat Market and ran it for a while. Now someone else manages the meat market, and he parks his trailer in the parking lot of the store. The truck he currently operates dates from 1994, and its walls reflect years of long, slow smoking. They may have been white at some point, but they long ago surrendered that color to a host of browns.

My first visit to Jake's was on a Tuesday, a day that Jake does not make any sides, so I had to stick with meat. His sausage is custom-made for him. "I use a blend of beef and pork with more pork because beef dries it out," he explained. The medium-grind filling gets nice and smoky, but not too much so, letting the flavor of the meat burst through.

Jake's sauce is thicker than most yet not gloppy, with the perfect balance of sweet and tangy. His pork ribs are the large kind and require some chewing to get all the meat off the bone; it doesn't just fall off by itself. The brisket is also firm. This reflects Jake's cooking style, which is to slow-cook the meat for 9 or 10 hours at 150 degrees. This is

PORK RIBS // BARBECUE BRISKET //
JAKE'S BEANS // HOMEMADE POTATO SALAD

considerably lower than the temperature used by most others. He also wraps his meat in silver foil at the beginning of the cooking process. He starts out with the fat down, then turns it after a couple of hours to let the fat drip through the meat and make it moist and juicy.

This reflects Jake's cooking style, which is to slow-cook the meat for 9 or 10 hours at 150 degrees.

My second trip, to sample the sides, was worth it. Jake's beans are warmed in the pit so they taste quite smoky, and their thick, sweet sauce is delicious. His potato salad is homemade, with mayo and lots of pickles.

❖ the ❖

ONIONS ARE

MARINATED

in lime juice

which softens their flavor

LOCATION
1521 Gessner

PHONE
713-365-0373

HOURS
Mon-Thur: 8:00am-11:00pm,
Fri-Sat: 8:00am-12:00pm

FOOD
Mexican

PRICES
$

OWNERS
Memo Piñeda

STARTED
2002

PAYMENT
All

SPECIAL SERVICES
Catering

WEBSITE
jarrocafe.com

JARRO CAFE

—

The **overstuffed tacos**, served on corn tortillas, are topped with the traditional lime wedges, cilantro and onions.

The sign on the truck says "Best tacos in town": a bold claim to make near Long Point, in the heart of one of the largest clusters of food trucks in Houston. But then, this is one of the oldest trucks in the city, and one of the most popular as well. The trailer is in the parking lot of the restaurant by the same name. ("*Jarro*" means a clay jug or pot.) Those who don't want to sit and eat inside the restaurant can grab a couple of tacos from the truck outside and quickly be on their way.

The overstuffed tacos, served on corn tortillas, are topped with the traditional lime wedges, cilantro and onions. (The onions have been marinated in lime juice, which softens their texture and flavor.) They also come with a radish garnish.

The truck also claims to have the best salsas in town, a claim with which I whole-heartedly agree. A tray containing six different salsas comes with

A tray containing six different salsas comes with every order.

every order. As you will see from the photo, the six include a bright orange-colored habanero salsa, which is quite hot. Next to this is a green tomatillo and smoky pepper salsa. Then there is the bright green jalapeño salsa. Next is a dry mixture of seven different, mostly smoky, peppers. Then there is the bright yellow carrot salsa, and finally a bowl of pink marinated onions with oregano.

CAMPECHANO TACOS // SIX DIFFERENT SALSAS
COCHINITA PIBIL TACOS // *SUADERO* TACOS
MEXICAN COCA-COLA //

Those onions are used for the *cochinita pibil* taco, which is simply outstanding. *Cochinita pibil* is slow-roasted pork from the Yucatan, where the meat is marinated in citrus juices and cooked in a banana leaf. There are

The excellent homemade chorizo has a strong taste of cinnamon.

also some tacos served here that you won't find anywhere else. The excellent homemade *chorizo* has a strong taste of cinnamon. The *campechano*, invented here, consists of beef mixed with *chorizo*. We also tried the *carnitas*, crispy fried cubes of pork that have been marinated in orange juice before being cooked, and the *suadero*, small chunks of beef that have been marinated in lemon juice before being cooked. Also available here are bottles of Mexican Coca-Cola, which is sweeter than the U.S. version, as well as being made with real cane sugar.

CARNITAS	Cooked pork chunk Puerco cocinado co
FAJITA	Fresh and juicy Fresca y jugosa
POLLO	Grilled juicy ch Jugosa pechuga de
CAMPECHANO	Mix of chorizo a Res y chorizo
SUADERO	Chopped and marinade b Original sabor est
CHORIZO	Home made pork saus Con todo el sabor me
PASTOR	Pork marinade in a Con todo el sabor
COCHINITA PIBIL	Cooked por Original y del

we tried
THE FLAMING
LIPS ZINGER
which had
watermelon, cucumber and lemon juices

LOCATION
Various

HOURS
Various

FOOD
Fresh juices, smoothies

PRICES
$$

STARTED
2011

PAYMENT
Cash only

OWNER
Gretchen Hawkins

FACEBOOK
txjuicegirl?sk

WEBSITE
txjuicegirl.com

JUICE GIRL

—

She is making all of her juices and smoothies in a commercial kitchen, using **nothing except organic** produce.

When Gretchen Hawkins worked the juice bar at the original Whole Foods on Shepherd many years ago, she dreamed of having her own place. Her food truck, painted with bright yellow-and-orange sun streaks, is the first

When we caught up with her late in June, she offered a Summer Cooler that consisted of watermelon, cucumber and lemon juices.

step on this journey. At the moment, she is making all of her juices and smoothies in a commercial kitchen, using nothing except organic produce. Her next step is to make them on

the truck, and the final step will be to open a brick-and-mortar place. She bottles her juices in glass, unless she is attending a festival where glass is prohibited. "I much prefer glass," she explains, "since plastic affects the enzymes in the juice."

She makes seasonal drinks. When we caught up with her late in June, she offered a Summer Cooler that consisted of watermelon, cucumber and lemon juices. It was extremely refreshing under the hot noonday sun. We also tried the Flaming Lips Zinger, which had carrot, orange and lemon juices at its base with ginger added for additional spiciness. It too was a re-

FLAMING LIPS ZINGER // APPLE'AID
SUMMER COOLER //

markable blend of flavors. Finally, one of her signature juices, which she calls Apple'aid, is superb. The simple blend of apple and lemon juices will bring a little pucker to your lips.

We also tried the Flaming Lips Zinger, which had carrot, orange and lemon juices at its base with ginger added for additional spiciness.

You can also order any of the following added to your juice: spiralina, echinacea, hemp protein powder or chia seeds.

Isn't it great that there's a truck serving nothing but juices and smoothies to add to the diversity of trucks available on the streets of Houston?

100% JUICE

ORGANIC & /OR LOCAL

$5

APPLE'ADE: APPLE

THE FLAMING LIP

CARROT, ORANGE, GIN

SUMMER COOLE

WATERMELON, CUCU

GREEN TEA $2

BOTTLED WATER

✻ the ✻

RIBS WERE

THE LARGE

kind

and quite firm

JUS SMOKEN

LOCATION
13803 South Post Oak

PHONE
832-277-3598

HOURS
Fri-Sat: 12:00pm-6:30pm

FOOD
Barbecue

PRICES
$$

OWNER
Will Evans

STARTED
2007

PAYMENT
Cash only

SPECIAL SERVICES
Catering

—

All in all, Will's years of experience made this some of the **best barbecue** I've had in the city.

"We smoke anything" is this truck's motto. Will, known to his friends as "the smoke doctor," has been smoking for some 15 years. He cuts his own wood, primarily oak and occasionally pecan. "I would use nothing but hickory, except that it's too expensive," said Will. "It's a dollar a stick." He uses a dry rub and cooks his brisket fat-up for about 10 hours at between 200 and 250 degrees. Though he does not make his own sausage, he has it made especially for him: a coarse-ground pork sausage with lots of garlic. Smoked, it is truly exceptional.

I skipped the beans and potato salad since neither was homemade, so I ended up with a three-meat platter of ribs, links and brisket. I also sampled his homemade boudin.

As I was chatting with Will about his rig, a good customer of his returned for

I particularly enjoyed the smaller, thinner ends of the ribs, which were especially smoky and tender.

the second batch of barbecue that day. He told me he was from East Texas, and that this was the best barbecue he's found in Houston. He also told me that he was the one who'd christened Will, "The Smoke Doctor".

COARSE-GROUND PORK SAUSAGE WITH LOTS OF GARLIC // BRISKET // RIBS // BOUDIN

My first glance at the sauce suggested that it was extremely dark, thick and had a gloss that resembled a store-bought version. But nothing could have

The brisket had the distinctive ring of smoke suggesting a good, long, slow cook.

been further from the truth. It clung to the meat but had a distinctive taste with hints of smoke and sweetness. The ribs were the large kind and quite firm. I particularly enjoyed the smaller, thinner ends of the ribs, which were especially smoky and tender. The brisket was also firm and did not fall apart as you ate it. It had the distinctive ring of smoke suggesting a good, long, slow cook. All in all, Will's years of experience made this some of the best barbecue I've had in the city.

the MEAT TAKES ON A rust-colored hue

perhaps from the red chile

LOCATION
620 Sheldon

PHONE
281-862-9968

HOURS
Tue-Sun, 5:00pm-11:00pm

FOOD
Mexican

PRICES
$

OWNER
Marcos Martinez

STARTED
2008

PAYMENT
Cash only

FACEBOOK
KaRaNcHoS/158812667464242?
sk=wall

WEBSITE
karanchos.net

KARANCHOS

—

As you might guess from all that orange, the signature dish, *tacos de trompo*, is definitely a must-have.

Almost any Houston taco-truck crawl includes a stop at this famous joint on the east side of town, in Channelview. Owner Marcos Martinez is from Nuevo Leon, and when he started the truck in 2008, he sold only charbroiled chicken. Today the business has expanded to include an extension to the original truck plus a large number of tables and chairs, a small juice bar and a large restroom facility, all on a sprawling complex.

Karanchos is famous for serving *tacos de trompo*, also known as *tacos arabes*. These are pork tacos cooked on a vertical spit. It's not easy to find these tacos since the regulations in the City of Houston prohibit this method of cooking on a truck. It takes quite a while to prepare the pork since each piece has to be coated in seasoning and marinated before it's placed on the spit and cooked on the vertical grill. On top of the *trompo* sits a whole peeled

pineapple which, when heated, allows its juices to flow onto the cooking meat for added flavor.

"*Trompo*" means "spinning top": a reference to the way in which the spit constantly turns. This method of cooking is similar to the way that meat is cooked on a spit all around the world. In Greece, they're known as *gyros*; in Turkey, *doner kebabs*; and in the Middle East, they're *shawarmas*. The meat is sliced off the outer edges, allowing the next layer to continue cooking. According to Barry Popik, an expert on food terms, the term *tacos arabes* dates from the 1930s and is attributed to an Iraqi immigrant to Puebla, Mexico.

The meat takes on a rust-colored hue, perhaps from the red chile or (more likely) from *achiote*, a common natural colorant used in Mexican cooking. The same color echoes throughout this place. The employees all wear bright

···

orange T-shirts; and the restrooms, which are adjacent to the truck, are also painted bright orange.

As you might guess from all that orange, the signature dish, *tacos de trompo*, is definitely a must-have. The meat is cut into small pieces and begs to be topped with cilantro and onions, a squeeze of lime and a dousing of the bright green *jalapeño* salsa. It is particularly juicy, and the faint hint of pineapple is a terrific background note.

For the *pirata*, they take a flour tortilla, then melt Mexican cheese on it and top it with beef that has been cooked over charcoal. This is yet another extremely tasty taco. As good as all these dishes were, my favorite was their *chicharron*, which they serve only by the pound. We bought a half-pound order, tore it into pieces and filled the corn tortillas with it, along with the rest of the relishes. These large chunks of pork are just like *carnitas* and taste exquisite. We also sampled their cheese-stuffed *poblano* peppers, which they dip in an egg batter before frying. They were served on corn tortillas, to which a smearing of refried beans had been applied. They were an excellent appetizer.

When you order your tacos to go, they come with a couple of plastic

bags. One contains limes, chopped onions, and cilantro; the other, tortilla chips. You also get small containers of *salsa verde*, a smooth *jalapeño* sauce that packs quite a punch. The *tacos de trompo* are available only on weekends. The rest of the week, they turn into *tacos al pastor*, and end up being somewhat drier than the meat that comes directly from the *trompo*.

If you visit on the weekends, you can also pick up meat by the pound: *barbacoa*, *chicharon prensado* (pork rinds in a spicy red sauce), *carnitas* and *fajitas*.

I asked Marcos the meaning of the name Karanchos. He told that it was used instead of *cabrones*, which he advised me, was a bad word. The word is also used in the phrase "No sea un karancho," which is often used to scold young children: "Don't be a pest."

the

FARM-RAISED

CATFISH

is covered

in a spicy seasoned cornmeal batter

LOCATION
14520 Memorial

HOURS
11:00am-7:00pm

FOOD
Seafood

PRICES
$

STARTED
2011

PAYMENT
All

PHONE
713-269-7272

SPECIAL SERVICES
Catering

OWNERS
Joe Barber and Jay Pirotte

FACEBOOK
KatfishKitchen?sk=inf

KATFISH KITCHEN

—

At present, the trailer, which is brand-new and **one of the largest** I found, can be found on Memorial near Dairy Ashford during the day.

Their slogan is "Fry it right or don't fry it at all," and you'd better believe that they do a good job. The shrimp are butterflied to maximize their surface

The shrimp are butterflied to maximize their surface area, then dipped in a seasoned egg batter before frying.

area, then dipped in a seasoned egg batter before frying. The result is crispy on the outside and tender on the inside — and the seasoning makes them taste terrific. The farm-raised catfish is

covered in a spicy seasoned cornmeal batter. The filet emerges from the fryer very moist and with no muddy taste. The Jumbo Combo platter includes five catfish filets, five shrimp, two hushpuppies and fries. Before you dismiss these fries as merely fries, let me assure you that they're some of the best you'll ever eat. They seem to be coated with flour before frying, rendering them super crisp. A sprinkle of Cajun seasoning adds a nice zest.

At present, the trailer, which is brand-new and one of the largest I found,

CATFISH FILETS // FRIED SHRIMP // FRIES COATED WITH FLOUR // HUSHPUPPIES

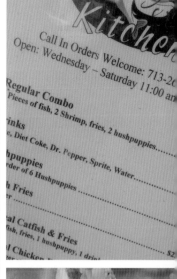

Call In Orders Welcome: 713-2
Open: Wednesday – Saturday 11:00 am

Regular Combo
Pieces of fish, 2 Shrimp, fries, 2 hushpuppies......

rinks
e, Diet Coke, Dr. Pepper, Sprite, Water......

hpuppies
der of 6 Hushpuppies ......

h Fries
er ......

al Catfish & Fries
fish, fries, 1 bushpuppy, 1 drint

l Chicken
$2

Before you dismiss these fries as merely fries, let me assure you that they're some of the best you'll ever eat.

can be found on Memorial near Dairy Ashford during the day. But when I spoke with owners Joe and Jay, they were planning to move: maybe to a spot on Washington in the evening, or one on West Gray during the day.

a

DRIZZLE OF

HOMEMADE

spicy mayo

finish off this spectacular burger

LOCATION
Various

PHONE
832-878-3103

HOURS
Various

FOOD
Chinese fusion

PRICES
$

OWNERS
Luong, Jerry Jan

STARTED
2012

PAYMENT
All

TWITTER
#!/kurbsideeatz

FACEBOOK
Kurbside-Eatz-kurb-ur-food-enthusi-
asm/28118149191282

KURBSIDE EATZ

—

It didn't take us very long to develop our menu, **it features things** we like to eat at home.

Nancy Luong and Jerry Jan are partners in the new Kurbside Eatz food truck serving Asian fusion comfort cuisine. The story about

Jerry was a sushi chef at Ra Sushi for many years while Nancy's family has been in the restaurant business during the years when Nancy was growing up.

how Nancy decided to open her truck starts when she visited New York and saw the vibrant street food scene there. Then last year, she attended Houston's first Haute Wheels Food Truck Festival and "something just clicked; it just felt right", said Nancy. She was inspired

by what she saw there and the rest, as they say...

Nancy and Jerry were already friends and both had been searching for an opportunity. Jerry was a sushi chef at Ra Sushi for many years while Nancy's family has been in the restaurant business during the years when Nancy was growing up. "I grew up in the biz," said Nancy. Her family is originally from China and they used to own a number of Chinese buffet restaurants in Houston. "It didn't take us very long to develop our menu," said Nancy. "It features things we like to eat at home," she said. The truck's graphics feature some really cool scenes of Houston. It is the food, however, that truly sets this truck apart.

The first thing I tried was the special for that day: Salt & Pepper Parmesan Calamari. They first dip the calamari into a mixture of flour, salt, black pepper and cayenne. A few minutes in the deep fryer and they turn into the crispiest calamari you'll probably ever eat. They're still quite chewy when served and because there are a lot of small pieces, they have a tendency to stick together when cooked. Don't bother trying to pull them apart; simply stuff as many as you can fit in your mouth at one time. You won't regret it. The first burst of flavor comes from the cayenne. As this dissipates, you get the flavor of the calamari. Just before serving, they add some slices of raw *jalapeño* for added heat and a sprinkling of Parmesan cheese, which is almost superfluous. They serve them with a homemade Thai Chili dipping sauce, which is both hot and sweet. Once you've tasted this homemade version, no commercially available sauce will ever do. This is one of those dishes that is so good that it should be a permanent addition to the menu.

Next up was the Triple Cheese Curry Beef Burger. Nancy recommended that I have it with a fried egg on top. It was an excellent recommendation. Curry is one of those flavors where even the slightest amount too much can overpower every other flavor around it, but here, Jerry's mixture of hand-formed, 100% beef with an 80/20 ratio of meat to fat was just

perfect, which means it's pretty high on the ooze scale, with the curry adding just a hint of background note as well as a soupçon of heat. Even the fried egg was cooked to perfection on the griddle with the white cooked through but the yolk still runny. This made for one helluva messy burger once you dug your teeth in for the first bite, permitting the yolk to break and run all over the place. All this meant was that, once you picked up the burger, you just could not put it down. The triple cheeses are in the form of sharp Cheddar, Parmesan and American but it is the addition of a crispy cheese chip, which Jerry makes by taking American and Monterrey Jack cheeses and melting them on the griddle until they cook to a crisp that adds an even

They first dip the calamari in flour to which salt, black pepper and cayenne have been added.

richer cheese flavor. Shredded lettuce and a drizzle of homemade, spicy mayo finish off this spectacular burger all stuffed in a sesame seed bun.

On my second visit, I decided to try their 'tacos' – all of them. I say 'tacos' because, instead of corn or flour tortillas, they use Indian *parathas*, which are thick and flaky rounds of wheat flour, that, when heated on the griddle actually add a nice flavor and greasiness to the tacos. The first one I sampled was the Shrimp Taco. The

shrimp are marinated in Asian spices and they're served with a miso-ginger slaw and some crumbles of *queso fresco*. Next up was the Chicken Taco, which has been steeping in a zesty garlic and soy marinade. It comes with shredded sharp Cheddar and jack cheeses, some homemade creamy cilantro spicy mayo and some chopped cilantro. Next, the Beef Taco, for which they use rib eye steak marinated in Asian spices. It, too, is served with the same accoutrements as the other ta-

Jerry's mixture of hand-formed, 100% beef with an 80/20 ratio of meat to fat was just perfect.

cos. Finally, and my favorite, the Crispy Taco Belly, where they take thin slices of pork belly and add some kimchi, lettuce and with shredded sharp Cheddar and jack cheeses, some homemade creamy cilantro, spicy mayo and some chopped cilantro. The *parathas* certainly add a lot o to these 'tacos' and even though they are small in diameter, they are plenty big enough to wrap around these delectable ingredients prepared by Nancy and Jerry.

It was on my second visit that I encountered the Braised Pork Belly Bun. Jerry had told me when I visited him the first time that I simply had to try it, but that he had already sold out. Since I thought I knew Chinese buns, the large, round, steamed kind, called simply *bao* or *bumbow*, which are mainly dough with very little filling, I was none

TRIPLE CHEESE CURRY BEEF BURGER //
SALT & PEPPER PARMESAN CALAMARI //
BRAISED PORK BELLY BUN

too excited. But then Jerry started to describe to me that they deep- fried the bun and that the pork belly had been slow-braised for six hours in Asian spices and sweet soy sauce, my ears perked up and it was obvious that I was thinking about something quite different. And, boy, was I. The first thing you notice when you bite into this thing of beauty for the first time, is just how giving the meat it. I swear this is something that can be eaten with no teeth at all it's so soft and juicy. Then there's the sweet and savory flavors that just go round and round in your mouth. On the menu, Jerry has written by this dish, "a party in your mouth". Nothing could be truer. Frying the bun

The shrimp are marinated in Asian spices and they're served with a miso ginger slaw and some crumbles of *queso fresco*

makes it slightly crispy on the outside, but it retains it softness everywhere else. Crispy fried onions, diced green onions and some chopped cilantro are all added just before serving.

❊ **they** ❊

WERE SERVED

WITH TRADITIONAL

curtido

which was topped with queso fresco

LOCATION
7910 Harrisburg

HOURS
Mon-Sun: 11:00am-11:00pm

FOOD
Honduran

PRICES
$

STARTED
2010

PAYMENT
Cash only

PHONE
(713) 875-4958

OWNER
Maria Rubios

SPECIAL SERVICES
Catering

LA POLLERA COLORA

—

La Pollera's business picks up later in the evening and **extends into the wee hours** as folks leave clubs, bars and dancehalls in search of sustenance.

The name of this truck refers to the colorful skirt used in Hispanic folkloric festivals. The truck is owned by Maria Rubios, who is from La Celba, on the northern coastline of Honduras. The Saturday that I visited her truck, her

The beef version consisted of seasoned ground beef, onions, carrots, tomatoes and potatoes. It reminded me of a Jamaican pasty.

two daughters were happily helping out. Since it was early afternoon, none of the *"Ricos Caldos"* advertised on a sign in the window were ready yet. Neither

were the *chuletas* nor the *yuca con chicharron*. Like many Hispanic trucks, La Pollera's business picks up later in the evening and extends into the wee hours as folks leave clubs, bars and dancehalls in search of sustenance.

I ordered the *pasteles* and *pescado frito*. The p*asteles*, two to an order, are basically large, thick corn tortillas that have been folded over, stuffed, sealed and then deep-fried. The beef version consisted of seasoned ground beef, onions, carrots, tomatoes and potatoes. It reminded me of a Jamaican pasty and of the fact that many cultures share something similar to the

YUCA CON CHICHARRON // PASTELES
PESCADO FRITO // SALTED, FRIED PLANTAINS

empanada. They were served with the traditional *curtido* or shredded cabbage, which was topped with *queso fresco* and a tomato-based sauce that kept the dish from being too dry. Pink pickled onions helped, too.

The *pescado frito* is a well-seasoned whole tilapia that has been deep fried. The seasoning includes lots of salt and garlic. The fish came with the same *curtido* and pink-colored onions,

The *pescado frito* is a well-seasoned whole tilapia that has been deep fried.

lying on a bed of *tajadas*, or slices of salted, fried plantains — a wonderful side dish.

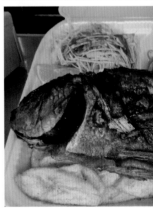

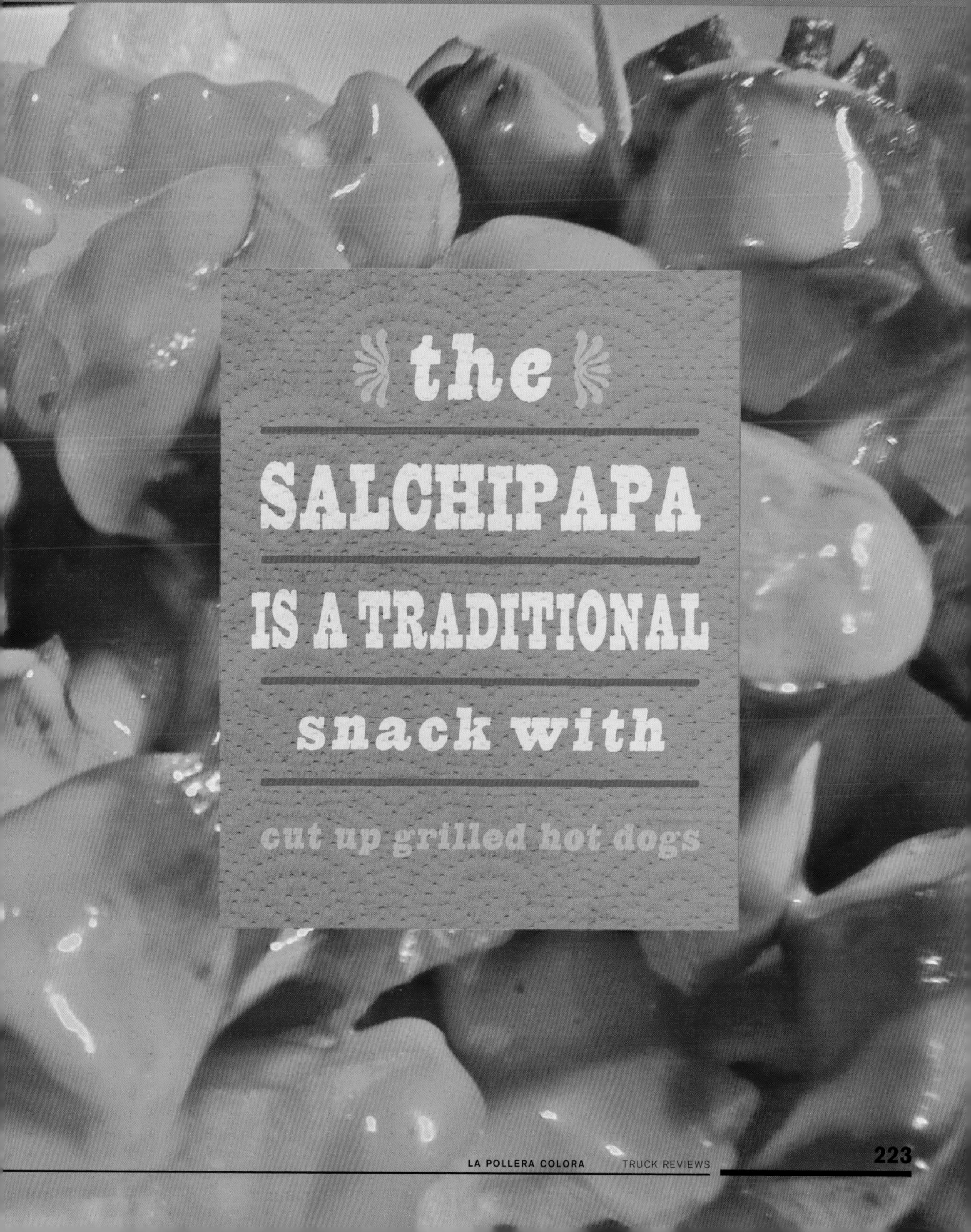

≽ **the** ≼

SALCHIPAPA

IS A TRADITIONAL

---

snack with

---

cut up grilled hot dogs

LOCATION
6100 Wilcrest

PHONE
713-344-4110

HOURS
Thurs-Sat: 6:30pm-2:45pm, Sun:
4:00pm-12:00pm, Mon: 7:00pm-
12:00pm

FOOD
Colombian

PRICES
$

OWNER
Joseph Gordon

STARTED
2010

PAYMENT
Cash only

FACEBOOK
home.php#!/profile.
php?id=100001337846053

LAS COLOMBIANITAS

—

An *aji salsa*, or hot sauce, consisting of chilies, onions, tomato and white vinegar, **adds a touch of heat** that enhances the flavor of this handmade empanada.

The name of this trailer means "the little Colombian girls." Parked in the parking lot of the Colombian club Mango's on Wilcrest at Harwin, it serves patrons of that establishment until the wee hours of the morning. When I mentioned to the owner, Joseph Gordon, that his name did not sound particularly Colombian, he told me that he is from a small island in the Caribbean, San Andres, which belongs to Colombia but is actually closer to Nicaragua, where people's names sound English and where Creole is spoken. British settlers arrived there from Barbados and England in the 17th century.

The Colombian *empanada* is made of the tuber, yuca, or cassava, and is deep-fried.

The Colombian *empanada* is made of the tuber, *yuca*, or cassava, and is deep-fried. It is stuffed with an extremely tasty mixture of beef, potatoes and onions. An *aji salsa*, or hot sauce, consisting of chilies, onions, tomato

EMPANADAS // ALCHIPAPA // BEEF KEBABS
COLOMBIANA (KOLA CHAMPAGNE) SOFT DRINK

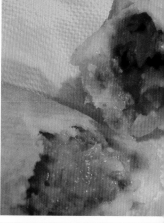

and white vinegar, adds a touch of heat that enhances the flavor of this handmade *empanada*. The *salchi-papa* is a traditional snack consisting of hot dogs heated on the griddle and cut up into small pieces and served with French fries. They mix everything together, then top it with a Colombian *salsa rosada*, or pink sauce, a simple mixture of mayonnaise and ketchup.

I also sampled a *chuzo* or kebab. Thin slices of beef are placed on a skewer along with slices of onions and red and green bell peppers. It is cooked on the griddle along with a mini *arepa*.

To complete the array of traditional tastes, order a golden-colored *Colombiana*™ (kola champagne) soft drink.

they

TOP IT WITH

CRUSHED

potato chips

which add a salty crunch

LOCATION
9413 Richmond

HOURS
Wed-Thur, Sun: 5:00pm-12:00am, Fri-
Sat: 5:00pm-5:00am

FOOD
Colombian

PRICES
$

STARTED
2004

PAYMENT
Cash only

PHONE
347-262-1682

OWNER
Lester Garcia

SPECIAL SERVICES
Catering

FACEBOOK
home.php#!/pages/Los-Perros-Hous-
ton/165637846785935

LOS PERROS

—

The *perro* we had is probably the **best hot dog** we found. The *perra*, a hot dog wrapped in bacon, may be even better.

Lester Garcia has been in Houston since 2005 and opened the first Colombian food truck in the city in 2008. He recently opened a second truck, which can be found on Washington Avenue. This was one of the most crowded trucks I visited. Open only in the evenings, it was in a parking lot with other Colombian restaurants. Salsa music blared from professional-looking speakers, people were dancing, and everybody was having a good time. On weekends, it's open until 5:00 a.m.!

Yes, *Los Perros* means "the dogs," and lest you think of calling the SPCA, you need to know that a *perro* signifies a hot dog, and that a *perra* is a hot dog wrapped in bacon. The *perro* we had is probably the best hot dog we found in Houston. We think that the *perra* would have been even better, but saw it on the menu only after we

had ordered the *perro*. What makes the *perro* so great are two things: First, they top the whole thing with crushed potato chips, which add an unexpected, salty crunch. Second are the seven different sauces with which they douse the *perro*: mayonnaise, ketchup, mustard, tartar, pink sauce (probably mayo and ketchup mixed together), pineapple sauce and raspberry sauce. The last two add a blast of sweetness that, when mixed with the salty potato chips, makes this dog hard to put down. You

This was one of the most crowded trucks I visited. It was in a parking lot with other Colombian restaurants.

will also find some *queso fresco* in there somewhere. Lester told me that these dogs normally come with two quail eggs on top. But that evening, they had already run out.

GRILLED *CHORIZO* // *PERRO* HOT DOG // *AREPAS*
PERRA BACON WRAPPED HOT DOG // *CHUZO*

The grilled *chorizo* is available in beef or chicken. I tried the beef version. It consists of very coarsely ground, rather

Next was the *chuzo*. This is a type of Colombian kabob, also available in chicken or beef.

chewy meat. Flavored with cumin, it has a greenish/yellowish tinge. It is served with a mini corn *arepa*.

Next was the *chuzo*. This is a type of Colombian kabob, also available in chicken or beef. We chose the chicken. On the wooden stick, pieces of onion and red and green peppers separated the large, grilled chicken pieces. It was extremely tasty.

I followed this with the *arepa*. Unlike Venezuelan *arepas*, made of ground corn, this one is made of whole corn. It is also larger and thinner than its Venezuelan cousin, and instead of being stuffed, the "stuffing" goes on top. At first glance, you think you're about to eat a *tostada*. When you pick it up, however, you soon realize that it is not crisp like a *tostada*, but soft. The shredded chicken version we chose was topped with a mayo/ketchup sauce, and was also extremely tasty.

the

LIST OF SYRUPS

SHE OFFERS

was staggering

over 50 flavors

LOCATION
Various

PHONE
832-265-1706

HOURS
Summer: 12:00pm-8:00pm,
Winter: 12:00pm-6:00pm

FOOD
Sno balls

PRICES
$

OWNER
Ariana Espinoza

STARTED
2009

PAYMENT
Cash only

WEBSITE
www.mamshouseofice.com

FACEBOOK
mamshouseoficesnoballs

TWITTER
mamshouseofice

MAM'S HOUSE OF ICE

—

I went to **New Orleans to learn how** to make these," she said, "and I get some of my syrups from there as well as make some of my own.

Ariana and her family are from Costa Rica. "In Costa Rica, sno-balls are called *granizadas*," she told me. She remembers when her dad used to make them by shaving the ice by hand back in California, from where the family moved. "He would also make all his

A sno-ball (which is what she makes) is fluffy. A snow cone is made with coarse ice particles and is crunchier.

syrup by hand. It used to take forever," she added. Those childhood memories must have stayed with her because she now owns one of the most popular

sno-ball trucks in the city. "I went to New Orleans to learn how to make these," she said, "and I get some of my syrups from there as well as make some of my own."

Ariana was also the first to explain to me the differences between a sno-ball, a snow cone and shaved ice. A sno-ball (which is what she makes) is fluffy. A snow cone is made with coarse ice particles and is crunchier. Shaved ice is coarser than a sno-ball and is typical of Hawaii.

The list of syrups she offers was staggering. The menu lists over 50 flavors, not

TIGER'S BLOOD COCONUT WITH THE CONDENSED MILK

// *GRANIZADAS* IN OVER 50 FLAVORS //

to mention the individual combinations that people come up with. I left myself in

> **The menu lists over 50 flavors, not to mention the individual combinations that people come up with.**

her capable hands. She asked me if I like coconut and, when I said that I did, she recommended the Tiger's Blood with the condensed milk. The blood-red sno-ball was fabulous. After I had finished about half, she gave me another shot of condensed milk to finish off the rest. Kids will undoubtedly love the color that the syrup leaves on your tongue.

❋ *fufu* ❋

IS A DISH

MADE OF

yam flour

it's a good base to soak up flavors

LOCATION
Taxi staging area, George Bush
Intercontinental Airport. (See below.)

FOOD
Nigerian

PRICES
$

PAYMENT
Cash only

MARISCO'S LA WENDY

—

Watching her make *the fufu* reminded me of when my father would make *polenta*.

This truck proved to be the most elusive included in this book. I had heard only that it served Nigerian food and was owned by someone called John Fred. I asked a Nigerian limo driver about it. He was familiar with the truck and thought that it parked at the taxi staging area at Intercontinental Airport.

One Saturday morning I set out for the airport, trying to follow the vague directions he'd given me. No success. My gut told me it had to be really close to the airport. As I meandered, I noticed a Shell station and decided, on the off chance, to stop in and ask if anyone had any clue as to the whereabouts of the taxi staging area. Luck was on my side. As I pulled into the station, I spotted a cab driver leaving it. He was Nigerian, and he was on his way to the taxi staging area. He knew of John Fred and told me that that he thought he no longer owned the truck and that a woman was now

running it. He also told me that she wasn't there on the weekends. I followed him to the taxi staging area and quickly determined that without his help, I would never have found it.

As you enter the airport from Will Clayton Blvd., in the 5500 block, there is a pink sign on the right hand side of the road that says, "Passenger Pick Up Waiting Lot." It is just before the overhead signs that describe the airlines and their terminals. You take a right here (there is no street name), then left at the first intersection, and there it is, on the right-hand side: the surprisingly secretive Taxi Staging Area.

Even after I found it, I had a problem: Only taxis are admitted. I followed my new friend into the lot and drove up to the guard shack. I asked about the food truck and was told that it is there during the week. I then asked, "What if a person who doesn't own a taxi wants to eat at the food truck? "Then you must park across the street and walk over," answered the attendant.

When I returned Monday, at lunchtime, that's exactly what I did. At first, I didn't notice this truck; the place was swarming with a couple of hundred taxis and their drivers. I did spot a couple of trucks not far from the entrance and went over to see what there was to have. The first truck I spotted was called Sufi's. It was run by Somalis for the Somali cab drivers. The truck parked next to it was a typical no-name *lonchera*, the kind of lunch truck that pulls into building sites and serves the construction workers. Since I didn't see anything of interest, I moved on. I was about to leave because I hadn't seen my quarry when I glanced towards the back of the lot, some 100 yards away, and spotted what I thought looked like a food truck. As I made my way past an impromptu basketball game and a group of cab drivers playing cards, I saw the name, Marisco's, and knew I'd found it.

The menu on the side of the truck lists Mexican items: *tacos, tortas, gorditas* and so on. But when I asked, the server told me that she served only Nigerian food. "What should I have?" I asked.

"What do you want?" she replied.

"Do you have a menu?" I asked.

"No," she said. I should have known.

The only Nigerian dish that immediately came to mind was *fufu*, so I asked if she had any. "Not right now, but I'm just making some and it will be about twenty minutes," she replied. *Fufu* is a dish made of yam flour. It has no discernable taste of its own, but it's a good base to soak up the flavor of whatever you put on it. The cook takes a large pot of boiling water, adds the *fufu* flour in bowlfuls, then stirs vigorously until the consistency is like that of a thick paste. Watching her make the *fufu* reminded me of when my father would make *polenta*. It is exactly the same process.

The offerings, I eventually determined, don't change a lot. Among them are a melon soup called *egusi*; what the server calls "beans," which are very flavorful black-eyed peas; beef stew; and *fufu*. I sampled the *egusi* but could not place any of the flavors. I asked what she normally served on the *fufu*, and when she told me *egusi*, I asked if she could substitute some of the beans and the beef stew. She did exactly as I requested.

The Nigerian cab drivers who surrounded me asked me what I was getting. When I told them *fufu*, a couple of them informed me that this was the best thing for my manhood. I expressed my appreciation for this information. When they saw that I had beans with it instead of the customary *egusi*, they shook their heads in disbelief.

❖ the ❖

MUSHROOM-
FILLED
crêpe

with greens was superb

LOCATION
403 Westheimer

PHONE
713-291-9933

HOURS
Mon, Thu-Fri: 7:00am-1:00pm; Wed,
Sat-Sun: 10:00am-2:00pm

FOOD
Crêpes

PRICES
$ $

OWNER
Sean Carroll

STARTED
2010

PAYMENT
Cash only

SPECIAL SERVICES
Catering

TWITTER
melangecreperie

FACEBOOK
people/melange-crepe-
rie/100000517719016

WEBSITE
http://melangecreperie.wordpress.com

MELANGE CRÊPERIE

—

When Sean and his new wife returned from their honeymoon in the City of Light, he wanted to bring **street-corner** *crêpes* to Houston.

When I asked Sean Carroll where he got his nickname, "Buffalo," he seemed surprised that I couldn't guess. "I'm from Buffalo," he said.

At his cart, though, he channels Paris. When Sean and his new wife returned from their honeymoon in the City of Light, he wanted to bring street-corner *crêpes* to Houston. An artist by training, he spent many months planning his *crêperie* cart.

He didn't overcomplicate things and says that he got in the business for "around $10 grand." When he's ap-

An artist by training, he spent many months planning his *crêperie* cart.

proached by people who want help going into business for themselves, he refers them to his wife: "She's better with the money side."

Buffalo Sean's cart is officially known as a "fixed location mobile unit," an oxymoron if there ever were one. This basically means that he can't roam the streets, but has to stay put in one place — in his case, in front of the restaurant Mango's on lower Westheimer.

He named his business Melange because he is developing 100 different *crêpe* recipes, fusing together all the different cultures he sees in Houston. Two recipes — ham, egg and cheese; and banana and Nutella™ — are always available, he says, because his customers threaten him when he tries to remove them. The day I visited, he also had a *duxelle* of mushrooms (finely-chopped mushrooms, cooked in butter with shallots and wine) with fresh greens; and a filling he called Italian cheesecake.

ITALIAN CHEESECAKE *CRÊPE* // *CRÊPE* FILLED WITH MUSHROOM AND GREENS // *CRÊPE* WITH A HOMEMADE STRAWBERRY COMPOTE //

Making a fresh *crêpe* takes just a few minutes. While making small talk, Sean removes a scoop of batter from a large plastic container and pours it on the hot, round griddle. He then uses a special spatula to even it all out, and draws the batter to the very edge of the griddle, maximizing the diameter of the *crêpe*. After 30 seconds or so, he places a large, flat spatula underneath the *crêpe*, freeing it from the griddle, then flips it on the other side to finish cooking. Next he adds the toppings. Once the *crêpe* is cooked, he folds it in half and then in half again and places it in a triangular paper holder, which makes it very easy to handle and eat.

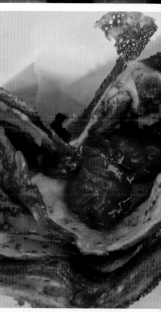

The *crêpe* filled with mushroom and greens was superb, with the creamy mélange of mushrooms (cremini and oyster) giving it an earthy taste that was accompanied well by the field greens. But it was the Italian cheesecake that took my breath away; after one bite, I could see why people threaten him over their favorite items. He makes the filling with a blend of ricotta and cream cheese, which he sweetens with sugar and local honey and adds crumbled graham crackers to fool you into believing it has a crust. He serves the *crêpe* with a homemade strawberry compote — a great way to top off a heavenly dessert.

yet ANOTHER FASCINATING snack

that no one should miss

LOCATION
9612 Beechnut

HOURS
Mon-Tue, Thur-Sun:
12:00pm-8:00pm

FOOD
Roasted corn, Mexican snacks

PRICES
$

OWNER
Melissa

STARTED
2006

PAYMENT
Cash only

MELISSA'S ROASTED CORN

—

When you order *un elote*, the server removes the ear of corn from **the roasting oven**, pulls back the husk and silk, then cuts the kernels from the corn with a large knife.

Mexican roasted corn makes a wonderful snack at any time of the day, and the roasted corn here is some of the best I've sampled in Houston. The corn is

The corn is cooked in its husk in a large roasting oven at the back of the trailer; the smoky flavor permeates every kernel.

cooked in its husk in a large roasting oven at the back of the trailer; the smoky flavor permeates every kernel.

When you order *un elote* (an ear of corn), the server removes the ear of corn from the roasting oven, pulls back the husk and silk, then cuts the kernels

from the corn with a large knife, positioning the cob over a large polystyrene cup so that, as she cuts, the kernels fall in. Already at bottom of the cup, she has added spoonfuls of margarine, mayonnaise and Parmesan cheese. She layers the corn with hot sauce, seasoned chili powder and sour cream. This process is repeated until the cup is completely filled, right up to the rim. The resulting multi-colored snack is hard to resist, but it's best if you wait a few minutes so the cheese and margarine have time to melt. You can help them along with a good stir, coating the kernels so that the spicy seasonings stick to each one.

MEXICAN ROASTED CORN // FRUIT COCKTAIL
// *CHICHARRON PREPARADO*

It's fun to watch the assembly of the *chicharron preparado*, because, just when you think she's through adding stuff to the crispy wheat cracker base, she pulls out another container with yet another ingredient and manages to find space for it all. She first tops the

This reflects Jake's cooking style, which is to slow-cook the meat for 9 or 10 hours at 150 degrees.

base with *cueritos* (long slices of pickled *chicharron*), which are quite rubbery and not unlike calamari in appearance and texture. Then comes shredded cabbage, diced tomatoes, sour cream and a good squeeze of lime. Like other versions I have tried, this *chicharron preparado* is difficult to eat. I managed by breaking off pieces small enough to fit in my mouth. The different textures, colors and tastes make this yet another fascinating snack that no one should miss.

❖ a ❖
TERRIFIC
MINI-EXAMPLE
of carrot cake
nice, fresh, and moist

LOCATION
Various

PHONE
832-398-8086

HOURS
Various

FOOD
Cupcakes

PRICES
$

OWNERS
Michelle Marie Marzoch, Justin Febbo

STARTED
2010

PAYMENT
Cash only

SPECIAL SERVICES
Delivery

TWITTER
mmmcupcaketruck

FACEBOOK
MMMCupcakeTruck

WEBSITE
mmmcupcake.net

MMM CUPCAKES

—

The truck's name is a play on words. Not only does MMM signify "good," the **three M's are also the initials** of one of the owners.

In a previous life, this truck was an ice cream truck. The team converted it themselves to a cupcake truck. Since they don't actually do any cooking on the truck, the amount of equipment they need is minimal.

The truck's name is a play on words. Not only does MMM signify "good," the three M's are also the initials of one of the owners.

Frequent posts on Twitter and Facebook make it easy to track this truck, which travels through downtown and the Rice Village, never spending more than a couple of hours in any one location. The first time I visited it in downtown Houston, they were exactly where their Twitter post said they were.

As I approached, I noticed quite a line, and one of the employees was outside the truck saying, "I'm sorry, but we sold out." While I was interview-

The four cupcakes I tried were all nice and moist, and you could tell that they had been made fresh that day

ing them, they turned away at least a dozen people.

They sell between 250 and 500 cupcakes a day, and they might have run out on that day because it was customer appreciation day, when they offer a buy-one-get-one-free deal.

After you order your cupcakes, the server packages them in a box with a

CRANBERRY-ORANGE // PUMPKIN-CINNAMON
CARROT CAKE // CHOCOLATE // RED VELVET

see-through top, where cut-outs hold them upright, preventing them from rolling around as you transport them.

The servers do not add the exceptionally smooth cream cheese, chocolate or buttermilk toppings to the cupcakes until you place your order; that way, it

Some varieties are seasonal; others, available all year round.

doesn't dry out. The four cupcakes I tried were all nice and moist, and you could tell that they had been made fresh that day. Some varieties are seasonal; others, available all year round. In the cranberry-orange version, I could most definitely taste both fruits. The chocolate version had a rich taste and had some crispy, slightly burnt edges, which added to the rich flavor. The pumpkin-cinnamon was the perfect fall treat; and the carrot version was a terrific mini-example of this classic cake.

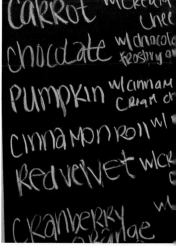

it was a

GOOEY MESS

TO EAT

with the filling

oozing out of every side

LOCATION
Various

FOOD
PBJ sandwiches

PRICES
$

STARTED
2012

PAYMENT
All

OWNER
Jill Butler, Will Lidwell

FACEBOOK
/Monsterpbj

WEBSITE
http://www.monsterpbj.com/

TWITTER
/monsterpbj

SPECIAL SERVICES
Gluten-free, vegan, vegetarian

MONSTER PBJ

—

All their bread comes from a small, local Houston bakery called the Best Bread Around Bakery and all their jams are **locally made**.

The Monster PBJ truck is hard to miss with bright graphics that are very inviting, especially for kids. The premise behind this truck is one of the all-time favorite comfort foods for both kids and adults – the peanut butter and jelly sandwich. This truck has some major following. Mention PBJ to adults and a gleam appears in their eyes as they're transported back to their childhood. Conjuring up the thought of a PBJ almost always evokes a happier time.

Jill Butler and her partner, Will Lidwell, owners of the truck, also own a design company. When Jill decided to become a vegan some years ago when she suffered some health problems, she was disappointed in the healthy food options available to her. "At that time, there was a void in the marketplace. There certainly weren't a lot of food trucks serving good, healthy food. That's changed somewhat now," said Jill. "The second void we noticed is that there were no

trucks that were family-friendly, where kids and adults could enjoy eating," added Jill. The team behind this successful concept is committed to quality and to making a healthy sandwich. They grind their own nuts and their jams and bread have no preservatives in them. This attention to detail is not without reward – quality ingredients do make better-tasting products.

You're probably thinking, OK, once I've tried one PBJ, I've tried everything this truck has to offer, right? Wrong. The many different variations available mean that you could customize your PBJ every day for a year and still not eat the same one twice. How so, you ask?

First is the size of sandwich you want. A 'junior' uses one slice of bread, folded in two. The 'classic', two slices and the 'monster', three slices. Then there's the type of bread. There's white, whole wheat and a nice touch: gluten-free bread. Next is the decision of the type

CUSTOMIZED PB&J SANDWICHS // PEANUT, ALMOND AND CASHEW BUTTER // THREE LOCAL MADE JELLIES

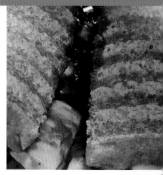

of nut butter you want spread on your bread. Naturally, there's peanut, but they also have almond and cashew available. Then you get to pick the jelly you'd like, ranging from apple and blueberry to strawberry. This is followed by the selection of slices of fruit, from choices of apple, banana and strawberry.

You're not done yet. If you want any sweetener, like agave or honey or perhaps you'd like some Nutella®, that's your next choice followed by the decision of whether you want the crust on or off, the type of cut you prefer from straight, diagonal, halved or quartered and finally, whether you want your sandwich plain or grilled.

At first, the choices may seem a little overwhelming but as soon as you arrive you are handed a brown paper bag, which has all of these choices printed on it and all you do is to write your name on the bag, then indicate your choices by checking the appropriate boxes. Your customized PB&J sandwich is served in the very same bag. Once you get the hang of it you will discover that it's really quite simple and efficient.

All their bread comes from a small, local Houston bakery called the Best Bread Around Bakery and all their jams are also locally made. My first PBJ sandwich was a 'classic', on whole wheat with cashew butter, blueberry jam, banana slices, and Nutella®. Since I did not completely fill out the answers to all

the choices, I was asked by the server "plain or grilled?" Since I had never had a PBJ grilled, I asked for his recommendation "I really like it grilled," he said. I took his advice and was glad that I did.

Since this truck invokes so much fun, my strategy for the second sandwich involved choosing all the ingredients that started with the letter "a". This just seemed like it was a fun thing to do. So, almond butter, apple slices, apple jam and agave sweetener all went in. My mistake, if you can call it one, was to choose gluten-free bread. Since I had never eaten gluten-free bread before, I decided that I had to give it a try. My heart goes out to people that cannot digest gluten because the gluten-free bread I tried was just too dry and really had no redeeming features. The fillings were great but could not quite make up for the insipid bread.

My last "classic" selection was outstanding and included white bread, peanut butter, strawberry jam, fresh strawberries and honey with the crust on and grilled. It was a gooey mess to eat with the filling oozing out of every side of the sandwich but the blend of strawberry flavors with peanut butter made me wish I had ordered the "monster" instead of just the "classic".

"We want to continue to work on our ingredients to ensure the best quality possible, plus make sure we're delivering our products as speedily as possible. Next we may add some more adult offerings," said Jill.

he

USES A DRY RUB

ON HIS RIBS

and brisket

and marinates them for four days

LOCATION
8042 Martin Luther King

PHONE
713-367-8114

HOURS
Fri-Sun: 9:30am-6:00pm

FOOD
Barbecue

PRICES
$

OWNER
Patricia Ann Johnson, Easter Aaron

STARTED
2010

PAYMENT
Cash only

SPECIAL SERVICES
Catering

MS. ANN'S KITCHEN

—

The trailer is a beauty, **decked out** in diamond-pattern stainless steel.

It wasn't hard to find this place as I drove south on MLK from Loop 610; I just had to look for the cars parked in every direction in a parking lot of an Autozone. Ms. Ann's attracts a crowd. At lunchtime, the cars line up as if at any drive-through, and Easter Aaron busily runs between them, taking and delivering orders.

The business card that Ms. Ann handed me stated: "We don't just do Bar-B-Que." She also makes gumbo, seafood chowder, pies and cakes, but most of that is for her catering business. For all intents and purposes, drivers waiting for their orders are here for one thing and one thing only: some of the best barbecue the city has to offer.

"We built the trailer from scratch," said Easter. "We started the business about nine months ago, and we thought we could just sell barbecue from the pit. Then we met the city authorities, so

for the last eight months, we've been fixing it up to make sure we're legal." The trailer is a beauty, decked out in diamond-pattern stainless steel, and the pit has an automatic opener for the top. When I pulled up, I noticed Ms. Ann polishing the window and counter, through which people place and receive their orders. And when I photographed Ms. Ann inside her trailer, I noticed how spotless things were. I bet if I visit again in six months, it'll be just as shiny and spotless.

The day I visited they had three items available: sausage on a stick (not homemade, so I passed); baby back ribs; and brisket. Easter uses only mesquite and cooks his brisket for seven hours at 275 degrees. He uses a dry rub on both his ribs and brisket, and also marinates them for four days. He starts out cooking the brisket fat down,

BABY BACK RIBS // BRISKET // SAUSAGE ON A STICK // POTATO SALAD // SWEET BAKED BEANS

then turns it and finishes it with the fat up, so that it seeps into the meat and keeps it nice and moist. He starts cooking at around 11 p.m. each night and comes back every hour to check on the temperature until 6 the next morning. "Are you serious?" I asked.

"Yes, sir," he said.

Whatever magic he uses, works. The brisket was extremely moist and tender and, unlike a lot of the barbecue I sampled, it was not overwhelmingly smoky. The red ring of fire was definitely present and thicker than many others I tried. The meat also had a lot of fat, undoubtedly making it moist and extremely tender. The brisket and the ribs were so well seasoned that I did not need to add sauce.

Which was a good thing: For my taste, the sauce had too much smoke flavor. Easter was honest enough to tell me that it was store-bought, then doctored up.

Now for the ribs. These tiny, baby back ribs were absolutely superb. They needed no chewing, merely nudging off the bone. They, too, were extremely tender and moist and very well seasoned: some of the best barbecue ribs I have ever had.

Finally to the sides. Usually at a barbecue place, the sides just get in the way of the meat, and they're rarely homemade. But since Ms. Ann goes to the

trouble of making all of her own sides, I figured I should try them. Am I glad I did.

The potato salad was heavy and thick with firm potatoes, hard-boiled eggs, pickles and mayo. It was remarkably good and disappeared even before the meat. The beans were sweet baked beans, swimming in dark brown liquid. It was evident that Ms. Ann used brown sugar, and a lot of it, although when I asked her about her recipe, she just laughed at me. I can understand why she would want to protect that secret.

I am always amazed by the quality of the food you can find at mobile food units, and especially from such an unassuming unit such as this one. There aren't too many signs on this trailer, but with barbecue this good, people are going to find you, signs or no signs.

we
CALL IT
A STUFFED
cone
when we put ice cream in it

LOCATION
14090 Bellaire

PHONE
504-319-1728

HOURS
Fri: 3:00pm-7:00pm, Sat: noon-
7:00pm, Sun: 1:00pm-5:00pm

FOOD
Sno cones

PRICES
$

OWNER
Terry Gaines

STARTED
2005

PAYMENT
Cash only

NEW ORLEANS STYLE SNO-BALLS

—

She caters to people from New Orleans who know what a true **New Orleans–style** sno-cone tastes like.

Terry Gaines, originally from New Orleans, came to Houston in 2005 after Hurricane Katrina devastated her hometown. She is a single mother who works full-time at a home improvement center but decided that she wanted to fulfill her childhood dream of owning a sno-cone store. So she opened this one, and on weekends she caters to people from

She doesn't just fill your cup, she keeps packing it down until no more will fit, then she adds the flavorings

New Orleans who know what a true New Orleans–style sno-cone tastes like. She has all of her concentrates shipped from New Orleans. "Even though it

costs more," she says, "they just taste better."

Terry lifts a large chunk of ice into the top of the ice shaver, and what emerges at the bottom is as white and as dense as packed snow. She doesn't just fill your cup, she keeps packing it down until no more will fit, then she adds the flavorings. Being a sno-cone virgin, I put myself in Terry's capable hands. When she asked what I'd like, I asked her which flavor was her favorite.

"Strawberry Cheesecake," she replied with a smile spreading across her face. As she was adding the flavoring, I noticed something fascinating on the menu in her window: Along with jars

STRAWBERRY CHEESECAKE SNO CONES //
SILVER FOX CONES // TIGER BLOOD SNO CONES
// WEDDING CAKE SNO CONES //

filled with pickles and pickled pigs' lips, which are available for sale, she also offers what she calls "extras" for the sno-cones. On that list was condensed milk. When I asked about it, she said, "You gotta try it."

Then I spotted ice cream on the list. Terry told me, "When we put ice cream in it, we call it a stuffed cone." She "stuffs" the scoop of vanilla ice cream right in the middle of the polystyrene cup, then covers it with the remaining shaved ice. Naturally, I ordered both.

If you close your eyes and taste a spoonful of the cheesecake sno-cone, you will swear you're eating a piece of strawberry cheesecake.

If you close your eyes and taste a spoonful of the cheesecake sno-cone, you will swear you're eating a piece of strawberry cheesecake; the flavoring is that good. And it doesn't hurt that the condensed milk and ice cream coat your mouth with a pleasant fatty layer. It is a strange yet wonderful experience.

And if, before ordering, you want to sample a flavor such as Silver Fox, Tiger Blood or Wedding Cake, Terry will let you.

all

SLOW-SMOKED

OVER

mesquite

with homemade flour tortillas

LOCATION
Various

HOURS
Various

FOOD
Gourmet Mexican

PRICES
$

STARTED
2010

PAYMENT
Cash only

PHONE
713-213-2409

OWNER
Sylvia Casares

TWITTER
/#!/sylviaenchilada

WEBSITE
sylviasenchiladakitchen.com

NO BORDERS ENCHILADA KITCHEN

—

She's taking to the streets with what she calls "*frontera* **cuisine**," food from either side of the Texas-Mexico border.

Sylvia Casares is famous for the enchiladas at her brick-and-mortar restaurant, Sylvia's Enchilada Kitchen. Now she's taking to the streets with what she calls "*frontera* cuisine," food from either side of the Texas-

Sylvia uses homemade flour tortillas, which are briefly browned on the griddle.

Mexico border. Sylvia, who grew up in Brownsville, is a perfectionist about such matters. "It took me two years to get the *fajitas* up to the level of my enchiladas," she told me.

For her, the truck is a chance to extend her brand, as well as to experiment. "We're trying things out on the truck that might end up on the menu at the restaurant," she said. She also installed a mesquite smoker on the truck to add additional flavor to some of her dishes.

Her *Frontera* Tacos come with chicken, pork or turkey, all slow-smoked over mesquite. Sylvia uses homemade flour tortillas, which are briefly browned on the griddle. I tried the smoked turkey with *mole*, which she tops with cilantro and chopped onion. Sylvia's version of this classic Mexican sauce, made with chocolate, is superb.

SMOKED TURKEY WITH *MOLE* TACOS // PORK WITH *HABANERO* SAUCE // *FAJITAS* // *ELOTE*

The burnt kernels of corn had the most flavor, but all the corn remained sweet throughout.

Next was the pork with *habanero* sauce that takes hold the moment it hits your tongue. And finally, I had the *fajitas* that she worked so hard to get right. (I can confirm that they were worth the trouble.) I also sampled an *elote*, or corn on the cob, which had also been grilled over mesquite. I particularly liked the burnt kernels of corn since they had the most flavor, but all the corn remained sweet throughout.

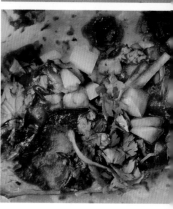

with

GRILLED
ONIONS AND
bell peppers

with homemade remoulade

LOCATION
Various

PHONE
281-402-6968

HOURS
Various

FOOD
Creole

PRICES
$

OWNERS
Richard Denegall

STARTED
2012

PAYMENT
All

TWITTER
intent/user?screen_
name=NOLAs2Geau

FACEBOOK
NOLAsCreole2Geaux

WEBSITE
nolas2geaux.com

NOLA'S CREOLE 2 GEAUX

—

Astonishingly good **Creole cooking** now made on the streets of Houston.

Brianne Sacco is not from here. She's not even from Louisiana. She's from New Jersey and Florida. But that's not going to stop her from turning out some fantastic Creole cuisine as the chef of the truck called Nola's Creole 2 Geaux.

Of course, she did work for Emeril's restaurant in Orlando for quite a while, where she picked up her liking for and knowledge of Creole cuisine, which led to in the astonishingly good Creole cooking she is now making on the streets of Houston. It's what she calls "Gourmet Creole Cuisine." Brianne has done quite a lot since graduating from the Orlando Culinary Academy. She has worked in casual-dining as well as fine-dining establishments. She butchered meat while working at Vito's Steakhouse in Orlando and when she managed the Lombardi's Seafood Market in Orlando, "I learned to cut up any kind of fish there is," said Brianne. Brianne's father grew up in Houston

and she spent a lot of time here when she was a child, so when she decided to try something different, she moved here.

The truck was already built for someone else. They had used it for a few months and then decided it was not for them. "It pretty much had everything in it I needed. All we had to do was wrap it in Mardi Gras colors and set up shop", said Brianne.

Brianne makes everything from scratch and this is apparent in the quality of everything she serves.

Maque Choux is one of the quintessentially Louisiana dishes that Brianne prepares very well. It is a dish you will find served everywhere in Louisiana. Its name, according to Wikipedia, probably came from the French interpretation of the name for a Native American dish. Made with plump kernels of corn, pieces of tomato and the holy trinity

MAQUE CHOUX // CRAB AND CRAWFISH ETOUFFÉE // RED BEANS & RICE // BLACKENED CATFISH

of celery, onions and bell pepper. Brianne seasons it with typical Cajun seasonings, including sassafras, which announces itself on the very first taste. Served over white rice, Brianne's Crab and Crawfish Etouffée is stuffed full of seafood in a thick, unctuous sauce, whose base is the holy trinity. Brianne's Red Beans & Rice is the stuff dreams are made of. She makes it with smoked ham hocks and chunks of ham but it is the addition of Andouille sausage that makes the dish for me. She also uses Andouille in her Shrimp, Chicken and Sausage Gumbo, which is thick with ingredients and uses a dark roux base. There are so many complex flavors in this dish that it's hard to pick out just one. I also tried her Andouille Sausage Po-Boy, which comes with grilled onions and bell peppers. The bread is Slow Dough's po-boy bread and Brianne serves it with her homemade *remoulade*, a slice of lettuce and some extra hot sauce for good measure. It is a terrific combination.

On my second visit, I encountered Brianne's Blackened Catfish. She serves this with any of the sides she has available. On that particular day she had her famous grits on the menu. "Right now I'm using smooth ground grits but I'm looking for a source for coarse, stone-ground, grits," Brianne told me. The grits are made with butter, heavy

cream, Cheddar cheese, garlic and some Louisiana hot sauce. Do I really need to say more? Needless to say, they were fantasticly creamy with an undertone of cheese and garlic that made you beg for more.

She dips her catfish filets in flour seasoned with cayenne and paprika. After pan-frying, she places them on top of the grits just before serving. Once the juice from the fish starts to drip all over the grits, adding even more flavor to them, it's hard to describe the pleasure of eating them, since they are so tasty to begin with. Let's just say once you start eating them, you won't come up, even for breath, until every last grit is gone.

Brianne's food is very well seasoned, something she learned while working for Emeril Lagasse.

Another nice thing to like about this truck is that they sell Valued Life Rainwater, of which a portion of the proceeds goes to help Houston's homeless.

the

CATFISH

IS COATED IN

seasoned cornmeal

and completely greaseless

LOCATION
Various

PHONE
832-454-7985

HOURS
Various

FOOD
Cajun-fried catfish and shrimp

PRICES
$$

OWNERS
Lee Smith

STARTED
2011

PAYMENT
Cash only

SPECIAL SERVICES
Catering

TWITTER
offthehookfish

FACEBOOK
php#!/pages/Off-the-Hook-Catfish-Shrimp/140809709280298

OFF THE HOOK CATFISH & SHRIMP

—

They season the fries liberally with a spice mix that, along with the dry corn-meal breading mixture and the liquid batter for the shrimp, are destined to remain **secret family recipes**.

Leave it to a Cajun to perfect the art of the fish fry. Lee Smith and his partner, Laryssa Lee, should know a thing or two about frying fish. Lee's sister Joanna is married to Greg Holmes, who for the past ten years has owned the Southern Express Seafood Truck, also reviewed in this book. Lee is from Tallulah, Louisiana, and worked offshore for years before moving to Houston and setting up shop. Lee uses the same source for his fish as Greg does and was sure to keep it a tight secret. They use only wild catfish, which has a fresh taste and does not taste in the least bit muddy.

I had the large fish-and-shrimp combo, which consisted of five catfish filets, five large shrimp and French fries. They season the fries liberally

They use only wild catfish, which has a fresh taste and does not taste in the least bit muddy.

with a spice mix that, along with the dry cornmeal breading mixture and the liquid batter for the shrimp, are destined to remain secret family recipes. Everything was well-seasoned and plentiful.

FISH-AND-SHRIMP COMBO // SEASONED FRIES // FRIED CATFISH FILETS // FRIED SHRIMP

The catfish is coated in seasoned cornmeal, and when it was served, it was completely greaseless on the outside while the plump filet remained juicy.

Because the shrimp are coated with a liquid batter, they have a thicker and more substantial exterior, making them almost crunchy.

Because the shrimp are coated with a liquid batter, they have a thicker and more substantial exterior, making them almost crunchy. Be warned: Once you start eating these, they are so tasty and go down so effortlessly, you will find it hard to stop.

At the conclusion of my meal, Lee insisted I try one shrimp coated in the same seasoned cornmeal he uses for the catfish and one coated in a combination of seasoned cornmeal and liquid batter. The former made the shrimp nice and crispy but the latter added a dimension of flavor and crispness that made this my absolute favorite.

32.454.

CALL IN OR

IRS: Wed – Sat: 11am – 8pm

REGULAR FISH PLATE
5 catfish filets, 2 hushpuppies & zesty fries

LARGE FISH PLATE
10 catfish filets, 2 hushpuppies & zesty fries

REGULAR SHRIMP PLATE
6 large butter-flied shrimp, 2 hushpuppies &

LARGE SHRIMP PLATE
12 large butter-flied shrimp, 2 hushpuppies

LARGE FISH/SHRIMP COMBO
5 filets, 5 shrimp, 2 hushpuppies & zesty fries

FAMILY FISH PLATTER
2 hushpuppies & large order

a

THREE-CHEESE

BLEND MELTS

over the hot fries

and turns them into one big mass

LOCATION
Various

FOOD
Korean BBQ/Mexican Fusion

PRICES
$

STARTED
2011

PAYMENT
All

OWNER
Eric Nguyen

TWITTER
OhMyGogi

FACEBOOK
OhMyGogi

WEBSITE
ohmygogi.com/

OH MY GOGI

—

There is only one word needed to describe the *quesadillas*: **Outstanding**.

Gogi means "meat" in Korean, so it should not be surprising that beef, chicken and pork are at the heart of everything served here. "I lived in L.A. and Austin, both of which have a lot of food trucks, so I got used to seeing and eating at trucks all the time," said Eric Nguyen.

I asked Eric why he chose to do Korean fusion as opposed to Vietnamese, the culture from which he hails. "You don't have to be from a culture in order to cook its food," he said. "I have a lot of Korean friends, plus I was inspired by Roy Choi. It took me six months of testing the recipes before I got them right. I

Each *quesadilla* is topped with two delectable sauces, carefully drizzled in thin lines on top of the tortilla.

kept making the recipes until I got them right." And get them right, he did.

Roy Choi owns the famous Kogi BBQ food truck in Los Angeles. He's credited with creating the first chef-driven truck, which led to the recent mobile

food revolution. Perhaps Eric named his truck in appreciation of what Roy has done for the food-truck community.

The first thing I tried was his *kimchi quesadilla*. First, Eric marinates thin strips of chicken in Korean spices. After you place your order, he cooks them on the griddle, then sandwiches them between two halves of a large flour tortilla. He also adds some Korean *kimchi* (spicy, fermented cabbage) and a blend of four cheeses. The half–moon shaped *quesadilla* is cut into four triangles just before being served, making it extremely easy to eat. Each *quesadilla* is topped with two delectable sauces, carefully drizzled in thin lines on top of the tortilla. The first is a Korean-Mexican *salsa rojo*, which looks like a typical Mexican red sauce but tastes of sesame, ginger and garlic. The second is the special house sauce, a spicy mayo whose pink color is achieved with the addition of chiles and hot sauce. By the time the *quesadillas* are served, the cheese has had

KIMCHI QUESADILLA // OMG FRIES // CHICKEN TACOS // BEEF TACOS // PORK TACOS

ample time to melt and unify all the flavors. There is only one word needed to describe these: Outstanding.

Next were the OMG (Oh My Gogi) fries, which reminded me vividly of nachos. The OMG fries have made a name for themselves as a dish that people crave.

The OMG fries have made a name for themselves as a dish that people crave.

First Eric takes seasoned fries, which, by themselves, taste nice and spicy, and tops them with so much stuff that they become almost unrecognizable. First, a three-cheese blend melts over the hot fries and turns them into one big mass. Next is *Sriracha* sauce, followed by the house sauce or spicy mayo. The most exciting thing is next: thin slices of Korean-seasoned beef. The only issue I had with these is the fact that I like my fries crispy; the toppings left these somewhat limp. This, however, is a very minor criticism. They were OMG great-tasting.

I also ordered the three-taco combination. I had one chicken, one beef and one pork taco. Each tasted vastly different from the next and, while there was no denying their Asian heritage, I enjoyed each of them for the diversity of flavors they provided. Each taco arrives in a corn tortilla and is topped

with the special house sauce and shredded lettuce, then a light vinaigrette made of Korean soy salsa and a sprinkling of sesame seeds. The best of the three? That's a difficult choice. But I'd say the beef.

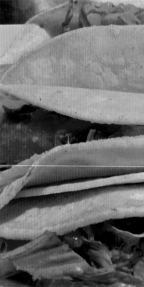

❖ **one** ❖

OF THE MOST

UNUSUAL

and best-tasting

sandwiches anywhere

LOCATION
Various

PHONE
281-902-9820

HOURS
Various

FOOD
Stuffed pies, similar to empanadas

PRICES
$

OWNER
Joe Phillips, Joanna Torok

STARTED
2010

PAYMENT
All

TWITTER
/#!/OhMyPocketPies

FACEBOOK
pages/Oh-my-Pocket-
Pies/156771461778

WEBSITE
ohmypocketpies.com

OH MY! POCKET PIES

The pies come with a selection of homemade **dipping** sauces.

Joe Phillips has been designing restaurants, menus and kitchen layouts for others for quite some time. Dry Creek, Cedar Creek and Mi Luna are among his projects. When he recently decided to open a food truck for himself, he adopted a simple philosophy: to use the finest local seasonal ingredients, to support local farmers and suppliers, and to do so in a sustainable manner.

The Breakfast Pie I ordered took a while to make. Joe's partner, Joanna Torok, explained that they make the half-moon pies to order, pinching the edges by hand, and that kind of freshness takes time. That wasn't a problem because

The generously filled pies are a perfect size to be eaten out of hand.

both Joe and Joanna enjoy chatting with their customers, many of whom are regulars. They use eggs and produce from local farmers and wanted me to be sure

to note that they fry everything in soybean oil. The Breakfast Pie comes stuffed with eggs plus two fillings. I picked bacon and onions, a perfect choice. The generously filled pies are a perfect size to be eaten with your hands.

The second pie I tried was the chicken chile *relleno*. Oven-roasted chicken, roasted poblano peppers, jack cheese and corn are mixed with their special sauce.

The pies come with a selection of homemade dipping sauces. My favorite was the roasted *tomatillo*, although the roasted red chile was a close second. They also make a mean ranch dressing.

My final selection was the Shrimp Burger. Boy, was that a treat. A challah bun from Slow Dough Bakery is filled with a fried patty made from ground shrimp, *panko* and spices. Add lettuce, a slice of onion and cucumber and spicy *Sriracha* mayo, and you have one of the most unusual and best-tasting sandwiches anywhere.

THE BREAKFAST PIES // CHICKEN CHILE RELLENO PIES // SHRIMP BURGER // BRISKET PIE

On my second visit, I tried one of Joe's seasonal pies, the Margherita, which is made with fresh, seasonal, local ingredients. It is stuffed with mozzarella, basil, tomatoes and homemade pesto. It tastes exactly like a Margherita pizza. Joe also made a Curried Butternut Squash with a preserved lemon *aioli*. It was outstanding. The filling includes potatoes, peas, cilantro and red onions along with a *masala* sauce that included ginger and turmeric.

The final savory pie I sampled was the barbecue one. Joe rubs the brisket with Katz's espresso coffee before cooking it.

Add lettuce, a slice of onion and cucumber and spicy *sriracha* mayo, and you have one of the most unusual and best-tasting sandwiches anywhere.

After cooking, he adds a red-eye gravy with a strong hint of vinegar. At first the gravy threw me for a moment, reminding me of the mustard and vinegar-based barbecue in South Carolina. But once I got over the shock, and the taste began to smooth out a little, it was quite good.

OMPP also offers a sweet pie each day. In this case it was a S'mores version. Two mini-pies make up an order, and each is filled with Nutella®, marshmallow whip and graham crackers. When it is served, Joe drizzles more Nutella® sauce on the top and dusts it with confectioner's sugar. The melted filling is delectable.

✳ *they* ✳

WERE SERVED

WITH TRADITIONAL

curtido

which was topped with queso fresco

LOCATION
4222 Richmond

HOURS
on-Fri: 11:30am-9:00pm,
Sat-Sun: 11:00am-7:00pm

FOOD
Thai

PRICES
$

STARTED
2011

PAYMENT
All

PHONE
(857) 205-9682

OWNERS
Alex Sears,
Thitinan "Bo" Chanchompoo

TWITTER
/#!/PadThaiBox

FACEBOOK
/pages/Pad-Thai-
Box/287160367988673?sk=wal

WEBSITE
/#!/PadThaiBox

PAD THAI BOX

—

With the exception of the egg rolls, all the food is prepared right in front of you, so it's **exceptionally fresh**.

Take a young American entrepreneur and an incredibly gifted young Thai chef, put them together as roommates in college, and you end up with Houston's first food truck selling Thai food. Thitinan, who goes by "Bo," worked in a fine-dining Japanese restaurant in Boston before coming to Houston, but his passion is for the cuisine of his

The mini rolls, wrapped in thin rice paper and stuffed with rice vermicelli noodles, shrimp, mint and cilantro, come with a sweet chili dipping sauce.

homeland. Bo is a graceful and hospitable host, wanting only that you enjoy his food. That is not difficult to do.

Except for the sweet chili sauce, he makes all his sauces from scratch. And with the exception of the egg rolls, all the food is prepared right in front of you, so it's exceptionally fresh.

The first dish I tried was the spring rolls. The mini rolls, wrapped in thin rice

paper and stuffed with rice vermicelli noodles, shrimp, mint and cilantro, come with a sweet chili dipping sauce. They were the perfect appetizer for the next course, the truck's signature dish, Pad Thai. Here, Bo uses thicker rice noodles, which he stir fries with chunks of chicken, an egg, tamarind juice, bean sprouts and scallions. Just before serving, he adds crushed peanuts and a lime wedge. "You should see Bo making the sauce," said Alex. "He weighs everything carefully before putting it all together." This kind of attention to detail yields a dish that has outstanding flavor, with everything exceedingly well-balanced.

Next was the Thai Basil Chicken. (While chicken is the protein of choice, all the dishes can also be ordered with shrimp.) Bo stir-fries chunks of chicken along with onions, green bell peppers, mushrooms, ultra-thin strips of carrots, fresh basil and kefir lime leaves. It is served on a base of Thai jasmine rice.

SPRING ROLLS // THAI BASIL CHICKEN
THAI FRIED RICE // THAI TEA AND THAI COFFEE

It is an extremely aromatic dish with a wonderfully herbal flavor that epitomizes Thai cooking. It is not to be missed.

Last was the Thai fried rice. Bo starts out by scrambling an egg, then adding steamed Thai jasmine rice, strips of chicken, onion, green onion and tomato. Slices of cucumber and a lime wedge are used as garnishes. It is a simple dish with an abundance of flavors.

As beverages, Bo also offers traditional Thai tea and Thai coffee made with half-and-half and evaporated milk. They are both sweet and superb.

❋ **warm** ❋

IT ON THE

GRIDDLE

until

the cheese melted

LOCATION
1919 West Alabama

PHONE
713-528-6874

HOURS
Mon-Fri: 10:00am-12:00am, Sat:
10:00am-1:00am, Sun: 12:00pm-
12:00am

FOOD
Greek

PRICES
$

OWNER
Frank Markantonis

STARTED
2011

PAYMENT
Cash only

FACEBOOK
/PapouJerry

TWITTER
/PapouJerry

PAPOU JERRY'S GYRO TRUCK

—

Since the Gyro is the signature dish of this truck, you'd expect it to be good. **It was**.

"I owned an Exxon gas station for sixteen years and was a mechanic. Last year's heat wave got too much for me so I sold the station and decided to look for something else to do," said Frank Markantonis, owner of Houston's first Greek food truck. "My brother, Petros, owns the West Alabama Ice House which our dad bought in the '70s. One day, as we were sitting around drinking beer, I mentioned to my brother that we needed to open a restaurant. We were staring at the taco truck in the parking lot and, "wham!", it hit me. The rest, as they say, is history," Frank went on to say. The taco truck they displaced is the Tierra Caliente truck, which has been an institution at the WAIH for ages. Fans of Tierra Caliente will be pleased to know that they won't have to travel very far to find them – they're set up in the parking lot of the Hollywood convenience store, right across the street from their old location.

"The truck is named in honor of my dad but how it got its name is an interesting story. Once we had decided on a truck, we obviously knew what type of food we were going to serve, I was having a hard time thinking of a name. I asked my daughter and she said, 'That's easy….Papou Jerry', so that was it" said Frank.

You can't miss this truck. It's all decked out in blue and white, the colors of the Greek flag, plus there's a huge picture of Jerry on one side. "My aunt passed by the other day and she told me she almost had an accident when she saw my dad on the side of the truck. He died ten years ago. Now he'll be immortalized forever," added Frank.

The first thing I tried was the Grilled Cheese Sandwich with Gyro meat. Frank told me it was one of his best sellers. My first bite told me why. It's a simple concept. Take a slice of American cheese, sandwich it, along

GRILLED CHEESE SANDWICH WITH GYRO MEAT // GREEK HAMBURGER // GREEK FRIES // GREEK PIZZA

with slices of the beef and lamb blend of gyro meat, between two slices of bread, coat it on the outside with some butter and warm it on the griddle until the cheese melts, binding everything together. The outside is toasty and crispy and the cheese melted over the meat tastes wonderful. It's a fusion version of the comfort food classic.

Next was the Greek hamburger. Frank uses a sesame-seeded bun, which he smears with his homemade *tzatziki* sauce, a delicious garlic-yogurt sauce. He uses a single beef patty, which he tops with some feta cheese. It is definitely worthwhile waiting for the feta to melt on top of the patty, since it adds a sharp creaminess. The burger can be had unadorned, meaning no lettuce or tomato, to give the cheese a chance to shine, but Frank is equally happy to add the standard accoutrements.

The burger came with Frank's Greek Fries. These are extra crispy fries and delicious thanks to Frank's dousing with his own Greek seasonings, the ingredients for which Frank guards as a family secret.

Since the Gyro is the signature dish of this truck, you'd expect it to be good. It was. Frank takes the gyro meat and the pita bread and puts them on the griddle to warm. He folds the pita in two, adds the meat, then his famous *tzatziki* sauce along with some chopped onion and parsley. It is a delightful sandwich. Equally delightful

is the Greek Pizza Frank has come up with. He lets the pita bread remain on the griddle until it forms a crust underneath, then tops it with some marinara sauce, feta, chopped tomatoes and Gyro meat. It is astonishingly good and I don't know why no one else has thought about making this before. Last was his Greek Salad, which he tops with a fat slice of salty feta cheese and a homemade vinaigrette with some great tasting olive oil. You can also get this salad with gyro meat, which turns it into a full meal.

it

LOOKED

TERRIFIC

and it was

firm and tender

LOCATION
13310 Cullen

HOURS
Tue-Sat: 5:00pm-2:00am

FOOD
BBQ

PRICES
$$

STARTED
2004

PAYMENT
Cash only

PHONE
832-588-8006

OWNER
Jim Daniels

SPECIAL SERVICES
Catering

PERFECTO PIT BBQ

—

He cooks mainly with oak, starting with his brisket fat-down for the first couple of hours, then fat-up for the rest of the eight to **ten hours** it takes to cook.

Jim is just getting back in the business of making barbecue, so the night we visited him outside the S&S Sports Bar on Cullen, he had only ribs and sausage — no brisket and no sides. What we sampled, however, made us wish he had everything else available. I vowed to return.

The *jalapeño* sausage, though commercial, was juicy, and the pepper gave it a nice kick. It had just the right amount of smoke flavor.

His delicious ribs were firm and did not come off the bone without some assistance. He uses a dry rub, but I couldn't pry his ingredients out of him. Same with his sauce. I noticed a bottle of commercial sauce in the truck, but he doctors it up. The result is a relatively thin, sweet and tangy sauce with a vinegar undertone.

He cooks mainly with oak, starting with his brisket fat-down for the first couple of hours, then fat-up for the rest of the

He starts out at 350 degrees, then reduces the temperature to an undisclosed lower setting. "I can't be giving away all my secrets," he said.

eight to ten hours it takes to cook. He starts out at 350 degrees, then reduces the temperature to an undisclosed lower setting. "I can't be giving away all my

BARBECUED RIBS // BARBECUED SAUSAGE // BBQ BRISKET SANDWICHES //

● ●

secrets," he said. Jim's dad barbecued, and he is keeping up the family tradition. "It's my passion," he added.

When we returned to try the brisket, we bought it in a sandwich. As soon as Jim removed the side of brisket from the smoker and started to slice into it,

As soon as Jim removed the side of brisket from the smoker and started to slice into it, I noticed the telltale red ring of fire that indicates slow cooking.

I noticed the telltale red ring of fire that indicates slow cooking. It looked terrific, and it was: firm and tender at the same time. It contained very little fat, and it was not too smoky. It was one of the best BBQ sandwiches I have eaten, and definitely worth returning for.

✦ the ✦

CLASSIC

VIETNAMESE

soup

is exceptionally good

PHAMILY BITES

LOCATION
Various

PHONE
832-598-8746

HOURS
Various

FOOD
Vietnamese

PRICES
$$

OWNER
Van Pham, Mark Tran, Manson Kan

STARTED
2011

PAYMENT
Cash only

WEBSITE
phamilybites.com

FACEBOOK
PhamilyBites

TWITTER
/PhamilyBites

—

"There's a lot of **passion** that goes into this *pho*. I don't use any premix or preservatives like some other people do.

When your mother is known in Houston as the Paula Deen of Vietnamese cooking, with her own cooking show on the radio, you know there's a good chance that you might end up in the food business. That's how Van Pham started out his culinary career as owner of the Phamily Bites food truck, along with his partners, Mark Tran and Manson Kan.

Van's mom, Xinh Nguyen, makes the pork and shrimp egg rolls by hand every day. The *pho*, a classic Vietnamese soup, is also her recipe, and is exceptionally good. "It takes 48 hours to make," said Van. "There's a lot of passion that goes into this *pho*. I don't use any premix or preservatives like some other people do. I use good quality, fatty brisket that I buy from this Vietnamese butcher that has been our family butcher ever since I can remember. We make a northern–Vietnamese type of *pho*," said Van

Phamily Bites offers three different kinds of *pho*: Brisket only, eye of round, and meat balls. You can also get a combination of all three meats. We tried both the brisket and the meat balls. The broth Van uses is the same for all his *pho*; it is the addition of the meat at the last minute that gives the different kinds of *pho* their individual flavor. All had a deep, rich flavor with star anise at their base. My only complaint is that the *pho* is lacking a little in the addition of fresh herbs and bean sprouts that usually accompany it. However, since it is served in a Styrofoam cup, albeit a large one, once the freshly made noodles are added, there isn't much room for anything else.

We also tried a *banh mi*, or Vietnamese sandwich, that Van calls *bo luc lac*, or shaking beef. At Vietnamese restaurants, *bo luc lac* is one of my favorite dishes: filet mignon served on a bed of watercress along with a salt -pepper-and-lime

SHAKING BEEF SANDWICH // *PHO* // SPAM *MUSUBI* // PORK EGGS ROLLS // VEGETARIAN EGGS ROLLS

dipping sauce. Van has turned the dish into a sandwich — with excellent results.

We visited this truck on its first real night of operation, just after it passed inspection. Things were hectic. They lost power on a regular basis because the location they were using wasn't prepared for the electric needs of a food truck. But once the problem was fixed, they were off and rolling.

We caught up with Van again one Saturday night on Washington Ave. I called ahead to make sure he had two dishes that we'd missed: the eggs rolls and Spam *musubi*, a dish that epitomizes Hawaiian cuisine. He said he did, so we headed his way.

His mom's egg rolls are amazing. She makes two kinds: one with pork filling, which he serves with the traditional spicy, garlicky fish sauce dipping sauce; and a vegetarian version, which he serves with a dipping sauce made from soy sauce and vinegar. The exterior was super crispy, as Van had cooked them to order.

Spam *musubi* is one of those foods that once you've had it, it's hard not to crave it all the time. Van makes it the traditional way, using a plastic mould made specifically for this dish. First he cuts a slice of Spam, then fries it on the griddle. While this is cooking, he preps the rice by adding *Nori Komi Furikake*, a sushi rice seasoning, along with sesame

seeds for texture. The assembly process is laborious, with the sheet of *nori*, or seaweed, being placed on the bottom of the mold, followed by the Spam, then the rice. He presses down on the rice with the top of the form, then rolls the *nori* around it, and seals it. This meaty sushi is about the size of a deck of cards and makes a great finger food, hot or cold. Van now makes it available with a fried egg, an addition that makes it even more craveable.

The menu at this truck is displayed on a digital screen. It, along with another digital screen, acts as a photo booth and was designed by Mark Tran, who owns Digital Memories. As you approach the screen, if you press on a button under the screen, it takes your photo and uploads it directly to Facebook.

he

FIRST SOAKS

BLUEBERRIES

and peaches

In a homemade whiskey syrup

LOCATION
Various

FOOD
Pizza

PRICES
$$

PAYMENT
All

STARTED
2011

OWNER
Anthony Calleo

FACEBOOK
/Pi.PizzaTruck

TWITTER
/#!/pipizzatruck

PHONE
713-478 0374

PI PIZZA

—

Anthony named the truck with a play on the word pi, the mathematical constant. In the truck's logo, the symbol (π) morphs into a one-eyed, clawed monster **devouring** a slice of pizza

This is the very first truck to serve pizza in Houston. Considering the technical difficulties involved in making pizza on a truck, we should marvel that anyone figured out how to do it. Not only does the pizza dough have to rise for a number of hours, but it has to be cooked in a large oven capable of reaching 700 degrees or more; and it takes four to six minutes to cook — a long time for someone to wait for food at a truck.

In June, when I first spoke to Anthony, he'd just purchased the truck, already equipped for pizza, from someone in Long Island. It was due to arrive, he said then, "any day now." He opened the last week in

October, having overcome any number of difficulties.

Anthony named the truck with a play on the word pi, the mathematical constant. In the truck's logo, the symbol (π) morphs into a

Anthony serves gourmet pizza by the slice as well as whole pies. They're some of the most creative and tastiest pizzas I've ever tried.

one-eyed, clawed monster devouring a slice of pizza. The theme is "Monster Pizza, Monster Truck." The symbol also appears on the décor of the truck, as well as on his social media sites. Anthony even has a pie cutter in the shape of the pi symbol.

Anthony serves gourmet pizza by the slice as well as whole pies. They're some of the most creative and tastiest pizzas I've ever tried. Anthony has worked in every mom-and-pop pizzeria in the city and has dreamed of owning his own place for ten years. He's a proud pizza nerd. He talks about the bite, chewiness, thickness and air-hole structure of the dough, the droopiness of the end of a slice when you pick it up. ("It needs to be able to take the weight of the toppings and have a slight droop, not be Viagra-straight," he said.) He makes everything from scratch. He spent two and a half years working on the dough recipe. "I do not use any dough conditioners or flavor agents, and I can tell it's done by the way it looks, feels and smells," he told me. "I let it sit between one and a half to two days before it's ready to use."

This kind of attention to detail makes the difference between a pizza and a Pi pizza. Anthony will not consider putting a pizza in the oven until the temperature reaches at least 650 degrees. This takes up to an hour and a half to achieve, starting from a cold oven. The dough has lots of air holes in the structure and had the wonderful bread-like flavor that can only come from a well-cured dough. Five to six minutes in the large Baker's Pride oven, and you have a perfect pizza.

Now for the toppings. Since Anthony rotates his specials each week, only three are available at any time. Cheese and pepperoni are always available. My first slice was The Grizzly Hawaiian, which starts with a scoop of his homemade red sauce, which has a rich herbal note in addition to a nice sweetness. He then tops this with slices of chicken that have been marinated in his sweet, smoky, hot "grizzly sauce," along with pieces of thick-cut bacon, pineapple and a custom cheese blend consisting of 70 percent mozzarella and 30 percent provolone. Chunks of pineapple and a drizzle of local honey just before serving turn it into a great-tasting slice, combining sweet, savory and hot.

Anthony is particularly proud of the Drunken Peach. He first soaks blueberries and peaches in a homemade

He makes everything from scratch. He spent two and a half years working on the dough recipe.

whiskey syrup for a day or two. He uses the same tomato sauce, but changes the cheese to local goat cheese with the addition of finely-diced habanero peppers. It is a fascinating blend of sweet, salty and hot, with the whiskey syrup adding an incredible depth of flavor. It is hard to eat just one slice of this great pie.

The last thing I tried on my first visit was the 420. It is, as Anthony

describes it, a "stoner's delight, wacky enough for any stoner." In keeping with its name, he charges $4.20 a slice. On top of the tomato sauce and custom cheese blend, he adds Chili Cheese Fritos corn chips, barbecue

Anthony will not consider putting a pizza in the oven until the temperature reaches at least 650 degrees. This takes up to an hour and a half to achieve.

sauce, a spicy wing sauce, and tops it with even more cheese. It is one of the wildest pizzas I've ever tried, but it works remarkably well.

When I ordered the Outdoorsman on my next visit, Anthony confided that this was his favorite pizza. A couple of bites into it, I shared his opinion. The first thing he does is marinate black cherries in port syrup for a few days. A smear of homemade tomato sauce and some thick-cut slices of venison sausage from Broken Arrow Ranch in Ingram, Texas, are followed by a light load of mozzarella. The resulting sweet-and-savory delight is an adult version of pepperoni pizza.

Anthony also offers specialty sandwiches, which he plans to change weekly. The one I tried was a Hill Country Heritage, made with a wild Texas venison bratwurst. It is cooked in Karbach Brewery's Weiss/Versa beer, which Anthony said "was made just for this brat," before being topped with sauerkraut. He stuffs

DRUNKEN PEACH PIZZA // THE 420 PIZZA
THE GRIZZLY HAWAIIAN PIZZA // HILL COUNTRY
HERITAGE SANDWICH // THE OUTDOORSMAN PIZZA

it into a Slow Dough Bakery pretzel bun, which he smears with a good dose of his homemade *Shaohsing*

It is a fascinating blend of sweet, salty and hot, with the whiskey syrup adding an incredible depth of flavor. It is hard to eat just one slice of this great pie.

(rice wine) honey mustard. Venison sausage can be very dry, so this one is mixed with pork for moisture. Anthony is still working on getting the mustard just right. The day I sampled it, it had a little too much bite. Knowing what a tinkerer he is, once he gets back into his lab, I am convinced he'll get it right.

His final offering was a seasonal dessert pizza made with a pumpkin-pie sauce as a base. He topped it with chocolate-covered bacon, white-chocolate shavings and ancho-chile roasted pecans. A dollop of cream to finish it off, and you've got a sweet deal that works incredibly well as a pizza.

the

SMOKED BEEF AND EGGS GO

incredibly well together

a terrific idea

LOCATION
519 East Highway 90A,
Richmond, Texas

HOURS
Mon-Sat: 6:00am-2:00pm

FOOD
Barbecue, Mexican

PRICES
$

OWNER
Lolo Garcia

STARTED
1987

PAYMENT
Cash only

PHONE
281-617-8600

SPECIAL SERVICES
Call ahead, brisket by the pound

PLANTATION BBQ

—

"We use oak and mainly pecan and slow cook it at no more that 250 degrees for at least 15 hours. That and my **secret** seasoning."

"When I first started this truck in the eighties, there was no one else around," said Lolo Garcia with a big smile. "I wanted to teach my children a trade.

Two items blew me away. The first is the smoked-brisket-and-eggs taco: chopped barbecue beef brisket fried it on the griddle with eggs.

And today both my son and daughter run this place, and my other daughter runs a second truck in Columbus."

Garcia has been doing this so long that the local Health Department refers to him as "The Godfather" and tells prospective mobile food truck owners

to visit him in order to find out how it's done. Today, his son Antonio and daughter Amanda keep the truck going six days a week, from the early hours in the morning.

"The secret is in the slow cooking," Lolo said about the juicy brisket he was removing from the smoker. "We use oak and mainly pecan and slow cook it at no more that 250 degrees for at least 15 hours. That and my secret seasoning." The other secret I learned was that Mrs. Garcia can be found at the truck every morning making homemade flour tortillas. One look at the large, irregular disc and you just knew these were made from scratch, right there in the tiny

SMOKED-BRISKET-AND-EGGS TACO // BRISKET AND RIB PLATE // *CHICHARRON* TACO

trailer. The food is a fascinating blend of traditional barbecue with Mexican food.

Two items blew me away. The first is the smoked-brisket-and-eggs taco: chopped barbecue beef brisket fried on the griddle with eggs. It is a terrific idea that I have since made with my own leftover barbecue brisket (only certainly not as good as the original). The smoked beef and eggs go incredibly well together. Next was the *chicharron* taco, which Amanda made with eggs and homemade skillet potatoes. This is served with their *pico de gallo* and a red salsa, which was remarkably spicy. It is a taco that will go down in the annals of great tacos.

They also serve a brisket taco with *pico de gallo*, which was also superb. The pairing seemed so natural that I wondered why I hadn't tried mixing Texas BBQ with Mexican cuisine before. Another interesting taco is their smoked sausage with *pico de gallo*.

Mr. Garcia wanted me to try almost everything they made, so he fixed me a brisket and rib plate and doused it with his barbecue sauce. The brisket was wonderfully juicy and smoky, a sure sign of patience with the smoker. The rib meat was firm and did not fall off the bone without some help. Sometimes, when ribs fall off the bone, it is a sign that the ribs have been boiled

before smoking to speed up the cooking process — something Garcia would never do.

he

MIXES THE

THE DRIED

and ground peppers

with olive oil, paprika, oregano,
salt and garlic

LOCATION
Various

PHONE
832-538-4777

HOURS
Various

FOOD
Portuguese/South African

PRICES
$

OWNER
Jorge Fife

STARTED
2011

PAYMENT
All

SPECIAL SERVICES
Catering

PIRI PIRI CHICKEN

—

He uses the **chili *pequin* peppers** that are readily available here and are similar in size, color, shape and potency to the peppers found back home in Mozambique or in South Africa.

I first met Jorge Fife many years ago when he operated Taste of Portugal, a tiny restaurant on Jones Road. He served amazing food there: from *feijoada* and *sardinhas* to *bacalhau* and *piri piri* chicken. But he finally gave up his restaurant and started a business selling doors.

Food, however, continued calling him. I'd occasionally get an email from him saying that he was serving something special or that he had just finished making some homemade *chourico* or Portuguese sausage. And recently, I was delighted by an e-mail saying that

he had opened a food truck serving *piri piri* chicken.

To make *piri piri* chicken, Jorge takes whole chickens and slow cooks them in an oven. Before they are completely done, he removes them to a grill and douses them liberally with his *piri piri* sauce.

Jorge was born in the former Portuguese colony Mozambique and moved to South Africa, where he was in the import/export business. He left South Africa because he felt it unsafe to raise a family there.

PIRI PIRI CHICKEN // LEMON-PEPPER CHICKEN // WHOLE CHICKENS AND HALF CHICKENS //

To make *piri piri* chicken, Jorge takes whole chickens and slow cooks them in an oven. Before they are completely done, he removes them to a grill and douses them liberally with his *piri piri* sauce.

He uses the chili *pequin* peppers that are readily available here and are similar in size, color, shape and potency to the peppers found back home in Mozambique or in South Africa. He mixes the dried and ground peppers with olive oil, paprika, oregano, salt and garlic, which together add a wonderful taste and a mild heat to the chicken. Jorge says he has toned down his recipe because "I don't want to overdo it. If it's too hot, you can't taste the chicken." Slow-cooking leaves the chicken extremely moist and tender.

Jorge also makes a lemon-pepper chicken, which is prepared in much the same way. This is a perfect offering for those who don't care for spicy food. It has a delicious balance of pepper and lemon flavors, and because it too has been slow-cooked, remains moist throughout.

Jorge sells whole chickens and half chickens. Both come with salad and a roll or tortillas.

the
MEAT
REMAINED
firm
yet tender

RIB TIME BBQ

—

Sherman uses oak and pecan for his smoker and cooks the brisket for eight to twelve hours at around **250 degrees** with the fat up.

LOCATION
15910 Old Richmond Road

PHONE
832-498-5476

HOURS
Fri-Sat: 11:00am-7:00pm

FOOD
BBQ

PRICES
$

OWNER
Sherman McDonald

STARTED
2009

PAYMENT
Cash only

SPECIAL SERVICES
Catering

Sherman McDonald owned a barbecue restaurant for 20 years in Mission Bend before he decided to kick back a little. "I still love to cook," he said, "so I decided to buy a trailer." We're glad he did. Sherman's barbecue is some of the best around.

Let's start with the boudin. "A friend of mine makes it," said Sherman. Apparently, the friend likes spicy food;

The brisket still had some fat on it and also had the ring of fire, indicating a nice, long, slow cook.

the boudin was one the spiciest I have ever tried. I got there around noon one Saturday, and Sherman told me that the

boudin wasn't quite ready and that it needed another 20 or 30 minutes. By the time I had finished my interview and taking photos, enough time had passed so that Sherman gave me a piece to try. In my opinion, had we left it any longer, it would have been too smoky, but as it was, it was perfect. The spicy warmth stayed with me for at least an hour after I had consumed it.

Sherman uses oak and pecan for his smoker and cooks the brisket for eight to twelve hours at around 250 degrees with the fat up. He uses a dry rub but would not reveal all his secret ingredients. The same was true of his ribs, which fell off the bone. "I use a

tenderizing process on the ribs," he said. But that was all he would say on the subject. The ribs cooked for three to four hours. The brisket still had some fat on it and also had the ring of fire, indicating a nice, long, slow cook. The meat remained firm yet tender. Sherman uses a spicy sausage made by Holmes Smokehouse, which had the right amount of fat in it, keeping it nicely moist. Sherman's homemade barbecue sauce was the perfect balance between sweet and tangy, and his beans were full of flavor, with pieces of onions, bell

"I use a tenderizing process on the ribs," he said. But that was all he would say on the subject.

pepper and bits of his smoky ribs. The potato salad was also excellent, with potatoes that were still firm, not mushy.

the

BRISKET IS

REMARKABLY

tender and juicy

you can really taste the flavor

LOCATION
7129 FM 1464

HOURS
Wed-Sat: 12:00pm-8:00pm

FOOD
Barbecue

PRICES
$

STARTED
2008

PAYMENT
All

PHONE
281-932-3886

OWNER
Wayne Lockhart

FACEBOOK
/RibsOnWheels?sk=info

WEBSITE
mmdzine.com/row/

RIBS ON WHEELS

—

"You can taste everything **for free** because we know you'll be back to buy some". Wayne Lockhart

Once you get close to this location, it's easy to spot this trailer: You'll see the smoke rising from the back of it. "This is Chicago-style barbecue," Wayne Lockhart said as I looked over the menu. Originally from Chicago, he proudly told me that he is a recovering addict, who moved here when he wanted to start a new life. "Thirteen years now and counting," he said. "Thank you, Houston, for your Southern hospitality and for not judging me."

He opened Ribs on Wheels right after Hurricane Ike. "Instead of raising pricing and gouging people, I took $1 off of each price.

He opened Ribs on Wheels right after Hurricane Ike. "The first thing I did was to cook for all the city workers and for the Centerpoint crew that were fixing the lights," he said. "Instead of raising pricing and gouging people, I took $1 off of each price. That helped me get started." He was about to drop $30,000 just on a trailer he found when he met another barbecue trailer owner who told him about the Pace America race trailers. He spent about the same $30,000, but this time it included all the appliances and interior he needed. Inside he has a four-door, open-pit barbecue at one end of the trailer, which has a black-and-white racing theme with winner's flags all around.

"We turn no one away," said Wayne. "If you can't pay today and have an honest face, we know you'll be back tomorrow. You can taste everything for free because we know you'll be back to buy some," he added.

PORK RIB TIPS // BARBECUED BRISKET // CZECH-STYLE SAUSAGE // BARBECUED RIBS

Wayne cooks all his meat over charcoal. Because of this, the barbecue does not have the strong smoky flavor we associate with Texas 'que. His ribs cook two hours; his brisket takes seven. On both, he uses a dry rub whose ingredients he keeps secret. I was able to taste salt, pepper and garlic, as well as a nice heat level from the rub. Wayne's sauce starts with a commercial sauce, to which he adds secret ingredients.

The brisket is remarkably tender and juicy, and because it's not super-smoky, you can really taste the flavor of the meat. The sausage, a commercially available, Czech-style link made from pork and beef, is nice and fatty, with a decent amount of heat.

New to me were the pork rib tips. Wayne told me they were a Chicago specialty. "We cut off the tops of the ribs, so there's just meat and gristle and no bones," he said. These, along with his ribs, were the best things I tried.

His baked beans have a terrific blending of sweet and tangy flavors in a thick, reddish-brown sauce. "My wife makes the 'tater salad and only she knows the ingredients," said Wayne. I could make out tiny pieces of red pepper and pickles among the large chunks of potatoes, which are combined with mashed potatoes. The potato salad is thick and tasty yet does not contain too much mayonnaise.

stuffed

WITH A

DELICIOUS

chicken mixture

topped with mayonnaise

LOCATION
7106 Bellaire

PHONE
281-690-3329

HOURS
Mon, Wed-Sun: 9:00am-10:00pm

FOOD
Honduran

PRICES
$$

OWNERS
Alvaro

STARTED
2009

PAYMENT
Cash only

SABOR CATRACHO

—

According to Wikipedia, Central Americans refer to a person from **Honduras** as a *catracho*.

As an insider might guess from the name, this converted school bus serves an extensive menu of Honduran dishes. According to Wikipedia, Central Americans refer to a person from Honduras as a *catracho*. The term was coined by Nicaraguans in the mid-19th century when Honduran General Florencio Xatruch returned from battle with his soldiers after defeating American freebooters who'd aimed to re-establish slavery and take over all of Central America. As the general and his soldiers returned, some Nicaraguans yelled out "¡*Vienen los xatruches!*" — "Here come Xatruch's boys!" But Nicaraguans had so much trouble pronouncing the general's last name that they altered the

The ground meat is well seasoned and mixed with tomatoes, carrots and small cubes of potatoes.

phrase to *los catruches* and ultimately settled on *los catrachos*.

We tried the *carne molida con tajadas*, ground beef with plantains. The ground meat is well seasoned and mixed with tomatoes, carrots and small cubes of potatoes. The mixture sits on top of *curtido*, pickled shredded

GROUND BEEF WITH PLANTAINS // ENCHILADAS
TACOS HONDUREÑOS // PASTELITOS DE CARNE

cabbage, which in turn sits on top of slices of fried unripe plantains (not the sweet kind). In one corner of the plate

Next were the tacos *hondure-ños*, Honduran tacos, which consist of two corn tortillas almost a foot across

there's a mix of pink pickled onions and carrots, and crumbly cheese is sprinkled on top of everything. This dish is also available with chicken, grilled beef or pork chops.

Next were the tacos *hondureños*, Honduran tacos, which consist of two corn tortillas almost a foot across. These were stuffed with a delicious chicken mixture, topped with mayonnaise, then rolled up *taquito*-style. The ubiquitous *curtido*, crumbly cheese and pink pickled onions and carrots sat on the side.

MENU
POLLO CON TAJADAS
CARNE ASADA CON TAJADAS
CHULETA CON TAJADAS
CARNE MOLIDA CON TAJADAS
TACOS HONDUREÑOS
BALEADAS
PASTELITOS DE CARNE
ENCHILADAS
PLATANO FRITO
REFRESCOS HONDUREÑOS
BANANA
UVA
MIRINDA
HORCHATA

✦ an ✦
EMPANADA
FILLED WITH
mechada
an excellent shredded beef

LOCATION
8621 Westheimer

PHONE
713-780-2663

HOURS
Mon-Thur: 7:00am-11:30pm, Fri-Sat:
7:00am-4:30pm, Sun: 10:00am-10:00pm

FOOD
Venezuelan

PRICES
$$

OWNERS
Jose and Iris Muñoz

STARTED
2003

PAYMENT
All

SABOR VENEZOLANO

—

"There are so many Venezuelans living in Katy," he says, "that the Venezuelans there call it **Katy-zuela**." Jose Muñoz

Jose Muñoz is from Maracay, Venezuela, and since 2003, his truck has served Houston's Venezuelan community. For years he was at the corner of Westheimer and Fondren. He moved a couple of years ago to a mechanic's shop one block east of Fondren, where he now parks two trucks, one for cooking and serving, the other for storage. In Katy, at 1818 Fry Road, his wife, Iris, manages another truck. "There are so many Venezuelans living in Katy," he says, "that the Venezuelans there call it Katy-zuela."

Arepas, or filled corn patties, are found everywhere in Venezuela. Jose offers 10 varieties. The one I tried was the *reina pepiada*, which consisted of shredded chicken, mayonnaise, avocado and potatoes. It tasted similar to a chicken salad, only better, with the crispy *arepa* not detracting from the filling. According to the website venezuelanfoodanddrinks.blogspot.com, the dish, whose name means something like "the curvaceous queen," is named after Venezuela's first international beauty queen, Susana Dujim.

Tequeños, or cheese sticks, come ten to an order. But since I was buying a lot of different things, Alicia, the server, let me have just five. They had been made earlier and kept hot under a heat lamp,

The dish, whose name means something like "the curvaceous queen," is named after Venezuela's first international beauty queen, Susana Dujim.

so they were somewhat rubbery, but the gooey cheese interior didn't suffer. I also had a greaseless handmade *empanada* filled with *mechada*, an excellent shredded

FILLED CORN PATTIES // CHEESE STICKS //
EMPANADA // CACHAPA // PABELLON

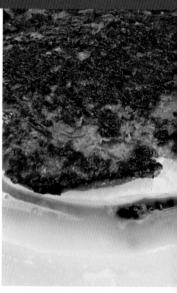

beef. The *empanada*, too, suffered from being precooked and kept in a warming oven — one of the downsides to street food, where speed of service is of the essence.

Next was the *cachapa*, which came close to being the best thing I had there. It is a thick corn fritter, made from the sweetest corn there is, fried until it turns black, then folded over and filled with *queso fresco* which melts just before being served. It's so sweet that at first you think sugar may have been added to the mix, but this is certainly not the case. The sweetness is from the corn.

But the best thing I had here was the *pabellon*, which consisted of two slices of *tostones*, green plantains that are placed in a special press to expose as much of their starch as possible, then fried to a crispy yellow. Between the two *tostones* were a layer of shredded beef, lettuce, tomato and avocado. The assemblage is too large to be eaten like a sandwich. But by using one of the slices of *toston* as a plate, you can easily eat some of the delectable filling by placing it on top of the *toston*.

the
BLARING
MUSIC AND
flashing lights
enthralled the kids

FOOD
Ice cream treats,
frozen doggie treats

PRICES
$

STARTED
2010

PAYMENT
All, including Paypal

OWNER
Shannon Holliday

SPECIAL SERVICES
Catering, parties

FACEBOOK
/people/Snowdog-Ice-
Cream/100000459942971

WEBSITE
snowdogicecream.com/

SNOW DOG ICE CREAM

—

Shannon makes organic frozen **doggie popsicles** using honey, yogurt and peanut butter with a small rawhide sausage stuck in them. She offers these to any of the dogs around.

Shannon Holliday does more than just sell ice cream treats out of her truck. She dresses up as a clown and caters

Shannon will drive her truck to your house fully loaded not just with ice-cream treats, but with enough toys, games and music to keep a bunch of screaming and unruly kids entertained.

kids' parties, providing cool treats for kids and dogs and entertaining the kids with games and music.

Let's talk dog first. Shannon travels to these parties with Miles, her six-year-old Malamute mix. Miles, the snow

dog, is exceedingly well-behaved, especially around kids. He stays in the truck, watching and hoping that some kid drops his ice cream inside the truck just as Shannon hands it to him. My bet is that if that ever happens, Miles quietly retreats with his booty to a corner of the truck. There again, he is so well-behaved that he may not.

Shannon makes organic frozen doggie popsicles using honey, yogurt and peanut butter with a small rawhide sausage stuck in them. She offers these to any of the dogs around. As you can see from the picture on the next page, Sophie, our German shepherd mix, made light work of the treat.

ICE CREAM TREATS // DOGGIE POPSICLES // TOYS // GAMES // MUSIC // FLASHING LIGHTS

Now for the kids: Shannon will drive her truck to your house fully loaded not just with ice-cream treats, but with enough toys, games and music to keep a bunch of screaming and unruly kids entertained. Plus she dresses up as a clown. The cost: Around $200, no matter how many ice creams are consumed.

Shannon used to work for an installation artist but when the recession hit, people stopped buying art and she got laid off. She remembered how one day, while she was visiting her father in New Orleans, they stopped by a sno-ball trailer and she noticed the line of about forty kids, all waiting for sno-balls. She quickly figured out that this business was recession-proof, so the day she got laid off was the day she bought her ice cream truck.

Since Snow Dog Ice Cream is not your typical ice cream truck, in order for me to meet up with Shannon, interview her and snap some pics, it was necessary for me to go to one of the parties she runs. I arrived at the moment Shannon was pulling into the house's driveway. The blaring music and flashing lights enthralled the kids right from the start. And ice cream can never go wrong.

Shannon's license plate: SNOWDG.

Footnote: During the writing of this book Miles passed away but his memory lives on.

❋ *the* ❋

CATFISH IS

COMPLETELY

without grease and

remarkably fresh and soft

LOCATION
11310 Homestead

PHONE
713-560-3540

HOURS
Wed-Sat: 11:00am-8:00pm

FOOD
Catfish, shrimp

PRICES
$$

OWNER
Greg Holmes

STARTED
2004

PAYMENT
Cash only

SPECIAL SERVICES
Catering

SOUTHERN SEAFOOD EXPRESS

—

"Mr. Holmes gets his fish only from a special distributor that catches them in the wild." Anthony Markowski

Greg Holmes owned the Catfish Café in Atascocita before buying this truck and opening it in 2004. Originally from Mississippi, he was a commercial fisherman for 20 years. His wife is from Louisiana, another place where people know a lot about seafood and how to cook it. He employs two servers, Anthony and Melissa Markowski, who help him with the truck. After I tasted his catfish and raved about it, Anthony told me one of his se-

We won't sell any farm-raised catfish because they have too much of a fishy taste.

crets: "Mr. Holmes gets his fish only from a special distributor that catches them in the wild. We won't sell any farm-raised catfish because they have too much of

a fishy taste." The five small filets that came with the catfish and shrimp combo were absolutely delicious.

When I arrived one Thursday around 12:30 p.m., quite a few people were waiting for their lunch plates. They assured me that I would not be disappointed. "We make everything fresh," said Anthony. If you come here on a Friday at lunch, you may have to wait 30 minutes for your food. We're that busy."

I most certainly was not disappointed. The catfish is completely without grease and doesn't really even need to be chewed. It is so remarkably fresh and soft, it falls apart in your mouth. No amount of coaxing would get them to reveal even one ingredient in the yellow

EXTRA-LARGE, BUTTERFLIED, FRIED SHRIMP //
CAUGHT-IN-THE-WILD FRIED CATFISH //

● ●

Call in orders: 713-560-3540
OPEN: Wednesday - Saturday 11:00- 8:00
CLOSED: Sunday – Tuesday

Regular Catfish & Fries $6.00
• 5 pieces Fish, Fries, & 2 Hushpuppies

2 Large Fish & Fries $10.00
• 10 pieces Fish, Fries, & 2 Hushpuppies

 # 3 Regular Shrimp & Fries
• 6 Large butterflied Shrimp, Fries, & $7.00
  2 Hushpuppies

 # 4 Large Shrimp & Fries
• 12 Large butterflied shrimp, Fries, & $10.00
  2 Hushpuppies

cornmeal crust's seasoning, and I can't say I blame them. I know I tasted salt and, judging by the tiny black specks, there's black pepper. Any more guessing may prove dangerous, so I'll quit.

Anthony regaled me with stories about pro football players turning up in Bentleys for this catfish treat. "We had a woman come all the way from Clear Lake just so she could get a friend to try it," he said.

The shrimp are likewise incredible: extra-large, butterflied and coated with seasoned flour. (Don't bother asking for

Anthony regaled me with stories about pro football players turning up in Bentleys for this catfish treat.

those ingredients, either.) There is not a lot of batter, but what there is makes them crispy and superb. My platter came with five pieces of catfish, five shrimp, rough-cut fries and two hushpuppies. The hushpuppies alone could make you drive all the way out there on a whim. "We used to serve a spicy *jalapeño* hushpuppy," said Anthony, "but a lot of our customers are older, and they don't like spicy food. So we changed to a sweet corn hushpuppy, and people really love them." After one bite, I understood why.

✻ and ✻

WHAT COULD

BE BETTER THAN

free beer?

from houston's oldest and
largest craft brewer

HANDCRAFTED BEERS & ALES

ST. ARNOLD'S

—

Imagine what fun it must be to be the events and marketing manager for St. Arnold's Brewery, in charge of giving out **free beer**. That's what Lenny Ambrose does.

LOCATION
Various

HOURS
Various

FOOD
Beer, Root Beer

PRICES
FREE. Really.

STARTED
2008

PAYMENT
N/A

SPECIAL SERVICES
Community events

OWNERS
St Arnold's Brewing Company

TWITTER
/#!/saintarnold

FACEBOOK
/saintarnold

WEBSITE
saintarnold.com/

Okay, so this is not technically a food truck. It doesn't serve food. But for many, beer is the stuff of life, and what could be better than free beer?

I first encountered the trailer belonging to Houston's oldest and largest craft brewer at an arts festival at the Menil Collection, when I was handed a free beer.

Imagine what fun it must be to be the events and marketing manager for St. Arnold's Brewery, in charge of giving out free beer. That's what Lenny Ambrose does. He was very quick to point out that St. Arnold's

The events they like to sponsor are things like Texans tailgating parties, charitable events, arts organizations and any event "that makes Houston or Texas a better place."

reviews all opportunities case by case, and that the events they like to sponsor are things like Texans tailgating parties, charitable events, arts organizations

SAINT ARNOLD ROOT BEER // SAINT ARNOLD AMBER ALE // SAINT ARNOLD SUMMER PILS

and any event "that makes Houston or Texas a better place."

What's particularly interesting is that there is no limit to the amount of beer they can give away. "We just can't sell any of our beer and the event must not

it astonished me that they don't control the distribution of free beer. We shall all be eternally grateful for this small pleasure.

be a licensed venue, but other than that, there are no restrictions," said Lenny. As tight a control as the TABC has on beer distribution, it astonished me that they don't control the distribution of free beer. We shall all be eternally grateful for this small pleasure.

Don't you just love the tap handles coming out the side of the trailer?

}on{
A STICK WITH
A HOMEMADE
shrimp and
french bread stuffing which is just outstanding.

LOCATION
Various

PHONE
713-502-1188

HOURS
Various

FOOD
American

PRICES
$

OWNER
Joel St. John

STARTED
2012

PAYMENT
All

FACEBOOK
/pages/St-Johns-
Fire/173341046106975

TWITTER
#!/firetrucktx

WEBSITE
stjohnsfire.com/

SPECIAL SERVICES
Catering

ST. JOHN'S FIRE

—

I can't say enough good things about Chef Joel's cuisine. **What a treat**!

Joel St. John, a Bellaire native, spent thirty years in the restaurant business before hanging out his own shingle at his truck, which he calls St. John's Fire. Joel cut his teeth in Louisiana, where he developed an appreciation for fine cuisine when he spent over thirteen years in the heart of the French Quarter at places like Commander's Palace, Mr. B's and the Hotel Monteleone. When he returned to Houston in 1991, he worked at Harry's Kenya and the Brownstone and Aramark and then, most recently, as the Executive Chef at Spencer's for Steaks and Chops in the Hilton Americas downtown.

This is most definitely a gourmet food truck. Chef Joel is doing the same kind of dishes that he did at the white tablecloth restaurants he worked at, only for in smaller portions, more quickly and at very reasonable prices. He calls the cuisine he is serving Southern, but that gives him a lot of leeway since he defines this as coming from anywhere between Florida and California.

Seafood plays an important role on his menu as do Creole spices and he does both exceptionally well. And speaking of spices, more than 30 years ago, he developed his own proprietary blend of spices called JSJ Spice Mix - what else? - which he also sells from his truck.

In 1995, Chef St. John won "Best in Show" at The Great Tastes of Houston with his Cajun Egg Roll and for good reason. Inside a standard eggroll wrapper he stuffs a mixture of shrimp, crawfish and tasso, a spicy smoked pork used extensively in South Louisiana cuisine, which adds a wonderful smoky and spicy note, along with the "holy trinity" of onions, bell peppers and celery, some spinach and some of his proprietary JSJ spices. A few minutes in the deep fryer, and the result is like having all the tastes of Louisiana in the palm of your hand. The chef warns everyone ordering one that it's piping hot inside, so he recommends waiting a few minutes before biting into it.

Staring at it, waiting for it to cool,

GRILLED CHEESE SANDWICH WITH GYRO MEAT // GREEK HAMBURGER // GREEK FRIES // GREEK PIZZA

seems like cruel and unusual punishment to me. When you do eventually bite into the crispy eggroll exterior, allowing the filling to ooze out, the flavors that hit your tongue shout out "Louisiana". It is served with a guava creole mustard dipping sauce, which adds sweetness, tartness and heat. St. John also makes a Southwest Grilled Chicken version of this eggroll, which he stuffs with pieces of chicken, poblano peppers, corn, black beans and some cheese which, when melted, helps to hold everything together.

For his Tortilla Crusted Fish, St. John used sway fish, which is a firm fish not unlike catfish. The crushed- up tortillas are blended with some of his special spice mix along with some cumin. They make for a very crispy coating. This is served with a mango *jalapeño* glaze, which adds sweetness and heat, and some cilantro-lime rice, which adds to the complex flavors of the dish. Some pico de gallo on top of it all makes it a very colorful dish.

St. John serves his Grilled Pork Loin on a stick with a homemade shrimp and French bread stuffing which is just outstanding. His homemade fig glaze puts this dish over the top. All he would say about his stuffing is that: "there's a lot of butter in there."

On my next visit, I tried the Seafood Martini. In a small plastic cup he puts a serving of his equivalent of a *campechana*. He

uses shrimp, crawfish and a crab claw, along with some chopped cilantro and diced tomatoes, cucumber and jicama for added texture. This all marinates in a Clamato and V8 blend, to which he adds a lot of fresh squeezed lime juice. This concoction adds a nice spicy flavor to the seafood. Some tortilla chips are served on the side.

I also tried the Shrimp Corndog, a sort of grown-up's version of a corndog. He takes four, large Gulf shrimp, which he dusts with his seasoning and skewers then rolls in his cornbread and flour coating before frying. The result is a fascinating mix of flavors with the spicy shrimp giving way to the blander coating. A dipping sauce made of Dijon mustard and mayonnaise is the perfect accompaniment.

I can't say enough good things about Chef Joel's cuisine. What a treat to be able to enjoy this type of gourmet food on the streets of Houston.

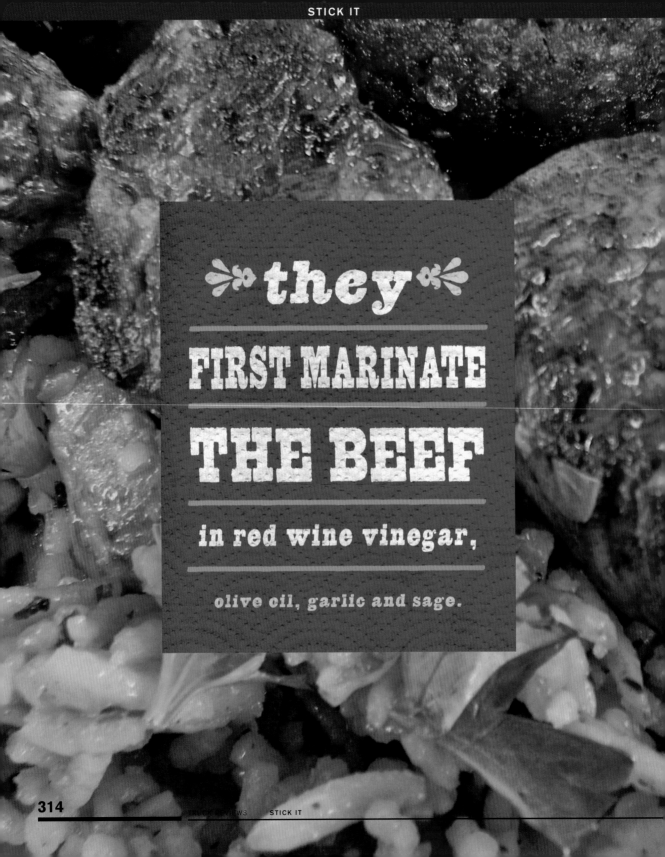

✣ they ✣

FIRST MARINATE

THE BEEF

in red wine vinegar,

olive oil, garlic and sage.

LOCATION
Various

HOURS
Various

FOOD
Anything on a skewer

PRICES
$$

STARTED
2011

PAYMENT
All

PHONE
832-589-7868

OWNER
Ruth Lipsky, Alberto Palmer

SPECIAL SERVICES
Catering

FACEBOOK
/pages/Stick-It-Food-
Truck/140313742731075

STICK IT

—

Ruth was inspired by many trips to the Renaissance Festival, where, as a child, she had feasted on lots of different things **on sticks**.

Ruth Lipsky and Alberto Palmer are both restaurant industry veterans who recently started the Stick It food truck. Their premise is simple – gourmet food served on a stick or skewer – a sort of universal and international kebab. They are both extremely creative and talented chefs and are always looking for new things to serve on a stick.

Ruth was born in Dallas and went to Le Cordon Bleu College of Culinary Arts in Arizona, then worked in Chicago at MOTO, a restaurant famous for molecular gastronomy.

When she left Chicago to come to Houston three years ago, Ruth was an executive chef, but left this position to allow her to have more of the renegade feeling and bring great food back to the people. Both Ruth and Alberto had tired of the rigidity of a traditional kitchen and yearned to open their own place.

Alberto was born in Puerto Rico but grew up in Houston. After stints at various fast and casual food joints, he worked at Jake's and at Dolce e Freddo, a place I still miss.

For the food they are serving on their truck, Ruth was inspired by many trips to the Renaissance Festival, where, as a child, she had feasted on lots of different things on sticks. But Ruth is not serving fair food, far from it; she is serving classical haute cuisine on a stick. Everything is made from scratch on this truck and it clearly shows.

You may think it would be hard to serve fish on a stick, but Ruth has mastered the technique. And if you're thinking that these fish sticks resemble those you may have had to eat as a child, think again. They bear absolutely no resemblance to those at all. For her Beer Battered Fish, Ruth takes filets of

BEER BATTERED FISH // GRILLED FILET ON A STICK // FUNNEL CAKE BATTERED BRIE //

catfish or sway and dips them in a beer batter before sliding them into the fryer for a few minutes. Ruth always uses a Texas beer in the batter, such as Karbach Brewery's Sympathy Lager or even good 'ole Lone Star. The batter is light and airy and extremely crispy, which contrasts well with the moist and flaky fish. The fish is not the only star in this dish, the accompanying hand-cut, super crispy, matchstick fries, sprinkled with sea salt, may well steal the show. Last but not least is a drizzle of homemade *aioli*, in which she uses malt vinegar as a secret ingredient. It's hard to say which is better, the malt *aioli* or the home-made ketchup, which serve as dipping sauces but if you use one on the fish and the other on the fries, you'll never have to make that decision.

One of their best sellers is the Grilled Filet on a stick. They first marinate the beef in red wine vinegar, olive oil, garlic and sage. This does two things. Firstly, it imparts rich and complex flavors to the meat and secondly, it keeps it very moist and tender. They serve it with button mushrooms stuffed with a vegetable mixture and a mushroom pilaf made with brown butter. This is the kind of dish for which you would gladly pay a lot of money at a fancy restaurant. It's nice to know you can also get this kind of food on the streets of Houston.

On my next visit, I tried the Korean BBQ Pork Belly Lettuce Wraps. Ruth marinates thick slices of pork belly, replete with lots of chewy rind, in Korean spices, soy sauce, sugar and a few other secret ingredients. A few minutes on the griddle is enough to caramelize the sugar, which remains on the surface, turning it crispy. They set the pork belly in slices of red leaf lettuce and serve it with Basmati rice with sesame *gastrique*, which means the addition of some of the juices from the pork belly along with the caramelized sugar, plus vinegar and sesame oil. In case you're wondering, the pork belly is on a stick and in order to eat it, you remove it from the stick and wrap it in the lettuce leaf along with some of the rice. What this does to the rice is to add a heavenly flavor, which marries perfectly with the slices of pork belly. It is a dish not to be missed.

The first bite of the Funnel Cake Battered Brie with Four Berry Compote will be enough to make anyone beg that this item never be removed from the menu. Ruth uses blueberries, strawberries, raspberries and blackberries along with a little honey to make the compote. The thing I like most about it is that it is quite tart and not at all too sweet and it works perfectly with the small balls of cheese that are covered in this delicious sauce. The cheese itself is covered in batter and briefly deep-fried, allowing it to melt until it is runny and gooey.

it's

COATED WITH

TINY CHOCOLATE

pieces,

along with crushed
walnuts and almonds

LOCATION
Various

PHONE
773-875-0880

HOURS
Various

FOOD
Italian ices, sno-cones,
sorbets, desserts

PRICES
$$

OWNER
Kim Clemmons, SeeLun Mak

STARTED
2011

PAYMENT
Cash only

WEBSITE
sweetridehouston.com/

FACEBOOK
/SweetRideHouston

TWITTER
/#!/SweetRideHoustn

SPECIAL SERVICES
Catering

SWEETRIDE

—

With Italian ice, the natural flavors are blended with the ice, which is so fine, it's **almost like a sorbet** in texture.

"In 2009, when I was laid off from an oil and gas company, I was done with corporate America," Kim Clemmons told me. "One day, a friend of mine asked if I would like to work with him

I asked Kim to explain the difference between Italian ices and sno-cones. "Sno-cones are typically kids' treats," she said, "whereas Italian ices are more for grown-ups."

in his ice cream truck. I loved it. It was fast-paced, and I got to deal with people directly." A gregarious soul, she soon decided she wanted her own business. She bought a truck and converted it herself with the help of friends. The first thing they did was to

add an extended top, to allow the servers to stand in the truck. White and red paint makes it look like an ambulance.

I asked Kim to explain the difference between Italian ices and sno-cones. "Sno-cones are typically kids' treats," she said, "whereas Italian ices are more for grown-ups." She reached into the small freezer and scooped up a cup of ice. "This is the crushed ice we use for the sno-cones. You can see it is quite coarse. We use this as the base, then add the liquid syrup that adds flavor and color." She then scooped out some blackberry-cabernet Italian ice. "With Italian ice, the natural flavors are blended with the ice, which is so fine, it's almost like a sorbet in texture," said Kim.

BARNABY CONE // DIP CLARKE // LAVERNE AND SWIRLEY // THE TREATS OF SAN FRANCISCO

The frozen mango dessert I tried is stuffed into a real mango, minus the stone in the middle, and tastes exactly like mango. The mango sorbet also tasted of real mango. Since Kim's sorbets are made with real fruit, and lots of it, this should come as no surprise. I also sampled a frozen chocolate truffle dessert, which Kim calls a "bomb." I chose the amaretto version. It is shaped like a dome, and Kim cuts it in half just before serving

You can see it is quite coarse. We use this as the base, then add the liquid syrup that adds flavor and color.

to make it easier to eat. Like the frozen mango dessert, it is extremely hard just after it is served. The exterior is coated with tiny chocolate pieces, along with crushed walnuts and almonds; in the center there's vanilla ice cream. It is a delightful dessert and sized so that you don't feel completely guilty when you consume one (or two).

"We're children of the '70s," added Kim, "and so we've come up with names for future items, names like Barnaby Cone, Dip Clarke, The Treats of San Francisco, and Laverne and Swirley." With this kind of creativity and passion, there should be little doubt that Sweet Ride will succeed.

the

THICK TORTILLA

MAKES THE

---

assemblage

---

easy to pick it up in one piece

LOCATION
5502 W. Airport

FOOD
Mexico City

PRICES
$

PAYMENT
Cash only

STARTED
2008

OWNER
Victor Buenrostro

TACOS GARIBALDI D.F.

—

Here they **serve specialties** you will not find anywhere else. Some items — the *torta capitalina*, the *alambres* and the *picaditos* — are unique to this truck.

This was one of the busiest trucks I visited. The reason is that Luis Buenrostro and his brother Victor specialize in food from the capital of Mexico, Mexico City, or *el Districto Federal* (D.F.). The truck is named for the Plaza Garibaldi, in the historic center of Mexico City. Here they serve specialties you will not find anywhere else. Some items — the *torta capita-lina*, the *alambres* and the *picaditos* — are unique to this truck. The *torta capitalina*, or sandwich from the capi-tal, is made on a very large sesame-seed roll, which they slice in two, cov-ering each side with a little oil before heating it quickly on the griddle. While the bread warms, they cut up a thinly sliced steak, a slice of ham and a hot dog and mix them together on the griddle as well. One side of the bread is covered in mayo, the other in refried beans. Between the two slices go the hot meats, along with slices of tomato, avocado and cheese. The resulting

One side of the bread is covered in mayo, the other in refried beans. Between the two slices go the hot meats

sandwich is delicious, a mammoth production that will satisfy even the hungriest of eaters.

Picaditos start with Luis taking a handful of *masa* and forming it in a tortilla press. He then fries the fresh-made tortilla on the griddle. When it's almost done, he removes it and presses

the edges up, forming a sort of plate, before laying on bright green *tomatillo* and cilantro salsa, sour cream, *queso fresco*, onion and your choice of meat. (I chose steak.) The thick tortilla makes the assemblage easy to pick it up in one piece and eat. It has the consistency and look of an *arepa*.

Finally, there were the *alambres*. At a food truck, the word can mean one of two things: either a skewer of meat like a shish kabob; or a mixture of chopped and fried meat, onions, cheese and other things. Here it means the latter, with

Picaditos start with Luis taking a handful of cornmeal masa and forming it in a tortilla press.

steak, ham, sausage, *chorizo*, grilled onions and Monterrey Jack cheese all mixed together on the griddle. Served with terrific refried beans and corn tortillas, it is simply sublime.

SAUCE THE

TRADITIONAL

pinkish-red color

of campbell's tomato soup

LOCATION
Highway 6 South (CROSS STREET?). In the parking lot of a Phillips 66 station.

PHONE
713-852-7642

HOURS
Wed-Mon: 5:30pm-12:00am

FOOD
Indian, Pakistani

PRICES
$$

OWNER
Vinod Mehra and
Sakun "Ginny" Mehra

PAYMENT
All

SPECIAL SERVICES
Halal

TANDOORI NITE DHABA

—

As soon as you approach the counter, the heady aroma of **Indian spices** convinces you that you're in the right place. And you are: It is astonishing how good the Indian food is from this truck.

Since this truck is outside Houston's city limits, it can have a semi-permanent set-up with chairs, communal tables and an awning — an arrangement acceptable in Harris County, but not inside the city limits. The truck is owned by the same family that owns another truck, Desi Grill & More, on Veteran's Memorial. The father, Vinod, runs Desi Grill, and the son, Sakun, runs this truck.

As soon as you approach the counter, the heady aroma of Indian spices convinces you that you're in the right place. And you are: It is astonishing how good the Indian food is from this

truck. They have a tandoor oven right on the truck; it appears to have been made out of an oil drum.

The word *dhaba* means a small, local restaurant in India and Pakistan, many times found on the side of the road.

We ordered the inevitable chicken *tikka masala* and a chicken curry with whole-wheat roti bread and basmati rice studded with lots of herbs and spices.

Everything is made to order, so it takes a while, but you get to watch your food being prepared. "How spicy do you like

TIKKA MASALA // CHICKEN MASALA // CHICKEN CURRY // VADA PAV // BHEL PURI

it?" the server asked. When we replied "hot," he smiled and more chilies went into the pot. When we first tasted the food, it did not seem excessively hot. But it was the kind of heat that builds up until it makes your nose run.

We ordered the inevitable chicken *tikka masala* and a chicken curry with whole-wheat *roti* bread and basmati rice studded with lots of herbs and spices. The two large pieces of chicken in the chicken *masala* came in a sauce the traditional pinkish-red color of Campbell's tomato soup; it was nice and creamy. The chicken curry contained more chicken, and its consistency was thinner; the spices were markedly different.

Tandoori
Nite

a
SLICE OF
AVOCADO

strips of cilantro,

crumbly cheese and grilled onions,

LOCATION
7403 Longpoint

HOURS
Mon-Sun: 8:00am-10:00pm

FOOD
Mexican

PRICES
$

OWNER
Frederico Montano

STARTED
2005

PAYMENT
Cash only

PHONE
713-859-7706

SPECIAL SERVICES
Catering

TAQUERIA EL ULTIMO

—

The three tacos we tried were outstanding, **each better than the one before it**. Each was topped with a slice of avocado, strips of cilantro, crumbly cheese and grilled onions.

"Look at my truck in this magazine," said Frederico as he handed me the January 2011 issue of Southern Living. There, along with trucks from other South-

The chicharron, which was almost like carnitas. The pulled pork, without fat or grease, was our favorite.

ern cities, was the Taqueria El Ultimo truck, which had made a list called "The South's Best Food Trucks."

Frederico Montano is from Hidalgo, and has owned this truck since 2005. He serves breakfast tacos as well as other tacos, and on weekends, he serves *menudo* (tripe stew) as well. He also does catering and told me that some schools contract with him to serve breakfast from his truck. This was the first I had ever heard of such an arrangement. Those are lucky kids.

The three tacos we tried were outstanding, each better than the one before it. Each was topped with a slice of avocado, strips of cilantro, crumbly cheese and grilled onions. The corn tortillas were crisped on the griddle, and two are served with every taco. The *tripa* (tripe) was cooked to a crisp. *Longaniza* turns out to be very similar to *chorizo* but slightly coarser and somewhat spicier. The last was the *chicharron*, which was almost like *carnitas*. The pulled pork, without fat or grease, was our favorite.

BREAKFAST TACOS // *MENUDO* // *LONGANIZA* // *CHICHARRON* // *CHARRO* BEANS

We also ordered the *charro* beans after we saw a hand-written sign on the window letting us know they were available. The beans were nice and spicy, and the liquid could be consumed like a soup. Chunks of pork skin added a lot to the flavor.

Note the sign for the beans below, with its picture of a cannon underneath. We wondered if this was to indicate the effect the beans might have after you consumed them.

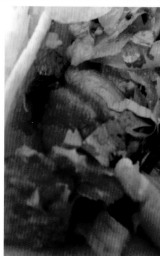

he

SPREAD

SOME BROTH

on top of the tortillas

to moisten them

LOCATION
6418 Windswept

HOURS
Mon-Sun 7:00am-10:00pm

FOOD
Guatemalan

PRICES
$

STARTED
2010

PAYMENT
Cash only

PHONE
281-236-1881

OWNER
Domingo Pocol

TAQUERIA GUATEMALA

—

Domingo, is from the town of Xela. He spent **five years cooking** for the Landry group at La Griglia and also at Cyclone Anaya.

Quite a few Guatemalan food trucks congregate along Windswept between Hillcroft and Fountainview and on streets to the north. This truck's owner, Domingo, is from the town of Xela. He spent five years cooking

These tamales are much larger than their Mexican counterparts; they contain a whole lot more *masa* and not a whole lot of filling.

for the Landry group at La Griglia and also at Cyclone Anaya. Earlier this year, he decided to be master of his own destiny. "The trailer cost me around $30,000 for absolutely everything," he said.

I asked him to give me the most typical dishes from his country. He immediately recommended the *tamal de pollo*, which was wrapped in a corn husk. These tamales are much larger than their Mexican counterparts; they contain a whole lot more *masa* and not a whole lot of filling. I was surprised to find that the chicken inside came with bones — something I later learned is typical.

A *tamal de arroz*, or rice tamale, Domingo told me, is a specialty that the Guatemalans make for the holidays, but he serves them every day. Rice flour is mixed with water or milk, then filled with chicken, red pepper and raisins, and wrapped

TAMAL DE POLLO // TAMAL DE ARROZ //
TACO DE GUATEMALA //

in a banana leaf, which keeps the contents exceedingly moist. It was extremely tasty and quite filling.

Last was the *taco de Guatemala*, which he prepared by putting a small amount of oil on the griddle, followed by four corn tortillas. He spread some broth on top of the tortillas to moisten them, then added toppings of pulled chicken and beef, grilled onions, cilantro, shredded cabbage and a spritz of lime juice. "It is customary to use four tortillas for this taco," Domingo said, "but some places use only two. It is also customary to make the tortillas by hand." Apparently that must be a little too much effort; he reached into a bag of pre-made corn tortillas.

The finished taco looked impossible to eat. It's flat and not folded together, so I did the only thing I could think of: took two of the tortillas and some filling in one hand, folded them over and ate. It worked perfectly.

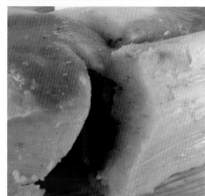

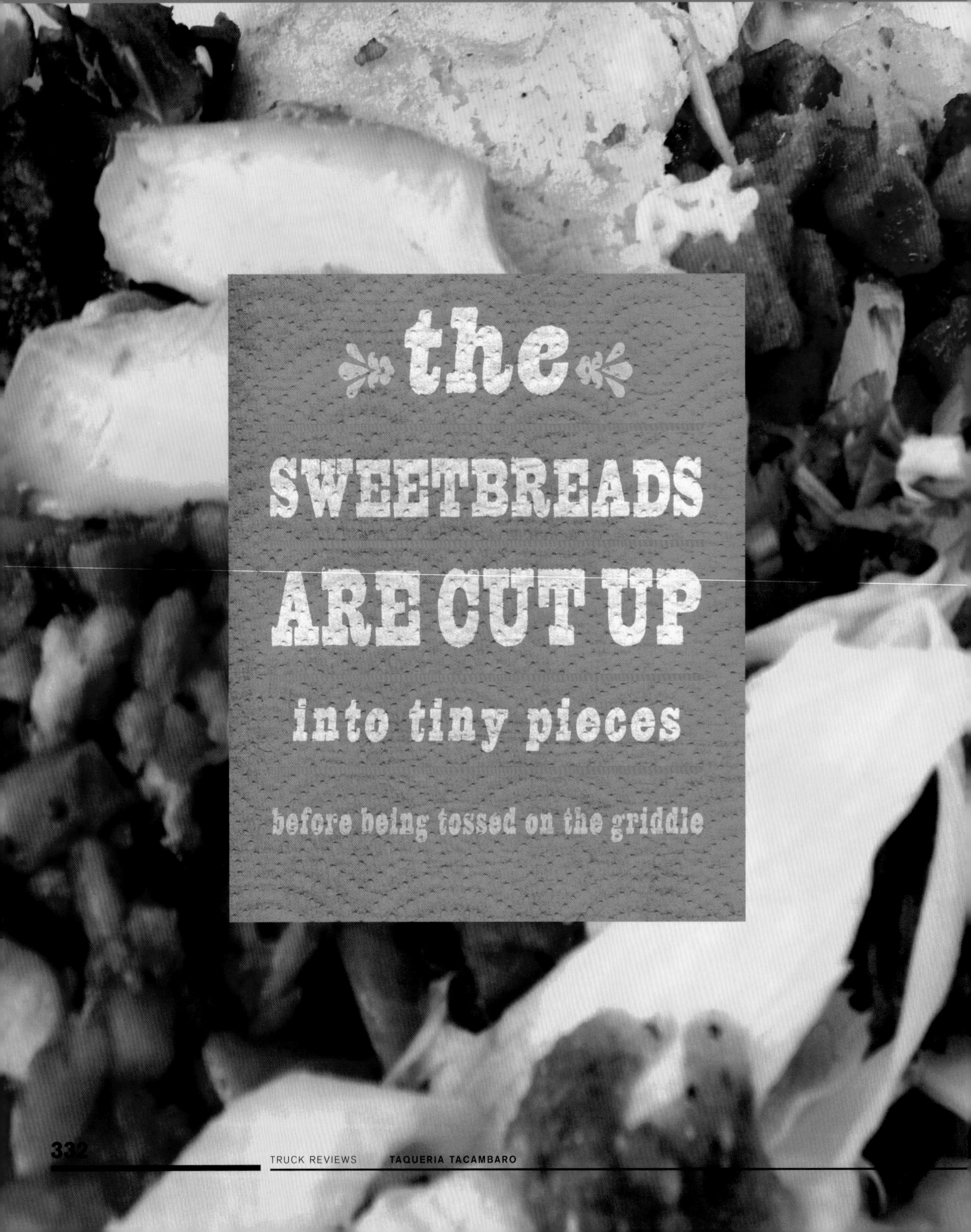

the
SWEETBREADS
ARE CUT UP
into tiny pieces
before being tossed on the griddle

TAQUERIA TACAMBARO

—

Tacambaro is a small town in **Michoacan**, in western Mexico, where owner Maria Rojas, is from.

This tiny, unassuming Mexican taco trailer turns out some very interesting tacos that are hard to find anywhere else in the city. Tacambaro is a small town in Michoacan, in western Mexico, where owner Maria Rojas, is from. She has been serving at this same location, tucked at the back of Canino's Produce on Airline, since 1997, a testament to the great food served here. Some of the more unusual tacos she prepares include *tripitas* (tripe), *mollejas* (sweetbreads), *buche* (stomach), *nopales* (cactus leaves), *lengua* (tongue) and *calabacitas* (squash). On weekends, she also prepares *barbacoa* (cow's cheek).

The sweetbreads are cut up into tiny pieces before being tossed on the griddle. This makes the exterior crispy and leaves the interior extremely soft and fluffy. They are served on some heated corn tortillas along with cilantro and some onions which have been slow cooked on the griddle and a slice of avocado.

On my next visit I tried a *gordita*. As you walk up to the trailer you may hear the unmistakable sound of *masa* being passed from one hand to the next as Maria hand forms a *gordita* before placing it on the griddle. This is a procedure she has done thousands of times, which means that she no longer has to watch what she is doing. The pit pat sound of the *masa* hitting her hands stops when the *masa* has reached the required thickness, then she turns her attention to forming the edges. All of this is done with an infectious smile that never seems to leave her face. The word *gordita* comes from *gordo* which

TRIPITAS TACOS // MOLLEJAS TACOS
NOPALES TACOS // CALABACITAS TACOS

means fat or thick and is the perfect description for this corn-based snack. It consists of a thick, round corn fritter, not unlike an *arepa*, which she opens up halfway by inserting a spatula on one side and peeling back the top surface as it is cooking, in order to stuff it with whatever meats you order. On her recommendation, I ordered the *pastor* or marinated pork. The orange-colored meat is diced into tiny cubes before being tossed on the griddle and covered with Mexican cheese which quickly melts. Slices of avocado, cilantro leaves, some diced tomatoes and some grilled jalapeños also accompany the meat on the side. It is served with some rust-colored, smoky cascabel pepper sauce, which adds some excitement to an already tasty snack. The cascabel pepper is also known as the rattle chili pepper because when it is dried, the seeds come off the pod and rattle around when shaken.

For those with a larger appetite, Maria can cook any of the meats she offers and put them in a *torta*. These large, oval-shaped *bolillos* or rolls are cut in two, smeared with grease and placed on the griddle to crispen slightly. As I normally do with Maria, I ask her to fill it with whatever is good. She offers me a 'mixta', or mixed meat combination. I nod in agreement. She chooses beef fajita and chicken fajita meat, which

are both superb. Slices of avocado, lettuce, tomato, slices of jalapeño, melted cheese and grilled onions also find their way in the roll. She presses it all down and cuts in two before serving it. She was also eager for me to try a vegetarian filling, for which she receives a number of requests. It was a tasty combination of *calabacitas*, or squash with *nopalitos*, or cactus pads. As with everything else I tried here, it was well-seasoned and had me wanting more.

♦ with ♦

TROMPO,

FAJITA MEAT,

avocado and green salsa

it, too, was delicious.

LOCATION
7975 Bellfort

PHONE
713-649-0539

HOURS
24/7

FOOD
Mexican

PRICES
$

STARTED
1998

PAYMENT
All

TAQUERIA TACONMADRE

—

You can just feel that this truck has been in business for a while. They seem to have everything in order and are built for **efficiency**.

This large truck wins prizes for most decorated, the largest menu and the fact that it's open 24/7. Really: It never closes. And the food is amazing. The sign on the side of the truck said that they specialize in *piratas*. These are large, handmade flour tortillas stuffed with fajita meat, bacon, avocado and green salsa. They are delicious.

Another sign touts *campechanas*. I think of *campechana* as a seafood cocktail in a tomato-based sauce, but here it is a taco made with a flour tortilla and stuffed with *trompo* (pork, similar to *tacos al pastor*), fajita

One taste made me long to sample other dishes from their extensive menu.

meat, *queso blanco* (Mexican white cheese), avocado and green salsa. It, too, was delicious. One taste made me long to sample other dishes from their extensive menu.

BREAKFAST TACOS // BARBACOA // CAMPECHANAS // PIRATAS // TOSTADAS

You can just feel that this truck has been in business for a while. They seem to have everything in order and are built for

This large truck wins prizes for most decorated, the largest menu and the fact that it's open 24/7. Really: It never closes.

efficiency. Their business cards say "*La casa del autentico taco Mexicano,*" or "the home of the authentic Mexican taco." Of this, you can be sure.

with

SHREDDED

LETTUCE,

tomatoes, sour cream,

and a whole jalapeño

LOCATION
5705 Fondren

FOOD
Mexican

PRICES
$

PAYMENT
Cash only

OWNER
Juan Jose Sanchez

PHONE
713-298-7707

HOURS
Mon-Sun: 9:30 am-9:30 pm

TAQUERIA TARIACURI

—

This truck is particularly notable for specialties not found elsewhere. This is the first time that I encountered *ceviche* on any food truck in Houston.

Tariacuri is a town in the Mexican state Michoacán. It is also a word the Purepecha Indians used for their king, who was born in the fourteenth century. This truck is particularly notable for specialties not found elsewhere. This was the first time that I encountered *ceviche* on any food truck in Houston. Some out there may think it risky to attempt to eat cured seafood from a food truck in the middle of Houston's hot summers. Think again. The *ceviche* was in a sealed plastic container and was removed from a refrigerator, so it posed no health threat. It was served on a crispy tortilla topped with *queso fresco* and cubed tomatoes.

Squeeze some lemon juice on top and add hot salsa from the selection available, and you have one of the most refreshing dishes I've ever had from a truck.

Next are the Chips Locos, for which the server takes two bags of Cheetos® and empties them into a Styrofoam container. She then heaps on top spoonfuls of *cueritos*, or pickled pig skins, from a large jar on the counter. The combination of chewy *cueritos* and crunchy Cheetos® is fascinating. Adding hot sauce to this snack makes it even more interesting as the liquid softens the Cheetos™®, turning them chewy towards the end, with a consistency not unlike the *cueritos*.

CEVICHE // CHIPS LOCOS // TOQUERE // FLAUTAS CON POLLO // ENCHILADAS // PAMBAZO

The third unusual dish was the *toquere*. No amount of research turned up much on the meaning or etymology of this word. It is a thick, sweet, corn patty not unlike an *arepa*. Instead of being stuffed like an *arepa*, it is simply fried on the griddle and then topped with sour cream and crumbly Mexican cheese. The corn makes it sweet, requiring hot sauce for balance.

Speaking of hot sauce, take note of the selection available here. Each comes in a tiny triangular plastic bag, ready for squeezing right onto the food. The red sauce is the Mexican Salsa Valentina™, which is available commercially in bottles.

The green salsa is a creamy *jalapeño* sauce, and the dark brown is a smoky *guajillo* pepper salsa that packs quite a punch. The dark green one, pure jalapeños, will definitely let you know when you've used a little too much.

Finally to the *pambazo*. The origin of this word appears to be from the words *pan* and *basso*, or low-class bread, and refers to simple white rolls. Some sources suggest it means brown bread. It is a specialty of Mexico City. Here, they make it by dipping a *bolillo*, or oval roll, in a red *guajillo* pepper sauce before placing it into a deep fryer to crispen the exterior before filling it with a smearing of refried beans, then the filling of choice. I picked a combination of fajita meat with *al pastor*

meat. It is topped with shredded lettuce, tomatoes, sour cream, *queso fresco* and a whole jalapeño. A more traditional filling would have been chorizo and potatoes, although those options were not available here. Nevertheless, it is a wonderful *torta*.

they

HEAT THEM ON

THE GRIDDLE

before filling them

with the meat of your choosing

341

LOCATION
7551 Bissonnet

PHONE
713-289-0149

HOURS
Mon-Sat: 12:00pm-10:00pm

FOOD
Mexican

PRICES
$

OWNER
Juan Vallejo

STARTED
2004

PAYMENT
Cash only

TAQUERIA VALLEJO

—

This particular truck is famous for its tacos with **salsa *Tlaquepaque***. For an order, they take ten small corn tortillas and briefly heat them on the griddle before filling them with the meat of your choosing.

This truck is owned by Juan Vallejo (hence the name), but Juan's brother Daniel and his wife run it. San Pedro Tlaquepaque, also known as

I also tried the *pirata*, which started with a flour tortilla that Daniel heated on the griddle until it turned a little burned and crispy

Tlaquepaque, is a city in the Mexican state of Jalisco, just outside Guadalajara. According to Wikipedia, the name Tlaquepaque means "place above clay land." The area is famous for pottery and blown glass.

This particular truck is famous for its tacos with salsa *Tlaquepaque*. For an order, they take ten small corn tortillas and briefly heat them on the griddle before filling them with the meat of your choosing. I chose *barbacoa*. Since they use two tortillas for each taco, you end up with five tacos in all. Next they pour over them a rather picante sauce made with tomatillos and *chile de arbol*. There is a lot of sauce used in this dish, so if you don't eat the tacos quickly enough, they will soon become soggy.

I also tried the *pirata*, which started with a flour tortilla that Daniel heated on

TACOS *TLAQUEPAQUE* // *PIRATA* // *GRINGA* HAMBURGUESAS // *GORDITAS* //*TACOS DE TROMPO*

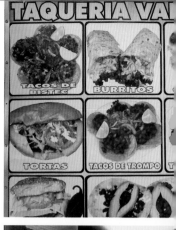

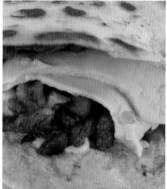

the griddle until it turned a little burned and crispy. He then topped it with

They also serve a *gringa*, which is similar to the *pirata* except that it is made with *al pastor* meat, seasoned pork.

beef fajitas, mozzarella and avocado, before folding it over and serving. It is extremely tasty, and the melted cheese does an excellent job of holding every-thing together.

They also serve a *gringa*, which is simi-lar to the *pirata* except that it is made with *al pastor* meat, or seasoned pork.

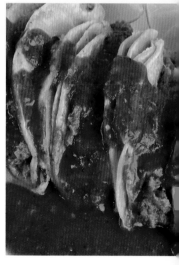

it
IS POSSIBLE
TO PICK THE
whole thing
up in your hands

LOCATION
554 ½ Aldine Mail Route

HOURS
Mon-Sun: 8:00am-9:00pm

FOOD
Mexican

PRICES
$$

STARTED
2009

PAYMENT
Cash only

OWNERS
Angeles

PHONE
832-630-1890

TAQUERIA Y FONDA MICHOACÁN

—

Even the faint possibility of a **dove enchilada** intrigued me so much that I decided to pay a second visit.

The sign on the side of the road said *cabrito en consome*: goat broth. I glanced behind the sign and saw a covered area that suggested outdoor seating, and behind that a food truck. I quickly turned the car around, parked and headed straight for the counter. As I entered the tiny makeshift seating area, I saw another sign on a small frame: "*Birria de Chivo*" (goat stew) and "*Tortillas Hechas a Mano*" (handmade tortillas). After a promising start, things were already looking up.

The menu turned out to be full of interesting dishes such as *sopes*, or thick pieces of *masa*; pork chops; *birria de chivo*; *menudo*; and enchiladas that they claim are *al estilo Tierra Caliente*. When I asked what that meant, the owner, Angeles, told me that it meant they were from Michoacán: The handmade tortillas are dipped in *adobo*, then briefly fried in a skillet, making them *dorado*, or golden in color. She also offered

enchiladas de mole (in a savory sauce), *enchiladas verde* (in a green sauce) and a plate called called *enchiladas con guilota*. I asked what the word "guilota" meant. "*Es una paloma*," said Angeles, meaning: "It's a dove." I found it hard to believe they were making enchiladas out of dove meat.

The bowl of goat broth arrived with a large bone with lots of meat on it, and included the marrow, which was stellar. The marrow had been sitting in the hot soup so long that it literally fell out of the bone. The homemade broth was thin and had a deep orange color, suggesting ample use of chilies. While it was noticeably spicy, it would not be considered hot. There were no vegetables in the broth, only meat, but on the table was a plastic *molcajete*, a bowl-like pestle full of chopped onion, cilantro and two lime wedges. The corn tortillas were homemade and quite thick. The soup was outstanding, and the meat fell off the bone, making it easy to fill the tortillas.

ENCHILADAS DE MOLE // ENCHILADAS VERDE // GOAT STEW // GOAT BROTH // DOVE ENCHILADAS

I also ordered a *sope*, which was also homemade. It is made from *masa* and is quite thick so that it almost looks like an *arepa*, except that *arepas* are filled and the *sope* has the ingredients on top. I had the fajita meat. First was a smearing of refried beans, followed by the meat, shredded lettuce, tomato, *queso fresco*, sour cream and cilantro. Because the *masa* is thick, it is possible to pick the whole thing up in your hands. But it is not crispy, so care must be taken that it does not fall apart.

Even the faint possibility of a dove enchilada intrigued me so much that I decided to pay a second visit. When I turned up again and ordered the *enchilada con guilota*, Angeles asked me twice if I really wanted that. When I insisted that I did, she came down from the truck and went to a refrigerator under the shelter for the small seating area. She pulled a tiny, plastic-wrapped dove out of the freezer and showed me what she was about to prepare: To my surprise, it was, in fact, a dove.

She defrosted the little bird in the microwave, then cooked in the deep fryer, we also ordered a *fajita* taco as well as a chicken *quesadilla* and a *guarache al pastor*. (*Guarache* is an alternate spelling of *Huarache*, a large, thick corn cake made in the shape of a shoe). The *fajita* taco was typical. It was well-seasoned with a lot of meat on it. We heard her making the *guarache* by patting it out and moving the *masa* from hand to hand until she had shaped into the typical long, oval shape reminiscent of the

sole of a shoe – hence its name. The result was a thick piece of *masa*, which she put on the griddle then topped with refried beans, *al pastor* pork, shredded lettuce, tomato, *queso fresco*, avocado and sour cream. The chicken *quesadilla* was superb with lots of gooey, melted cheese on top and a goodly amount of shredded chicken on the bottom.

Then came the dove. Angeles brings these in directly from Michoacán. I had visions of this bird flying down there for the winter, being shot and then finding its way back to Houston in the back of a pickup truck. It appeared in front of me spread-eagled, perched on the very top of the plate, fried to a crisp. There is not a lot of meat on this little thing, which tastes a lot like — wait for it — chicken. (Dark meat, to be precise.) But it was worth the trip, if for the story alone.

The *enchiladas* from Tierra Caliente did not look like any enchilada I'd ever seen before. Angeles told us that she serves what she calls "*enchiladas de Mexico*," which she also described as Tex-Mex *enchiladas*, and those would be the *enchiladas verde*; but the rest of her *enchiladas* use the corn tortillas *doradas*, which she folds in half and layers on the bottom of the plate. The *enchiladas* are served with the same toppings as most of the other dishes here: shredded lettuce, tomatoes, radish and *jalapeño* slices, *queso fresco* and avocado. They also include homestyle potatoes, which have been seasoned and fried with onions.

the

SINGLE, LARGE FILET

of catfish

had a cornmeal coating, fried to a crisp

THE LUNCH BAG

—

She co-owned a restaurant called Blu Monday Café downtown, but the partnership didn't work out, so she decided to open what she calls **"a kitchen on wheels."**

After 18 years of working in the field of mental health, Autherine Smith decided to change careers. "After working 24/7 for so long," she said, "I decided I wanted to try something new. Since I practically grew up in the food business, with all of my family owning different

It was excellent. The batter tasted nicely of garlic. You can also get the pork chop sandwich with a fried egg.

cafés, I knew that's where I would end up." She co-owned a restaurant called Blu Monday Café downtown, but the partnership didn't work out, so she de-

cided to open what she calls "a kitchen on wheels." She calls her truck the "mobile kitchen that cooks like home." She also delivers.

I tried the pork chop sandwich, which consists of a bone-in pork chop on a standard-looking bun, which she covers in mayo and lettuce and tomato. It was excellent. The batter tasted nicely of garlic. You can also get the pork chop sandwich with a fried egg. I also tried the catfish po-boy, which she serves on either a regular or whole-wheat hoagie. The single, large filet of catfish had a cornmeal coating, fried

PORK CHOP SANDWICH // CATFISH PO-BOY // FISH AND FRIES // FISH TACOS // FRIED-EGG SANDWICH

to a crisp. It, too, is served with mayo, lettuce and tomato.

Her menu includes fish and fries as well as fish tacos. She can prepare anything from blackened filet of tilapia to something as comforting as a simple fried-egg sandwich. In addition, Autherine does catering and event planning, and the brochure she uses to promote her

She can prepare anything from blackened filet of tilapia to something as comforting as a simple fried-egg sandwich.

business lists hors d'oeuvres, such as bacon-wrapped shrimp, crab puffs and lobster dip. Maybe one day she'll try these out in her truck as well.

※ *he tops* ※

THIS WITH

PICKLED RED

onions and

a slice of green apple for crispness

LOCATION
Various

HOURS
Various

FOOD
Asian/American fusion

PRICES
$

STARTED
2011

PAYMENT
Cash only

PHONE
713-550-3823

OWNER
Josh Martinez

FACEBOOK
/The-modular/112541498836694?sk=wall

THE MODULAR

—

"We spent a lot of time on the name of the truck," said Josh. '**Modular**' refers to modern cooking techniques and also to molecular cooking.

Josh Martinez has a great brick-and-mortar resumé. Josh is currently the general manager at Kata Robata. He previously owned a wine bar in Kansas City and worked at Kenichi, one of the best sushi restaurants in Austin, as well as with the Truluck's group. Together with Benjamin Rabbani, a chef with experience including Stella Sola and Bootsie's, under Randy Rucker, they have crafted a menu that would be intriguing in a posh restaurant but is unheard-of in a food truck.

"We spent a lot of time on the name of the truck," said Josh. "'Modular' refers to modern cooking techniques and also to molecular cooking." For example, all of the protein they're preparing is cooked *sous vide* – a method of cooking that involves sealing food in a vacuum-packed bag, then slow-cooking it in a low- temperature water bath.

The pork belly cooks for 48 hours; the chicken takes between eight and twelve. This cooking process gives the meats — pork, chicken and duck — a smooth and very tender texture, not to mention a deep flavor. "I actually don't add anything to the meat while it's cooking," said Josh. "The juices from the meat add all the flavor, and since the juices have nowhere to go other than back into the meat, it is very flavorful."

The first dish I tried was the crispy tuna *poke* tacos. *Poke*, pronounced poh-kay, is a traditional Hawaiian way of cutting raw fish into tiny bits and then seasoning them. The mini taco shells are made from *gyasa* skins (used to make wontons) and are exceptionally crispy. It is the filling, however, that most deserves attention. Tiny cubes of sashimi-grade fresh ahi tuna are combined with green onions, black sesame

CRISPY TUNA *POKE* TACOS // PORK BELLY UP // SHRIMP AND GRITS // THAT CHICKEN GOT THIGHS

seeds, tamari soy sauce and sesame and chile oils. Josh then tops the three mini-tacos with a *wasabi-Kewpie*™ mayo. (*Kewpie* is a popular brand of Japanese mayo.) The result is so tasty that one order may not suffice.

Next was the Pork Belly Up, which involves a good-sized slice of pork belly finished in a pan with *yakitori* sauce to form a nice glaze. Josh tops this with pickled red onions and a slice of green apple for crispness.

His shrimp and grits are among the best I've tried anywhere. For his shrimp, Josh uses a hard-to-find seasonal French pepper called an *espellete*, from southwestern France, near the Spanish border. The shrimp are well seasoned and sit on a bed of coarse-ground yellow grits, which come from the Homestead Gristmill in Waco. Josh makes the grits with whole milk from the Way Back When Dairy, just outside Austin. The grits have a wonderful texture, creamy and coarse at the same time.

The last dish we tried was That Chicken Got Thighs: chicken thighs that are also finished in the pan with *yakitori* sauce and topped with chicken crackling. Josh makes the crackling by taking chicken skin, removing the fat and dehydrating it until it becomes incredibly crispy and tasty. He also tops it with pickled

cucumber and radish and peanuts for added texture. This is exciting street food, and we can't wait to see what Josh will cook up in the future.

The theme of this truck is "bringing the restaurant to a parking lot near you." They're doing that exceptionally well.

✦ **the** ✦

CHUNKS ARE

LARGE, WHICH

means that

you're getting more meat than batter

LOCATION
Various

PHONE
832-643-7994

HOURS
Various

FOOD
Chinese

PRICES
$$

OWNER
John Peterson, Arthur Wentworth

STARTED
2011

PAYMENT
All

WEBSITE
riceboxtruck.com

FACEBOOK
/pages/The-Rice-Box-Truck/1405595
29385589?ref=ts&sk=info

TWITTER
/#!/RICEBOXTRUCK

THE RICE BOX

—

"We are both big fans of **Asian food**, and we both have a passion for our product".

John Peterson speaks Mandarin. He studied it at the University of Houston and spent a summer in Beijing. Now he's running Houston's first Chinese food truck.

And what a beautifully decorated truck it is. John had previously worked in the automotive industry (in tune-ups, to be precise), so he knew his way around. He also did all the work on the truck himself: design, build-out and decoration.

At present they offer the dishes that you would find at any American Chinese restaurant. But three things set them apart.

The truck is painted in traditional Chinese colors — bright red with black and gold accents — and decked out with Chinese pendants and paper lanterns. All the lettering on the truck is in a stylized Asian font. On the front of the truck is the phrase: "Powered by Rice." On the serving counter, you will find a golden *Doomba* figure. (More on that later.)

"I have always been such a big fan of Asian food, and I have a real passion for my product," said John. At present he offers the dishes that you would find at any American Chinese restaurant. But three things set him apart. First, the food is very high-quality. Second, they make all their sauces from scratch. And third, the portions are huge.

The first dish I tried was General Tso's chicken. Large chunks of chicken are coated in a batter, then fried, tossed with dried red peppers and served on a bed of rice. A sweet and savory sauce is poured on top. It's served, like all their dishes, in a traditional Chinese take-out box.

The first thing you notice about the chicken is that the chunks are large, which means that you're getting more meat than batter. The second thing you notice is that the chicken has no fat or additional strange pieces on it: It's pure meat. This makes it a pleasure to eat. As with all the dishes served here, you also get

EGG ROLLS // SWEET-AND-SOUR CHICKEN // GOLDEN *DOOMBA* // GENERAL TSO'S CHICKEN

an egg roll with every meal. The egg rolls are from Houston's own Lee's Eggroll Company.

The next dish I tried was called Golden *Doomba*. "*Doomba* was a nickname that I was given many years ago," John explained. "It's also my Twitter handle, as well as the golden bull figure on the serving counter." For this dish, he takes chicken drumsticks and coats them in a batter made of potato starch, flour, water and

Since you're eating the dish as it comes off the griddle, the flavors are exceptionally fresh and vibrant.

Asian spices before frying. The drumsticks are served over rice with a sauce made of ginger, soy, vinegar and scallions that John prepares fresh for each customer.

The last dish I tried was the sweet-and-sour chicken. Large chunks of chicken are dipped in the homemade batter, then fried on the griddle with chunks of pineapple, onions, green bell peppers, thin slices of cabbage and celery. John's sauce consists of rice wine vinegar, garlic, sugar, ginger and a few secret ingredients. Since you're eating the dish as it comes off the griddle, the flavors are exceptionally fresh and vibrant.

the

SAVORY CHICKEN

AND THE SWEET

and smoky sauce

a combination that works remarkably well.

LOCATION
Various

FOOD
Gourmet waffles

PRICES
$$

PAYMENT
All

STARTED
2011

OWNER
Phi Nguyen

FACEBOOK
/thewafflebus

TWITTER
/thewafflebus

PHONE
832-640-5494

WEBSITE
thewafflebus.com

SPECIAL SERVICES
Catering

THE WAFFLE BUS

——

Since this is street food, I turned the **waffle** into a sandwich.

Phi Nguyen may have been born in the Philippines but he was quick to point out to me that he is Vietnamese and grew up in Houston. He was in the IT business but got laid off and couldn't find a job for a year. "It was either: continue in the corporate world or follow my dream," said Phi. We're glad he decided to follow his dream. "I went to LA and NY and visited a lot of trucks to see how they did things," Phi told me. "I wanted to bring something totally different to Houston, something Houston did not already have on its streets, so I settled on waffles. I did not want to do just the same old waffles with just different toppings. Since this is street food, I turned the waffle into a sandwich," added Phi. And what a great series of sandwiches he has designed!

Phi has crafted an extremely creative menu – one that will please even the most jaded of foodies and one that makes it very hard to choose what to have. As you read the first description on the menu, you are tempted to stop

right there, but then you read the next and the next until you reach the bottom of the menu and still haven't decided.

It's easy to see that Phi is quite the perfectionist. Not only has he paired ingredients in a creative way, he has also perfected the homemade batter he uses for the waffles." I went through hundreds and hundreds of different batters and months of research until I got it just right – crispy on the outside and light and airy on the inside. I did not want a dense waffle because that would detract from the fillings," said Phi.

No amount of coaxing would get Phi even to hint at his waffle batter recipe. Understandably, it is a closely-guarded trade secret. The first one I tried was the Smoked Salmon Waffle. The freshly-made, golden-brown waffle was first smeared with some lemon-caper cream cheese, then filled with slices of smoked salmon along with baby spinach leaves and slices of tomatoes which have drizzled with some balsamic vinegar. The crispy and

SMOKED SALMON WAFFLE // WAFFLE FRYDERS //
DESSERT WAFFLES // CHICKEN AND WAFFLE //

crunchy exterior of the waffle soon gave way to a wonderfully soft interior and when the salmon hit my tastes buds along with a hint of lemon, balsamic and capers, it brought back vivid memories of some of the best lox and bagels I've eaten in NYC.

On my next visit, I tried the waffle sandwich that has many in Houston talking, the Chicken and Waffle. Phi marinates a chicken breast in a butter-milk brine for twenty-four hours. What this does is to ensure that the breast is particularly moist and juicy. A quick dip in some seasoned flour batter (you know he wasn't going to tell me what's in it, didn't you?) followed by a few minutes in the fryer. I was asked what sauce I would like with it. When I asked what kind they recommended, the answer from the truck came in unison: "*Ancho* chile, honey butter". It was most definitely the right choice, adding a slight smokiness and just the right amount of sweetness to the sandwich. The savory chicken and the sweet and smoky sauce is a combina-tion that works remarkably well.

Phi also invented something he calls Waffle Fryders. They are his take on sliders. Instead of merely buying a pre-seasoned patty, he grinds his own meat and seasons it directly on the grill. When almost cooked, he tops it with a slice of American cheese. He smears

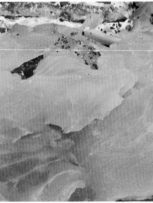

the waffle fries with a spicy mayo, which he makes by adding Sriracha™ sauce to mayonnaise. The patty gets cut into four and sandwiched between the very crispy waffle fries. It's a great combination and could give new meaning to burger and fries.

Phi also makes sweet or dessert waffles. Phi's favorite, (and now mine as well) The Strawberry Irish Cream *Crème Brulée*. He starts out by mak-ing a typical *crème brulée* filling and spikes it with a noticeable amount of Irish Cream liqueur. They spread a goodly amount of this on the waffle and top it with some sugar, which is then flamed to caramelize it. It is stuffed with slices of fresh strawberries before it is folded in half and sprinkled with confectioner's sugar. The groans start as you take your first bite and don't end until you've finished it. It is a remarkable waffle whose taste remains with you for quite a while.

✦ a ✦

COARSE-GROUND

BEEF LINK

with plenty

of well-seasoned flavor

LOCATION
12803 Hiram Clarke

PHONE
832-875-9951

HOURS
Tue-Wed: 10:30am-8:30pm, Thur:
10:30am-9:00pm, Fri: 10:30am-
10:00pm, Sat: 10:30am-1:00am

FOOD
Barbecue

PRICES
$$

OWNER
Charles Wilson

PAYMENT
All

SPECIAL SERVICES
Catering

STARTED
1996

FACEBOOK
/home.php#!/pages/Two-Brothers-
Smokin-Oak-Kitchen/231426830871

TWO BROTHERS SMOKIN' OAK KITCHEN

—

His **love and passion** is barbecue. What-ever I thought of his barbecue, he said, "It's never good enough for me."

According to the City of Houston records, this is one of the oldest con-tinuously operating trucks in Houston. Charles Wilson and his brother, Elton, started out on the corner of Ennis and Cleburne near the campus of Texas Southern University. I'd tried one of their brisket sandwiches years ago, when they were at their old location, but when I tried to locate them again for this book, I was at first unable to find them. One day, while driving in Katy, I spotted a BBQ truck with the name Two Brothers, and I was convinced that that's where they had ended up. The truck was closed, just as it was every subsequent time I vis-ited. I began to think I was out of luck when the name Two Brothers showed up on the list of trucks registered with the City of Houston. This time, I had an address on Hiram Clarke.

Elton left the business in 2004 to pursue other interests, and Charles moved to his current location in 2005, when the owner of the building on Ennis

"This ain't the place to be if you don't like spice," said Charles.

wanted to change the building and the parking lot where the truck used to operate. Charles Junior now works the truck with his father, Charles Senior, a retired Metro bus driver. His love and passion is barbecue. Whatever I

BARBECUED BRISKET // BARBECUED SAUSAGE

thought of his barbecue, he said, "It's never good enough for me."

It's hard to describe the feeling I had when I tried Two Brothers again after so many years. One bite of the brisket revealed the slow cooking that Charles puts it through. The pink smoke ring so sought after by BBQ aficionados was there in all its glory. So was the fat. "I always cook my brisket with all the fat on it and with the fat on top, so that it just seeps through the meat and makes it juicy and tender," said Charles. That's exactly how the meat was: juicy, tender and extremely smoky.

Charles led me to the end of his trailer, where his pit and smoke box are located. "There's my baby," he said. He uses a special dry rub on his brisket before it spends 14 or 15 hours at 250 degrees. That dry rub is one of the things that sets Charles's brisket apart from others; you taste it on the first bite. "This ain't the place to be if you don't like spice," said Charles.

The seasonings he uses are so secret that he wouldn't let me anywhere near the inside of the truck lest I give them away. In fact, I was honored that he let me photograph his "baby." The sausage he cooks is a coarse-ground beef link with plenty of flavor, and the

ribs are also well-seasoned, thanks to that dry rub. Charles cuts the ribs into bite-size pieces before serving, and they are superb. The potato salad and beans are good, though not homemade, and the barbecue sauce, though thin, is tasty.

The unmistakable taste of smoke permeates all his meats. When you buy a platter, it is so full that no more will fit in the Styrofoam container. We should all be grateful that Charles Junior is following in his father's footsteps.

i

STARTED TO MIX

THE CHOCOLATE ICE

with the ice cream

to form a creamy, icy concoction

LOCATION
Various

HOURS
Various

FOOD
Sno cones, hot dogs, nachos,
Frito pies

PRICES
$

OWNER
Spencer Gauthier

STARTED
2010

PAYMENT
Cash only

PHONE
832-221-2864

SPECIAL SERVICES
Catering

WEBSITE
unclepoppasnewolreansstyles-
noballs.vpweb.com/

UNCLE POPPA'S NEW ORLEANS STYLE SNO-CONES

—

A few minutes later I was digging into a terrifically creamy sno-cone like there was no tomorrow. I wondered whether a liquid chocolate flavor would taste artificial. **Absolutely not.**

This is one of the newest and shiniest trailers I found. I visited it twice, and on both occasions, it was spotless. Its bright green color also makes it hard

The Frito pie uses the same chili and cheese as the hot dog, but this time they're on top of crunchy Fritos®.

to miss. Since this was my second experience with sno-cones, I knew how to order. The only question was, which flavor? I saw two flavor offerings I had not come across before: chocolate

and orange, so I asked Spencer what he thought I should have. "Chocolate stuffed with vanilla ice cream and condensed milk," he said, and I did not hesitate one moment. A few minutes later I was digging into a terrifically creamy sno-cone like there was no tomorrow. I wondered whether a liquid chocolate flavor would taste artificial. Absolutely not. It had a rich chocolatey taste. When I met the vanilla ice cream, about halfway down the Styrofoam cup, I started to mix the chocolate ice with the ice cream to form a creamy, icy

concoction, which was not only tasty and refreshing, but incredibly rich as well.

The first time we met Spencer, he was serving only sno-cones, so we had to plan another visit to try his hot food. That occurred a few weeks later.

Sometimes you just want some old-fashioned comfort food with no pretensions, no fancy name, no fancy ingredients. That's where Spencer's hot dog and Frito pie come in. The dog is on a standard bun, which contains a boiled sausage along with chili and gloppy cheese. It hit the spot perfectly. The Frito pie uses the same chili and cheese as the hot dog, but this time they're on top of crunchy Fritos®. Spencer is not shy about using either the chili or the cheese.

> **{ a }**
>
> # CHOCOLATE CREAM
>
> # CREAM CHEESE ICING,
>
> ## to which chocolate
>
> ## sprinkles have been added

LOCATION
1123 Yale

PHONE
713-594-8685

HOURS
Various

FOOD
Cupcakes

PRICES
$

OWNERS
Millie Wallace

STARTED
2010

PAYMENT
Cash only

SPECIAL SERVICES
Catering

TWITTER
/whatupcupcake

FACEBOOK
/pages/Whats-Up-Cup-
cake/173004882732096

WEBSITE
whatsupcupcakehouston.com

WHAT'S UP CUPCAKES

—

The trailer itself is a beauty, a 1950s-era **Boles Aero**, with lots of chrome and a beautiful, classic design.

When Yvonne Cavazos started the What's Up Cupcakes trailer in 2011, it was one of the first trailers to sell cupcakes in Houston. Since Yvonne also has a full-time job, she decided toward the end of the year to sell the truck, including her recipes, to Millie Wallace, a former teacher who loves to cook.

The trailer itself is a beauty, a 1950s-era Boles Aero, with lots of chrome and a beautiful, classic design. I'd heard that Yvonne had sold it, and was delighted to spot it and its new owner one day as I was driving in the Heights.

Millie does not bake the cupcakes on the truck. She bakes them in a commercial kitchen, then transports them to the truck, where she sells them.

There's also a feel-good aspect to buying Millie's cupcakes. Millie is a recovering alcoholic, and she employs other recovering addicts. In addition, a portion of the proceeds from the business goes to an animal shelter. All of her cupcakes are made with organic ingredients, and she buys as many of her supplies locally as she can.

I tried the chocolate truffle, the peanut butter and the red velvet. The chocolate truffle is topped with a chocolate cream cheese icing, to which choco-

Millie puts a chocolate truffle into the molten cup cake when it comes out of the oven so that it falls to the bottom of and melts.

late sprinkles have been added. This delectable cupcake also hides a surprise when you reach the bottom. Millie puts a chocolate truffle into the molten cup cake

CHOCOLATE TRUFFLE CUPCAKES // PEANUT
BUTTER CUPCAKES // RED VELVET CUPCAKES

when it comes out of the oven so that it falls to the bottom and melts, except for a small piece which remains almost intact and firm and is an absolute pleasure to eat. It's a nice finish to a fine cupcake. The same is true of the peanut butter cupcake, which has a Reese's Pieces™ in the middle of it. It, too, is topped with a cream cheese, butter-cream icing, to which peanut butter has been added. A smattering of pink and red sprinkles on top adds a dash of color. The red velvet cupcake is deep red, with a vanilla-flavored cream cheese icing. The same pink and red sprinkles she uses for the peanut butter cupcake are used here, but don't hold Millie to the sprinkles. As she told me "We use whatever we feel like."

your FIRST BITE INTO IT, YOU you get

an explosion of different flavors

LOCATION
Various

PHONE
713-897 8272

HOURS
Various

FOOD
Asian fusion

PRICES
$

OWNER
Spectrum Catering

STARTED
2011

PAYMENT
All

SPECIAL SERVICES
Catering

WEBSITE
wickedwhiskcatering.com/

FACEBOOK
/pages/Wicked-
Whisk/237732012928769

TWITTER
/wicked_food

THE WICKED WHISK

—

The *Bolillo* is stuffed with pulled pork that has been braised in **St. Arnold's Santo** beer, a dark, malty brew.

The Wicked Whisk food truck is the brainchild of Executive Head Chef Jay Stone, who was hired a couple of years ago by Spectrum Catering and Concessions, a company with over 20 years' experience in the event and hospitality industry. Jay was hired to revamp their entire menu and to bring the catering experience to Houston by way of a food truck.

He has just taken the food truck experience to a whole new level, creating Asian-inspired dishes unsurpassed in Houston. Jay is originally from Nebraska and has been in the business for over twenty years. He gained a lot of experience working in Scottsdale at country clubs and at restaurants such as Boa. He also spent time on the road with Cirque Du Soleil, preparing food for VIPs and the like. The truck is built on a Mercedes delivery base, and although it appears quite compact, it is surprisingly roomy inside and contains everything they need to turn out some outstanding dishes.

On my first visit, I tried two dishes that have won accolades online. The *Bolillo* is stuffed with pulled pork that has been braised in St. Arnold's Santo beer, a dark, malty brew. Fried plantains,

It all hits you at once and rather than one flavor dominating, the mélange of flavors all work together to create a wonderful experience.

cooked until they are caramelized, fall apart and yield all their sweetness, line the bottom of the roll. This is followed by the pork, which is topped with a homemade *ancho-aioli* and some shredded smoked Cheddar cheese.

When you first bite into it, you get an explosion of different flavors –the sweetness of the plantains, the pork, the cheese and the spike of the *aioli*. It all hits you at once and rather than one flavor dominating, the mélange of flavors all work together to create a wonderful experience.

Next was the *Kimchi* Fried Chicken Wings. "We use a *mochiko* breading, which is sweet rice flour. We then fry and dust them with some dried *kimchi*. The *kimchi* takes fifteen hours to dehydrate. When it's finished, I add some Korean peppers and a touch of

"We use a *mochiko* breading, which is sweet rice flour. We then fry and dust them with some dried *kimchi*

nutmeg," said Jay. Six wings are served in a paper bucket. We also tried the Wicked Chips, wafer thin, hand-cut potato chips that have been fried until they're extra crispy and topped with more of the *kimchi* dust. Jay confessed his love affair with Korean food, which influences his cuisine, was inspired by his Korean wife.

Another influence for one of his dishes was the time he spent in Canada with the Cirque Du Soleil. *Poutine* is Canadian national junk food," said Jay. Indeed it is. It's very easy to find there since almost everyone serves it. It's French fries with gravy and cheddar cheese curds plus any other ingredient they feel like putting on them. Jay puts his own

twist on this classic. Instead of Cheddar cheese curds, he uses Maytag blue cheese crumbles which melt all over the fries, giving them a nice tangy taste. The traditional brown gravy is replaced with a porter beer *demiglace*, which is poured on top and settles on the bottom of the plate making the bottom layer of fries soggy. Fret not, since this is all part of the experience - plus the fries on top remain crispy. The fries are hand-cut and have the skin on. Chopped green onions and applewood-smoked *lardons* (thick chunks of bacon) round out the dish and make it quite a substantial meal.

With a name like the Texas Melt, you might imagine this burger would have lots of cheese on it. You would be wrong. The melt comes in the form of peanut butter, a large scoop of which is placed on top of the patty. Now I can already hear you say, "Oh no, not

He uses Maytag blue cheese crumbles which melt all over the fries, giving them a nice tangy taste.

another one of those 'creative chefs' that will mix any ingredient together just for effect". Don't worry, I was in the exact same place until I took my first bite. Now, peanut butter alone does not make for the best ingredient in a burger but, when mixed with the heat of a neon-green, home-made *jalapeño* jelly – now we're talking. Sweet, salty and hot! I hit the trifecta of flavors. Here you have Jay's rendition of a PB&J burger. Add that to a half-pound (and that's

AFTER cooking) of Angus beef with an 80/20 blend of meat to fat, made fresh daily and hand-formed into a thick patty. Put all of this on a Sheila Partin's Bakery *jalapeño* cheese bun, which already has sweetness and a little heat

With a name like the Texas Melt, you might imagine this burger would have lots of cheese on it. You would be wrong. The melt comes in the form of peanut butter, a large scoop of which is placed on top of the patty

built in, then add a couple of thick-cut slices of applewood-smoked bacon and then tell me it's not one of the tastiest burgers you've ever had, not to mention how gorgeous it is just to look at. The outside of the burger was well charred yet the inside was cooked exactly as I like it, medium rare. It's a messy burger to eat but one definitely worth every messy bite.

Jay told me the story behind the next dish I tried, the '*Chapagetti*'. "This is a late night Korean junk food fix that became famous when all the Korean soap operas showed people coming home from working late and fixing this dish." The name comes from the *cha-jang* (udon) noodles used in this dish, crossed with the word spaghetti. Jay likens the dish to Ramen noodles. He takes fully-cooked noodles out of a bag and tosses them in a wok along with a sweet black bean sauce, which he makes with *mirin*, (Japanese rice wine),

BOLILLO // *KIMCHI* FRIED CHICKEN WINGS
WICKED CHIPS // *POUTINE* // TEXAS MELT

sugar and water. He also adds very finely diced carrots, zucchini, onion and chicken. Sesame seeds and chopped

The outside of the burger was well charred yet the inside was cooked exactly as I like it, medium rare. It's a messy burger to eat but one definitely worth every messy bite.

scallions are used to top off the dish. The sauce colors the noodles black and the result reminds me of squid ink *risotto*. The taste is an interesting mix of bean paste with a sweetness coming from the sugar and *mirin*. This is a fascinating dish that sells out quickly whenever it's on the menu.

he

DIPS A

COOKIE INTO

malted

vanilla waffle batter

LOCATION
Various

FOOD
American

PRICES
$

STARTED
2010

PAYMENT
All

OWNER
Jason Kerr

SPECIAL SERVICES
Catering

FACEBOOK
/zillastreeteats

WEBSITE
zillastreeteats.com/

TWITTER
zillastreeteats.com/

ZILLA STREET EATS

—

"We wanted to **create a monster**," he said, "and I think we succeeded." The monster, of course, is the fire-breathing Godzilla-like monster on the side of his truck, devouring the city.

"It was an old Doritos™ delivery truck that we found and had converted in Florida," said Jason Kerr of his Zilla truck. I asked what was behind the name. "We wanted to create a

You will often find Jason's truck at the Wednesday farmers' market in front of City Hall. One of the items that he makes only when he's there is the Big Al Sandwich, which he makes using only local ingredients.

monster," he said, "and I think we succeeded." The monster, of course, is the fire-breathing Godzilla-like monster on the side of his truck, devouring the city.

Jason has had a long and distinguished career in Houston, both a chef and contributor to the Houston Press. He has worked at the now-defunct Zula, as well as at t'afia and Café Rabelais. He also consulted on the menu and kitchen at the champagne bar Cha.

You will often find Jason's truck at the Wednesday farmers' market in front of City Hall. One of the items that he makes only when he's there is the Big Al Sandwich, which he makes using only local ingredients. The roll is from Kraftsmen Baking, the arugula

from Animal Farm, and the sausage from Harrison Hog Farm. He stews the sausage along with onions and jalapeños in St. Arnold's Amber beer. The Ghost Pepper Jack cheese is from Pola Cheese.

Another item that Jason has developed a reputation for is the fried Nutter Butters. "I was going to develop a series of different things to fry," he said, "but

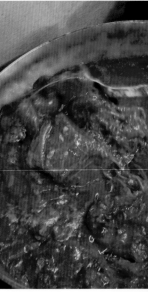

Another item that Jason has developed a reputation for is the fried Nutter Butters™. "I was going to develop a series of different things to fry," he said, "but these tasted so good, I thought I'd just perfect them.

these tasted so good, I thought I'd just perfect them." He dips a Nutter Butter™ cookie into malted vanilla waffle batter, then briefly deep fries it. He eliminates any grease with paper towel before dusting the concoction with confectioner's sugar and serving it with syrup — the same syrup he uses for his chicken and waffles. Biting into one, you can definitely taste the vanilla in the batter as well as the peanut butter in the cookie. It's a decadent treat, worth every calorie.

A

A la parilla	grilled
A la plancha	on the griddle
Adobo	sauce, marinade or seasoning
Agua frescas	cold waters. Combination of blended fruits and water.
Aguacate	avocado
Ahumada	smoked
Aji	hot pepper
Al Pastor	shepherd style. Derived from doner kebab style of cooking
Alambres	mix of grilled onions, steak, sausage, chorizo , cheese
Almuerzo	lunch
Amarillo	yellow
Antojitos	little cravings or snacks
Arepa	corn cake
Arroz	rice
Asado	roasted
Asador	grill
Atole	thick, corn-based drink

B

Bacalhau	Portuguese word for salted, dried codfish. Considered as national dish of Portugal
Banh Mi	Vietnamese sandwich made with a crusty French roll, various meats, carrot and cucumber strips, jalapeno and mayo
Baklava	layers of filo pastry filled with chopped nuts and sweetened with syrup or honey
Baleada mixta	Honduran specialty. Thick, wheat flour tortilla stuffed with eggs, *chicharron* and cheese
Barbacoa	cow's cheek
Batido	Also *Liquado*. Drink similar to a smoothie
Bhaji	curry
Bhel Puri	puffed rice smack with potatoes and tamarind sauce from Mumbai
Birria	stew made with goat and sometimes lamb
Bistek	steak
Blanco	white

Bo Luc Lak	Vietnamese Shaking Beef served with rice and watercress. The name refers to the constant shaking of the wok required during cooking
Bolillo	roll
Borracho beans	drunken pinto beans made with beer
Borrego	lamb
Bote	can
Boti	meat from the leg, shank or thigh
Boudin	Cajun sausage filled with spicy rice dressing
Buche	pig's esophagus
Burrito	Mexican filled flour tortilla, Typically refried beans, rice and some kind of protein
Burros	abbreviation for burritos

C

Cabeza	head
Cabrito	goat
Cachapas	Venezuelan corn patty filled with cheese

Cachete	beef cheek	**Carnitas**	Mexican roasted and fried pork
Cajet	caramel made from condensed milk	**Catracho**	slang for someone from Honduras.
Calabasitas	small squash	**Cazon**	shark
Caldo	soup	**Cebolla**	onion
Caldo de res	beef soup	**Cebolla encurtida**	pickled onions
Camaron	shrimp	**Cesina**	thin beef steak
Campechana	Mexican seafood cocktail with oysters, octopus, mussels, shrimp, squid in a tomato-based sauce	**Chaat**	spicy Indian street snack made from variety of ingredients
Campechano	mixture of beef and *chorizo*	**Chamoyada**	savory sauce made from pickled fruit, used in *raspas*
Capitalina	a sandwich from the capital, Mexico City , consisting of ham, sausage, tomato, avocado, refried beans, mayo	**Champurrado**	chocolate-based *atole* drink made with hominy flour
Caracol	conch	**Chana**	chickpeas
Caraotas	black beans	**Charga**	Pakistani spice mix used to coat chicken before frying
Carnaza	low-grade meat. (It seems strange that a truck would advertise this, however, this is the only definition I could find)	**Charro Beans**	soupy pinto beans A.K.A. cowboy beans
		Cheveres	hot dogs
		Chicharron	pork crackling
Carne	meat or beef	**Chicharron Preparado**	crunchy corn and wheat flour puff layered with shredded cabbage, avocado, queso fresco, sour cream, salsa
Carne asada	grilled meat		
Carne mechada	shredded beef skirt		
Carne molida	ground beef		

Chicken saagwala	Indian curry made with spinach and chicken
Chicken Tikka Masala	curry dish of roasted chicken chunks in a red or orange-colored sauce
Chico	small
Chilango style	Mexico city style
Chilaquiles	corn tortillas cut in quarters and fried, salsa is added along with eggs and pulled chicken then topped with cheese
Chile de arbol	bright red, thin, long chili pepper
Chiltepe	Guatemalan hot pepper
Chipotle	smoked, dried jalapeño
Chivo	baby goat
Chorizo	Mexican sausage
Chouriço	Portuguese pork sausage made with paprika, garlic, black pepper
Chuchita	Guatemalan tamale
Chuleta	pork chop
Churro	long, ridged pieces of fried dough with a donut consistency
Chuzo	Colombian kebab
Chuzo	kebab

Cochinita Pibil	suckling pig marinated in citrus juice wrapped in banana leaf then roasted
Cocktel	cocktail
Coco	coconut
Coltillo	knife
Comer	to eat
Comida	food
Consome	thin soup
Cordero	lamb
Cortado	chopped cabbage in Guatemala used to top many dishes
Costillas	ribs
Crema	sour cream
Cuchara	spoon
Cueritos	pickled pig skins
Cueros	pig's skin
Curtido	pickled cabbage, jalapeños, onions and carrots popular in central America

D

Daal	also 'dal', lentils
Dabeli	spicy Indian potato patty served on bun
Dahi	yoghurt

Dahi Puri	Indian mini pastry shells filled with savory chickpeas, potatoes, yogurt
Dal	also 'daal', lentils
Desayuno	breakfast
Desebrada	shredded
Desi	people from the Indian sub-continent
Dhaba	small, roadside restaurants in India and Pakistan
Diablitos	a spicy flavoring for shaved ice
Doblada	doubled. Refers ro a tortilla that has been doubled over and stuffed
Doble	double
Dorada	golden
Dorilocos	snack made with Doritos™ similar to a Frito™ Pie
Dulce	sweet

E

Elote	roasted corn on the cob
Empanada	filled pastry pocket
Entero	full, whole

F

Falafel	fried patty made from ground chickpeas and/or fava beans
Feijoiada	Portuguese stew of beans with beef and pork. Considered as Brazilian national dish
Flan	crème caramel
Flauta	flute. A flour tortilla that is rolled up around a filling and deep fried
Fresa	strawberry
Frijoles	beans
Frijoles criollos	black beans
Frito	fried
Fruta	fruit
Fufu	yam flour

G

Garnachas	stuffed, crispy corn tortilla similar to a *gordita*
Gola	Indian ice candy
Gordita	fatty. A small, thick Mexican corn cake similar to an *arepa*
Gram flour	flour made from ground chickpeas

Grande	large
Gringa	type of corn or flour tortilla taco filled with meat and cheese
Grosella	red currant
Guajillo chile	chile with a deep-red flesh, normally dried
Guarache	also *Huarache*. Flat heeled sandle. Flat corn cake
Guasacaca	guacamole (Venezuela)
Guayaba	guava
Guilota	dove
Guisada	stewed

H

Hallaca	Venezuelan tamale popular for Christmas
Hamburguesa	hamburger
Harina	flour
Higado	liver
Hongo	mushroom
Horchata	traditional Mexican drink made of ground rice, sugar and cinnamon
Huarache	also *Guarache*. Flat heeled sandle. Thick corn cake

Huevo	egg
Huevos	eggs
Hummus	chickpea dip

J

Jamaica	hibiscus
Jamon	ham
Jericalla	cinnamon egg custard from Guadalajara

K

Kadal	village in Nepal
Kala Khatta	tangy flavored syrup poured over crushed ice in Indian drink to make a *gola*
Korma	curry made with yogurt or coconut milk

L

Labios	lips
Lata	can
Lechera	condensed milk. Brand name belonging to Nestle™.
Lechoza	papaya
Lechuga	lettuce

Lengua	tongue
Limonada	lemonade
Liquado	Also *Batido*. Drink similar to a smoothie
Lonche	lunch
Loncheros	typical food truck that caters to workers at construction sites, especially for lunch
Longaniza	sausage, similar to *chorizo* but spicier and meat more coarsely cut

M

Machacado	dried shredded beef
Machito	goat
Maiz	corn
Makhni	buttery mix of butter and yogurt
Mango	mango
Marañon	tropical fruit whose seed is the cashew nut
Masa	flour, normally corn
Masala	mixture (of spices)
Mattar	also 'mutter', peas
Mayonesa	mayonnaise
Mechada	pulled
Mediano	medium
Medio	half

Melon	melon
Menudo	tripe soup
Milanesa	breaded meat
Mirinda	an orange-flavored drink sold in Central America
Mixto	mixed
Molcajete	traditional Mexican mortar and pestle made from volcanic rock
Mole	savory, thick Mexican sauce made with chocolate
Molida	ground
Mollejas	sweetbreads
Mondongo	tripe soup in Central America AKA *menudo* in Mexico
Mora	blackberry
Mutter	also '*mattar*', peas

N

Naan	Indian flatbread
Naranja	orange
Natilla	egg custard
Nopales	cactus leaves
Nopalitos	small cactus leaves
Nori	dried seaweed

O

Orejas	ears

P

Pabellon	stewed meat, rice and beans. Venezuelan national dish
Pacaya	*pacaya* palm
Pache	Guatemalan tamale specially for Christmas, wrapped in a banana leaf
Paleta	small stick. Fruit popsicle
Paleteria	stand selling fruit popsicles
Pastelito	half-moon shaped stuffed pastry
Patelito de perro	Honduran beef-stuffed pastry made of corn flour
Pambazo	dipped sandwiches (Mexico)
Pan	bread
Paneer	Indian cheese
Papas	potatoes
Para aqui	for here
Para llevar	take out
Parillada	mixed grill

Pasteles	sweet or savory fried pies
Pastelitos	sweet or savory fried mini-pies
Pastor	shepherd. Derived from *doner kebab* style of cooking
Patacones	plantain sandwich
Pav	bread
Pav Bhaji	potato-based curry served with bread
Pechuga	breast
Pepitos	pumpkin seeds
Pernil	roasted pork shoulder
Perra	bacon-wrapped hot dog
Perro	hot dog
Pescado	fish
Pho	Vietnamese noodle soup
Picadillo	shredded beef, beef hash
Picaditos	fried, thick corn torilla topped with salsa, sour cream, cheese, onion and meat
Pierna	leg
Piezas	pieces
Piloncillo	unrefined brown sugar
Piña	pineapple

Pirata	flour tortilla filled with fajita meat, bacon, cheese
Piri-Piri	AKA Peri-Peri, Pili-Pili. Swahili term for a small, potent red chili pepper used in Portuguese and African cooking
Platano	plantain
Platillo	small plate
Plato	plate
Pollo	chicken
Por embargo	to go
Potosinas	enchilada that comes from San Luis Potosi
Preparados	prepared
Puerco	pork
Pulpa	pulp
Pupusa	Salvadoran thick corn tortilla with a variety of fillings
Puri	unlevened bread

Q

Queso	cheese
Queso fresco	crumbly fresh cheese

R

Ragda Patties	savory Indian snack fritter made with potatoes and yellow peas
Rajas	roasted chile strips with onions and seasonings
Ranchera	ranch style. Generally a sauce made with tomatoes, onions, cilantro and oil and vinegar
Raspa	shaved ice
Refacciones	snack, pick-me-up
Refresqueria	stand selling refreshing drinks, normally made with fruit and water
Refritos	refried beans
Regulares	regular
Relleno	stuffed
Repollo	cabbage
Res	ribs, beef
Rostizado	roasted
Roti	Indian flat bread

S

Saag	also 'sag', spinach or mustard green
Saag paneer	normally spinach with cheese
Sag	also 'saag', spinach or mustard green
Salchicha	sausage
Salchipapa	sausage and French fries with salsa *rosada*
Salsa rosada	pink sauce consisting of mixture of mayonnaise and ketchup
Salsa verde	spicy green sauce made with *tomatillos*
Samosa	Indian stuffed pastry snack triangular in shape and filled with potatoes and sometimes, meat
Sandia	watermelon
Satay	marinated, skewered and grilled meat
Seekh kabob	variant of shish kabob. Ground meat and spices formed around skewer cooked in tandoor
Sencilla	single
Servilleta	napkin
Sesos	brains

Sev	crispy, salty Indian snack made with gram flour used to top a number of dishes	**Tajin**	dry, seasoned, chile mixture used for fruit, vegetables etc.	**Tlacoyo**	thick, oval-shaped corn tortilla
Shawarma	Middle-Eastern sandwich made with pita bread stuffed with meat grilled on a spit	**Tamales**	dish made of corn-based *masa* and cooked in a leaf wrapper served all over Mexico, Central and South America	**Tlayudas**	Oaxacan snack on a large, fried tortilla with beans, lettuce, meat, avocado
Sopa	soup			**Tocino**	bacon
Sope	traditional Mexican dish from Culiacan. Thick *masa* disk topped with beans, meat, cheese, etc	**Tamarindo**	tamarind	**Tomar**	to drink
		Tandoor	Indian cylindrical clay oven heat by wood or charcoal	**Tomate**	tomato
				Tomatillo	green tomato covered in a husk. Used for making salsa verde
Spam musubi	Spam topped with seasoned rice and covered in nori	**Tandoori**	a cooking methods using marinated meat cooked in a Tandoor	**Toquere**	thick, sweet Mexican corn patty similar to an *arepa*
Suadero	beef brisket	**Tarka**	Indian word for seasoning	**Toreado**	grilled
		Tayuyo	tamale cooked in corn husk	**Toronja**	grapefruit
		Telera	roll	**Torta**	sandwich
T		**Tempeh**	a fermented soybean cake	**Torta ahogada**	drowned sandwich
Tabbouleh	a salad made of bulgur, finely chopped parsley and mint, tomato and spring onion, seasoned with lemon juice and olive oil	**Tenedor**	fork	**Tostadas**	toasted. Refers to a corn tortilla, which has been toasted or fried until hard
		Tequenos	cheese sticks		
		Tequero	thick corn tortilla	**Trailero**	food truck
		Tikka	cutlet. Also the sauce used in chicken *tikka masala*	**Tripas**	tripe
				Tripitas	small pieces of tripe
Taco	traditional Mexican dish composed of a corn or wheat tortilla folded or rolled around a filling	**Tinga**	Mexican dish made with shredded chicken or beef simmered in chipotle sauce	**Troca**	truck
				Trompo	literally 'spinning top'. Refers to the shape of the meat once it has been packed onto the spit used to grill it. A.K.A. tacos *Arabes*
Tajadas	fried plaintains				

Tuetano	marrow
Tzatziki	Greek sauce made with yogurt, cucumbers, garlic, lemon juice, parsley

U

Unidades	units/pieces
Uva	grape

V

Vada Pav	savory Indian fritter made from lentils or potatoes
Vapor	steam
Vaso	cup
Verde	green
Vidrio	glass bottle

Y

Yuca	cassava

INDEX